from dynasties to dotcoms

the rise, fall and reinvention of British business in the past 100 years

Carol Kennedy

First published in Great Britain, 2003, by Director Publications Ltd
for the Institute of Directors, 116 Pall Mall, London SW1Y 5ED

Distributed by Kogan Page Ltd
120 Pentonville Road, London N1 9JN

This book has been commissioned to mark the Centenary of the Institute of Directors.
The IoD accepts no responsibility for the views expressed in it, which are those of the author.

A CIP record for this book is available from the British Library.

ISBN 0 7494 4127 5

Designed by Halo Design, London. Printed and bound in Great Britain by ABC Printers.

In producing this book to mark the Institute of Directors' Centenary, I have been fortunate in having the help of a dedicated and enthusiastic team.

Caroline Proud sub-edited my text with meticulous care and a deep knowledge of historical and current events. She also unearthed a mass of fascinating facts, from the launch of now-familiar brands to historical landmarks in science, innovation, politics and economics. Jane Moss, Director Publications' picture editor, tracked down many rarely seen archive photographs. Gary Parfitt, creative director for the IoD, exercised his professional magic on turning words and pictures into a superbly designed book in record time. Tom Nash, editorial director of Director Publications, master-minded the project with enthusiasm throughout, and both the IoD's director-general George Cox and chief operating officer Andrew Main Wilson have given it their unstinting support.

Also greatly appreciated was the extensive research undertaken by my fellow management writer Michel Syrett, who brought professional skill and judgment to the task of extracting and distilling information from business libraries and scratchy microfiche documents. A special acknowledgement, too, to the Frank Cass publication Business History, without which I would have been unable to piece together much of Britain's industrial and commercial story in the early 20th century.

Carol Kennedy
London, September 2003

a century of change

In one sense a century is a mighty long time. You only have to look at the world of 1903 to see how different things were then. Such is the pace of development that it seems an entirely different world. At the same time, a hundred years increasingly represents no more than a single lifetime. The last hundred years may already be part of history but it is history firmly linked to today. We can see how it has shaped our lives.

To celebrate the IoD's Centenary we thought it would be interesting to look at how British business, and its management, has developed over this period. It is a story never before presented with such clarity: a picture which is both fascinating and full of lessons.

George Cox, Director General
Institute of Directors

INSTITUTE OF DIRECTORS

00 years of business leadership

903   23 leading businessmen form the first Council of the Institute of Directors

906   The Institute of Directors gains the Royal Charter. Membership increases to 700

947   First edition of Director magazine published. The IoD's Policy & Executive Committee is established

955   2,500 members attend the first IoD Annual Convention held at the Royal Festival Hall

978   116 Pall Mall, London becomes the prestigious new home of the IoD. UK membership increases to 21,300

987   Margaret Thatcher, Britain's first female Prime Minister, addresses the IoD Annual Convention

999   The world's first independently accredited qualification for directors, Chartered Director, is launched

2001   Prime Minister Tony Blair officially opens the IoD's new 'young entrepreneur' premises, at 123 Pall Mall

2002   IoD UK membership increases 50% in 5 years to 55,000. Member premises now open in 7 UK cities

2003   The IoD's commitment to business excellence expands globally, with the launch of IoD International

ve are the
champions

66 Compared to the achievements of other countries, our (industrial) establishments are as backyard workshops to colossal factories. 99

Gustav Byng, chairman of the General Electric Company, warning against British business hubris in the early 1900s

1

n the opening years of the 20th century, Britain was still predominantly a land of family businesses, most of them small and proudly skills-based, basking in the fading Victorian glow of the nation's reputation as "workshop of the world". British manufacturing was associated with craftsmanship, as if even then there was a "heritage" quality about British goods. That, it was believed, was what the domestic market wanted, and the huge captive imperial markets followed where the motherland led. American ideas of standardisation and mass production, just beginning to revolutionise industry across the Atlantic, were anathema. When Ford opened its first UK plant at Manchester's Trafford Park in 1911 to manufacture the Model T, Britain's many craftsman car makers snorted that no-one would want to buy these cheaply produced "Tin Lizzies". One of them, the Talbot company, went so far as to boast in advertisements that its cars were produced "regardless of cost".

The ill-fated Titanic being completed at Harland and Wolff in 1912

The coming of big corporations, however, had been foreshadowed for decades by the time the Victorian age died along with the Queen in 1901. From 1844 onwards, and certainly by the mid-1860s, a wave of joint-stock and limited liability legislation had removed the boundaries to a firm's growth along with the link to its owner's personal finances – that long-established concept of partnership liability "to the last shilling and the last acre". But it was not until the expansive 1890s that giant companies began to be created by merger and a growing appetite for share ownership among the prosperous middle class, even if flotations continued to favour the upper levels of society. In his history of the City of London, David Kynaston records that in the Liptons share issue of 1898, dukes and marquesses received a full allocation of shares; earls, viscounts and barons 50 per cent; baronets and honourables 25 per cent, "and the general members of the public, nil". Even so, some of the best-known large companies remained in private hands until the First World War, among them the biscuit manufacturer Huntley and Palmer, soup maker Crosse and Blackwell, J. & J. Colman of mustard fame, glassmakers Pilkington Brothers and the Belfast shipyard Harland and Wolff, builders of the Titanic.

A rush of cheap money in the mid-1890s, with bank rate steady at two per cent for two years, precipitated a boom in new company registrations. The annual rate doubled from 2,515 in 1893 to 5,148 in 1897, and the next four years saw an explosion of mergers and amalgamations, although in a curiously narrow range of industries, principally textiles, brewing, iron and steel and tobacco. A fifth of the 52 biggest industrial companies in 1905 were in textiles and allied trades: 14 firms had come together in 1897 to form the English Sewing Cotton Co. Ltd., and in 1900 two enormous amalgamations took place in the industry with one set of 46 companies merging to form the British Cotton and Wool Dyers and another 53 joining in the Bleachers' Association. In 1901, American competition in the tobacco industry, driven by the monopolistic activities of James B.

Duke (heiress Doris Duke's buccaneering father), prompted the formation of Imperial Tobacco out of 13 UK companies headed by the Wills family business in Bristol.

By 1907, the 100 largest companies together were employing one and a half million people, 8.2 per cent of the working population, and about a fifth of them were located in "Outer Britain", with substantial industrial enterprises in Scotland, south Wales, Northumberland and County Durham.

The magnetic pull of London and the south east would not begin until the explosion of light industry in the 1920s.

The big-corporation phenomenon brought new disciplines into management: in 1901, the vice-chairman of the English Sewing Cotton Co. confessed that it had been "an awful mistake" to leave the vendors of acquired businesses in control of them, because they could not change the way they had always done things. Boards became top-heavy with directors, and reporting lines suffered.

J. & P. Coats, which dominated the sewing thread industry, was a rare model of how to manage an amalgamation of individually successful units. Formed in 1896, it had strong central direction, accurate statistical information, properly functioning departments that centralised buying and selling, and famously rigorous cost control. Its boast was that "every halfpenny stamp could be traced". No wonder it continued through decades to generate fortunes for its founding families, up to and including Lord (Kenneth) Clark, the art historian and owner of Saltwood Castle in Kent, and his son, the maverick Tory MP and diarist, Alan Clark.

Stanley Baldwin, of the family steel business, as President of the Board of Trade in 1922. He was Prime Minister by 1924

A clear need was emerging for directors to be guided through the legal maze of Companies Acts, of which seven had appeared between 1844 and 1900, with a flurry of lesser measures since the 1860s. A famous court case of 1897, Salomon v. Salomon, had established the corporation as a separate legal entity. Directors were held personally liable for the accuracy of their company's annual accounts. The Companies Act of 1900 brought in the compulsory independent audit and barred directors from involvement in auditing their own companies. In late 1902, a group of leading businessmen held meetings in the City of London to decide whether and how they should form their own professional organisation, and a committee of five was set up to work out proposals for an "institute of directors".

Women making cigarettes: the First World War hugely boosted smoking and it was deemed patriotic to support the industry

The meetings had been instigated by Arthur Addinsell, a chartered accountant and merchant with plantations and mining interests in Malaya, and some six months later, on April 29, 1903, in a room at the Institute of Chartered Accountants in Moorgate Place in the City, 23 eminent businessmen were chosen by their peers to form the founding council of the Institute of Directors. They included chairmen and senior directors of insurance companies, banks, iron and steel firms, railway companies, the Union Castle Mail Steamship Co. and several leading London retailers, headed by Mr. D. H. Evans of the eponymous Oxford Street department store. Addinsell became the first secretary. Apart from a firm of rolling-stock suppliers and Baldwin's Ltd., a family-run steel business with a future prime minister on its board – Stanley Baldwin would become a member of the IoD Council in 1908 – there was a curious lack of manufacturing representation, given its importance in the business world of 1903.

FLASHBACK TO 1903

In the year the Institute of Directors was born:

- ☐ the Conservative Arthur Balfour was prime minister
- ☐ the Republican Theodore Roosevelt was president
- ☐ Edward VII was king
- ☐ Emmeline and Christabel Pankhurst founded the Women's Social and Political Union
- ☐ the Russian Social Democratic Labour Party, led by Vladimir Ilyich Ulyanov (Lenin), met in London and Brussels; Lenin's supporters, the Bolsheviks, decided on military-led revolution
- ☐ Marconi transmitted the world's first two-way transatlantic radio message – between Roosevelt and Edward VII
- ☐ Wilbur and Orville Wright made the world's first powered flight – at Kitty Hawk, North Carolina
- ☐ Henry Ford started making cheap cars for the mass American market
- ☐ the first motor taxis and the first electric trams appeared on London streets
- ☐ a new thoroughfare, Kingsway, named after Edward VII, opened in the West End

- ☐ Robert Falcon Scott, Ernest Shackleton and Edward Wilson attempted to reach the South Pole
- ☐ Marie Curie was awarded the Nobel prize for physics for her work on radioactivity

- ☐ the UK population was about 38 million*
- ☐ average life expectancy was 48*
- ☐ the school leaving age was 12
- ☐ GDP was just under £125bn**
- ☐ manufacturing accounted for 28 per cent of output, agriculture, forestry and fishing 11 per cent, services 50 per cent*
- ☐ around 10 per cent of 10 to 14-year-old boys (140,000) had jobs***
- ☐ women accounted for 29 per cent of the workforce*
- ☐ around two million people were in domestic service***
- ☐ full-time average earnings were £1.40 a week****
- ☐ a second-class return from London to Glasgow cost about £1.66
- ☐ a four-course dinner at the Savoy cost about £0.38

*1900 figures **at constant 1995 market prices ***1901 census figures ****1902 figure

Sources: Office for National Statistics; Oxford Review of Economic Policy; The Economist: Pocket Britain in Figures, 1997; Christopher Lee: This Sceptred Isle, Twentieth Century, BBC Worldwide and Penguin Books, 1999; Patrick Robertson: The New Shell Book of Firsts, 1994, Headline Book Publishing

Note: An updated fact box, "100 years later", appears on page 206

Lord Avebury, a leading banker and first President of the Institute of Directors in 1903

The first president of the new institute was Lord Avebury, formerly Sir John Lubbock, who had been ennobled in 1900 for services to banking. (His grandson, the MP Eric Lubbock, who sparked the Liberal Party's post-war revival with a famous 1962 by-election victory over the Conservatives at commuter-belt Orpington, later revived the title for his life peerage.) Within its first year, the institute had a membership of 420 and occupied offices at 4 Corbet Court, Gracechurch Street, rented from the Mercers Corporation at £400 a year. It published a newsletter advising members on directors' responsibilities and legal liabilities, and in 1906 gained a Royal Charter and began lobbying Parliament on company legislation. By 1910, its membership stood at 1,348, a peak it was not to attain again until after the Second World War: the depression of the 1930s would see the organisation with barely 200-300 members, many of whom had not bothered to pay their subscriptions.

Along with textiles, the big British industries as the 20th century began were brewing, iron and steel (especially armaments and shipbuilding) and tobacco. One third of Britain's 50 biggest companies were in brewing, all controlled by socially powerful families, which had so many titles between them that they were collectively known as "the Beerage". Family interests also predominated in the Midlands iron and steel industry, which produced a number of political figures, chiefly Stanley Baldwin and the Chamberlains (Joseph, Austen and Neville), who were associated with the Birmingham nuts and bolts manufacturer, Guest, Keen and Nettlefold (now GKN). Even when companies became incorporated, family links persisted in the boardroom, not always with beneficial results. The iron and steel industry was self-evidently of national importance, yet steel makers were still stuck in the

THE CHANGING CENTURY

Facts from the business archives:

1900: The Net Book Agreement was introduced. The agreement, which fixed the prices of books sold in British shops, was to remain unbroken for 92 years

1900: The Daily Mail became the first British paper to sell a million copies a day

1901: Meccano was patented by Liverpool-based inventor Frank Hornby

1901: Britain's first cinema, The Mohawks' Hall, Upper Street, Islington, was opened, showing primitive "talkies" featuring music hall stars

1901: H. J. Heinz introduced tinned baked beans to Britain. Its test market consisted mainly of working-class housewives in the north of England

1902: Marmite was first manufactured in a factory in Burton on Trent

1902: The British road-haulage business was born; the Road

Carrying Co. was formed to carry cotton and other bulk commodities between Liverpool and the Lancashire mill towns

1903: The world's first public relations consultant, Ivy Ledbetter Lee, set up in New York. Lee, a former financial journalist, was to give Standard Oil boss John D. Rockefeller, vilified as a capitalist oppressor, a new image by filling his pockets with dimes to distribute among the poor

1904: Car maker Argyll unveiled the first British-made two-door saloon

1904: The North Eastern Railway company introduced the first electric passenger trains – between Newcastle Bridge Street and Benton on the riverside branch line

1905: The first British motor ambulance was commissioned for civilian service. It cost £465 and was built by Messrs. James and Browne of Oxford Street

1906: London Underground introduced season tickets for travellers on the Piccadilly Line

era of beehive coke ovens and the Bessemer process, and in 1910 Britain was producing barely half the German tonnage (as was also the case with electrical equipment). Iron production, as the historian Corelli Barnett has observed, remained largely "in the hands of little Dickensian family firms", operating out-of-date foundries with furnaces sometimes 70 years old.[1]

Yet it remained a confident, even swaggering time. Technological and scientific progress was in the air. As if to typify the energising spirit of the age, the hormone adrenalin was first commercially manufactured in 1901. In the same year, modern long-distance communications were born: Marconi's wireless station in Newfoundland received the first transatlantic signal – the three-dot Morse code letter "S" tapped out from Poldhu in Cornwall. The fact that Britain had been progressively losing industrial supremacy to Germany – and latterly the United States – since 1870 was comfortably hidden from view. Shipbuilding was at its zenith in British yards, as government spending rose on warship production, making it a highly profitable business for the five leading yards that built more than 63

Wireless pioneer Guglielmo Marconi with his apparatus in 1901, the year it transmitted the first radio message across the Atlantic

per cent of them – Vickers of Barrow-in-Furness, John Brown of Clydebank, Armstrong Whitworth of Elswick, Fairfield of Glasgow and Palmers of Jarrow. All five also did a massive export business, with Armstrongs producing almost as much for foreign navies as for the Admiralty.

1907: Britain's first aircraft manufacturer, Howard T. Wright, set up in business; two years later, he unveiled his first biplane at the Olympia Aero Show

1908: Malted milk was marketed by Horlick's Malted Milk Company of Slough

1909: Maynards Wine Gums were launched

1909: A factory in Hertfordshire started making Ovaltine. The original Swiss product was known as Ovomaltine. The name had to

be changed following a transcription error by the clerk registering the trademark

1911: John D. Rockefeller became the world's first billionaire

1911: HMS Africa became the first British naval vessel to be fitted with a flight deck

1911: The London General Omnibus Company withdrew its last horse-drawn bus

1911: The first stepped escalator in Britain was installed at Earl's Court Underground Station. To instil

public confidence, the District Railway company employed a man with a wooden leg, Bumper Harris, to ride the "moving staircase" all day long – "if he can do it, so can you" was the message.

1912: Hoover started exporting upright vacuum cleaners to Britain

1913: The first castings of stainless steel were made by Harry Brearley in Sheffield

1913: Potato crisps were launched commercially in Britain by Carter's Crisps of London. Among Mr

Carter's employees: one Frank Smith, who subsequently founded his own company and took Carter's over

1914: W. J. Bush & Co. became the first British company to manufacture Aspirin as the war cut off supplies from Germany's Bayer

1914: Two reinforced Rolls-Royce tourers became the first armoured motor vehicles to be used in warfare; the E. B. 5 Gunbus, built by Vickers, became the first aircraft

Source: Patrick Robertson, The New Shell Book of Firsts, 1994, Headline Book Publishing

partnership and the happiness principle

John Spedan Lewis (right), elder son of the founder of the John Lewis stores, was unlike his tyrannical father in every way. Thoughtful and idealistic, whereas his father treated employees like a Victorian mill-owner, he gave up a place at Oxford to go into the business in 1904, aged 19. Soon afterwards, he was sitting in a traffic jam on the top of a London horse-omnibus when it suddenly struck him that "extreme happiness" could result from renouncing personal wealth for some greater cause. He doubted, however, whether he had the strength of character to do it.

Six years later, when recovering from operations following a riding accident, he found what seemed the perfect compromise. When he inherited the business he would distribute his wealth by giving the employees co-ownership with non-voting shares (in order to prevent control passing to an outsider who might change the system).

He broached the plan to his father, who at first reacted with predictable scorn, but later agreed that Spedan could try out his ideas at the ailing Peter Jones store. This had been acquired for £20,000 in 1906 and by early 1914 was on the point of collapse. (Typically, old John Lewis insisted that Spedan first put in a full day's work at the Oxford Street store.)

Spedan immediately introduced shorter hours, new sales incentives and staff committees through which elected representatives of the rank and file could meet and question the chairman regularly. After six months, sales had grown by 12 per cent, but some of the older buyers complained to Spedan's father.

A monumental family row ensued, with old

Lewis threatening to terminate his son's quarter-partnership in the flourishing Oxford Street store. Spedan called his bluff, agreeing to give it up in return for the rest of his father's interest in Peter Jones. Against advice from his mother, the auditors and the Midland Bank – which said it would refuse the Peter Jones account if Spedan's plan went ahead – he persisted and eventually won. By the end of the First World War, turnover had increased fivefold – Peter Jones was one of the few London stores to increase its revenue in wartime – and by 1920 an annual loss of £8,000 had become a profit of £20,000.

The first profit-sharing scheme was introduced in 1918, along with a third week's paid holiday – unheard of at the time in retailing – and the recruitment of university graduates, including women (one of whom Spedan married). Spedan was convinced that business as a whole would never be truly efficient until it could attract the same well-qualified candidates as the professions.

His mission statement remains unique in business: "The supreme purpose of the John Lewis Partnership is simply the happiness of its members". His concept of Fairer Shares, the title of one of his (unreadable) books, included the sharing of knowledge and information with employees, a management idea that still generally owes more to lip-service than reality. (The stores' famous pledge "never knowingly undersold" was personally introduced by Spedan in 1926.)

Old John Lewis clung to life and his hands-on control of the business until he died in 1928, aged 92. Now at last the son could fully realise his partnership vision. He floated the business on the stock market as John Lewis and Co, raising over £1.5m in preference shares, and shortly afterwards formed the John Lewis Partnership Ltd. with a capital of

£312,000. A tightly-drafted "settlement in trust" sold to the employees the right to all his and his wife's present and future income from the stores, with repayment spread over 30 years. In 1950, ownership of the capital in the company was irrevocably handed to the people who worked in it. The Partnership is still listed on the Stock Exchange for its preference shares but because of its unusual capital structure cannot issue equity.

For over 70 years the John Lewis experiment has been widely hailed as a success, bringing decades of increasing profit and dividends to its "partners", along with a raft of shared benefits such as corporate country houses, company yachts and sporting facilities. Trouble loomed in 2000 when a number of partners dreamed of windfall riches if the trust could be disbanded and John Lewis sold off. The trust proved watertight and the revolt was seen off.

Though few family companies have followed his vision, Spedan deserves to be a business hero for the 21st century. His idea of leadership was being "the good captain of a well-run ship", and his nephew Peter Lewis, the last family chairman, says his uncle's biggest single contribution was to make it possible for more people "to enjoy business". The current chairman, Sir Stuart Hampson, still holds "happy hours" with his directors asking them how the business is doing in terms of happiness. "I am convinced that it is the secret of sustainable success," he says.

(Source: Carol Kennedy: Business Pioneers, 2001)

The smaller British family businesses were still predominantly in the first generation, with all the "push and go" (the admiring term used of the colonial secretary Joe Chamberlain) which that implied. In a survey of British business wealth between 1870 and 1914, nearly 83 per cent came from first and second generation businesses combined, contradicting the popular theory that Britain's industrial decline in this period was partly due to the propensity of the third generation for cashing in and retiring into the life of country squires – not so much clogs to clogs in three generations as "shirtsleeves to hunting jacket", as one distinguished economic historian has put it.[2]

Business wealth-creation was also more evenly distributed around the country than it would be later in the century, when the south-east corner of England took a disproportionate slice. Industrial magnates abounded in the provinces, their names synonymous with great industries – names such as Keen and Nettlefold, Cadbury, Elkington, Armitage, Armstrong, Whitworth, Crossley, Fry, Wills, Rowntree and Lever. In terms of personal wealth, the provinces as a group equalled London, and the provincial cities were filled with well-heeled businessmen: in Birmingham, the average personal fortune was around £106,000; in Manchester £146,000 and in Bristol £209,000. (Multiply by around 60 for today's numerical

Gordon Selfridge in 1910, the year after opening Selfridges on London's Oxford Street with crowd-pulling displays such as Bleriot's plane

equivalent, although purchasing power in the 1900s was exponentially greater.)

Retailing was becoming a major part of the economy, led by the growth of department stores and multiple chains around the country. Marks and Spencer had more than 100 "Penny Bazaars" by 1914. Motor transport and improved distribution systems were leading an explosion of grocery chains – Liptons, the Home and Colonial, the second-generation J. Sainsbury, the Maypole Dairy and many others. Outside the provisions business, leading multiples included G. A. Dunn in menswear, Boots the Chemist and W. H. Smith, which moved into shops from railway bookstalls in 1905. The shoe chain Freeman, Hardy and Willis and the Singer Sewing Machine Company each had more than 500 shops by 1914. The multiples' growth – from 1,564 shops in 1880 to 15,242 in 1905 and more than 25,000 by 1915 – was fuelled by rising middle-class economic power.

Department stores became ever more palatial – the shopping experience of their day. Gordon Selfridge opened his magnificent Doric temple on Oxford Street in 1909 with headline-grabbing publicity stunts such as exhibiting Louis Bleriot's travel-stained monoplane just after its pioneer Channel crossing. The store kings often made the papers for their private lives: Selfridge was a flamboyant, high-living

Whiteley's of Bayswater, London's first true department store
(opened 1863), pictured in 1912

An early W.H. Smith shop in Dorking,
Surrey. Smiths branched out from railway
bookstalls in 1905

Tea magnate Sir Thomas
Lipton as seen by the
cartoonist Spy

American (he had run Marshall Field in Chicago) who
bought an English castle and frequented nightclubs with
his cabaret-singer companions, Hungarian-born twins the
Dolly Sisters; William Whiteley was shot dead in his west
London emporium in 1907 by his unacknowledged son; Sir
Thomas Lipton, the tea tycoon, hob-nobbed with Edward VII
and spent most of his fortune trying to win the America's
Cup for Britain with a series of yachts called Shamrock.

At the grindstone of industry, meanwhile, in a workshop
in Oxford, one of England's greatest entrepreneurs, car
maker William Morris, was repairing cycles, tinkering with a
new patent petrol engine for a motor-bicycle and struggling
against financial difficulties. His cycle business collapsed in
1904, but he already had a vision of affordable motor cars,
which were still the preserve of a few wealthy hobbyists.
Within 20 years, that vision would make him Britain's
nearest equivalent to Henry Ford and in time, as Lord
Nuffield, the greatest philanthropist of his age.

Yet alongside this energy and business creativity

marched several factors that were leading British
manufacturers into a dangerously complacent and short-
term state of mind. Britain's industrial decline between
1880 and 1930 is often attributed to the deadening effect
of many family companies being content with sufficient
profit to give the family a comfortable living while reinvesting
at a minimal level and failing to push out the boundaries of
the business. Time and again, British manufacturers fell
back on the assured markets of the empire, reducing
costs such as wages when the pressure was on instead of
pursuing more efficient technical practices. One historian
has written of "a wanton disregard for the commercial
aspects of business life".[3]

Failure to adopt modern technology was visible to
anyone visiting many industrial offices. An historical account
of the works office of a major engineering firm, Stewart and
Lloyds Clyde Tube Works in 1905 – staffed, of course, only
by men – reported that "the only piece of modern
equipment was the telephone, with a private line to the

Lord Nuffield, the car-maker William Morris, in 1941. One of Britain's greatest innovators, he introduced mass production to the UK

A steel foundry in 1905. Iron and steel production still used 19th-century technology, unlike the US and Germany

Glasgow office… there was no other office machinery of any kind – no typewriters, adding machines, comptometers, payroll listing machines… Everything was handwritten and the only duplication was by letterpress copying."

Steel making was not the only key industry stuck fast in old technology. The same was true of sectors in which Britain prided itself on being supreme, such as cotton, footwear and coal-mining. The "not-invented-here" syndrome was rife, and in some products such as machine tools and chemicals it was to lead to a near-fatal dependence on German imports. Everywhere there was a stubborn unwillingness to adopt the techniques of mass production and standardisation of components that were propelling US companies into 20th-century efficiency. As early as 1901, Gustav Byng, chairman of the General Electric Company, challenged anyone to point to a single industry that had taken root and grown in Britain since 1881. "Compared to the achievements of other countries, our (industrial) establishments are as backyard workshops

to colossal factories." Frederick Lanchester, who built the first British petrol car in 1896 and was one of the few British manufacturers to respond willingly to modern production practices, commented acidly how, in the early days, when one of his craftsmen was asked to work to drawings, gauges or templates, "he gave a sullen look such as one might expect from a Royal Academician if asked to colour an engineering drawing".

Lack of standardised components, cheap and easy to replace, lost British exporters many overseas markets. British-made locomotives and rolling stock, though admirably engineered and built to last, were fitted with no fewer than 200 types of axle boxes and more than 40 types of handbrake. Paradoxically, the very quality of their build worked against them in developing markets such as South America, where the heavy British locomotives often jumped or buckled the cheap, lightweight track. US engine makers, using lighter construction and standard, mass-produced components, cleaned up in competition.[4]

THE REFLECTION

SWEATED LABOUR

Sweated labour was a burning issue for reformers and cartoonists in the 1900s

American manufacturers were being healthily exposed to the disciplines of early management theory with its emphasis on planning, co-ordination and efficiency. This was the "scientific management" pioneered by Frederick W. Taylor with his stopwatch observations of manual tasks at the Bethlehem Steel Works in Philadelphia and his followers, notably the husband-and-wife engineering team of Frank and Lillian Gilbreth, who developed time and motion study in industry. American exporters quickly established footholds in products that particularly benefited from scientific manufacturing techniques – typewriters, sewing machines (the Singer Sewing Machine Company was the first direct US investment into Britain after the General Electric Company set up in Birmingham in 1900), firearms, watches and agricultural machinery. Even in such a British-dominated industry as boots and shoes, US mechanisation was leading to an alarming influx of well-made footwear in British shops, cheaper and sometimes more fashionable than the domestic products.

Three powerful economic reasons fuelled the British reluctance to modernise production methods: cheap and abundant supplies of finance and energy, and skilled craft labour. The last was probably the single biggest block to British manufacturers adopting mechanisation; unlike the US, labour was cheap and plentiful relative to land costs. By 1910, the US was producing the same amount of tinplate as Britain, with a workforce just over one-quarter of the British total. It was the same with energy: coal was still the dominant fuel, and Britain was literally built on it. Steam continued to reign supreme: in 1912, only a quarter of the power supplied to British industrial businesses was driven by electricity, which remained expensive because there was little incentive to make its generation more efficient. For at least two years after world war broke out in 1914, when sea power was still the commanding factor, British warships continued to be fired by coal rather than oil. Capital was also cheap and readily accessible, so manufacturers were under no discipline to save on costs.

Nowhere was the contrast between the comfortable complacency of British manufacturing compared with the US more marked than in the fledgling automobile industry. Where US firms were busy developing the assembly line, with F. W. Taylor himself advising the Packard and Franklin companies and Henry Ford, who made the principle the core of his manufacturing, allegedly gleaning the idea from watching carcasses being "dis-assembled" on a moving belt in Chicago meat-packing factories, the small British companies persisted in their craftsman approach. Far from standardising components, many took pride in making their own. In 1914, Wolseley was boasting that it made everything down to the castings. The only exceptions were coils and tyres.

It was William Morris, a mechanic to his fingertips who could perform any technical task as well as his workmen, who would break this mould and buy in everything including the engine and body, thereby becoming the most commercially successful motor manufacturer in Britain. Morris and, to a lesser extent, Austin were the only British manufacturers to realise with Ford that the future market for motor cars, as Ford declared in 1908, lay with "the great multitude". Yet as late as the outbreak of the Second World War, many British car makers were still aiming their over-engineered, expensively finished products at professional and middle-class buyers.

The inevitable outcome was that British cars were from the beginning overpriced compared with Fords, which also out-performed them. In 1913, the Model T sold for £135 – £200 and had a rating of 22.4hp: the Austin Ten was £325 and rated only 14.3hp. It was ironic that, apart from Morris, the only Briton before 1913 to recognise the coming democratisation of the car market was the man who persuaded Henry Ford to set up his UK assembly plant and ran it for him – Percival (later Lord) Perry. By 1906, the US had overtaken France as the world's premier car maker, but Britain's industry was growing fast, even if it had started under German auspices. Daimler was the first registered UK car company, financed by a group of speculators under Harry J. Lawson, the man responsible for the campaign to abolish the walking-pace speed limit behind the red flag. It was founded in 1896 in Coventry, in the West Midlands region, which would remain the key motor manufacturing centre for a century, and was soon followed by Lanchester, one of the few companies to start from scratch making cars; most others, like Rover, Morris, Humber, Riley and Sunbeam, graduated from the bicycle

trade, or, like Wolseley and Napier, were spin-offs from other engineering activities.

As the century turned, car companies were starting up at the rate of about a dozen a year, most of them now faint historical memories such as Crossley, Standard, Alldays and Onions, Star, Swift, Singer, Riley, Belsize and the Scottish firm of Arrol Johnston. By the outbreak of the Great War, it was estimated that some 400 new car companies had been created in Britain on a wave of optimistic investment, but 300 of them had already disappeared, many through rash over-spending. The Argyll plant on the banks of the Clyde at Alexandria was a prime example, designed as a lavish model factory, with marble floors and 500 washbasins for the workers. The company collapsed in the depression of 1907, which wrecked many car makers' business plans.[5]

The most successful founders were themselves mechanics and engineers who had served apprenticeships in allied industries after first undergoing a good school education. Several were from middle-class backgrounds and had attended public schools. R. W. Maudslay, the founder of Standard Motors, went to Marlborough College and the Crystal Palace School of Engineering before being apprenticed in the railway industry. Henry Royce, who would make his first car in 1904 in partnership with the Hon. Charles Stewart Rolls, attended the City and Guilds Technical College, served a railway apprenticeship with

Herbert Austin foresaw the mass market like Morris, but proved less successful in production terms

the Great Northern Railway Company, and worked as a fitter at a Leeds machine tool company. John Marston, who founded Sunbeam, went to Christ's Hospital and was apprenticed to a maker of japan ware, a sort of decorative enamel. Like Royce and his great rival W. O. Bentley, Herbert Austin also served an apprenticeship with the Great Northern before emigrating at the age of 17 to Australia with an uncle. George Singer and William Hillman were both marine engineers who turned to cycle making and other engineering trades before moving into cars: Hillman made roller skates and sewing machines and pioneered the mass production of ball and roller bearings in Britain. Sir William Arrol of Arrol Johnston came from an eminent Scottish family of consulting engineers who had built the Forth Bridge.

Coventry and the Midlands became the natural home for the new industry because the area was the centre of cycle manufacture as well as other machine trades. Wolseley, an Australian maker of sheep shearing machinery, appointed young Herbert Austin, who had

worked for it in Australia, to manage its new UK operation in Birmingham. It was not long, however, before Austin, who had caught the motor bug, built his first car, a three-wheeler steered by tiller. He turned out a number of models for Wolseley, which by this time had started its own motor division, but in 1905 quit to set up his own business in a derelict printing works. His first badged model, a handsome 25 – 30hp car called the Endcliffe Phaeton, was on sale by the spring of 1906 for £650.

Morris, by contrast, was convinced from the start that there would be huge demand for a popularly priced light car, as there had been for bicycles in the 1890s. Unlike Austin, who fell into the trap common to early British car makers of trying to produce too many models of varying designs and finishes, and making all the parts themselves, Morris perceived that the path to profit lay in buying in everything needed to build a car, engine and body included. "The work is better and more cheaply done while the cost and worry of more plant is avoided," he wrote some years later in a trade magazine. "Money is

The most famous pairing in automotive history: left to right, the Hon. Charles Stewart Rolls in 1908, Rolls and Royce aboard a 1905 model, and Henry Royce, the master engineer, c. 1920. The cars were traditionally called "Royces" by their makers

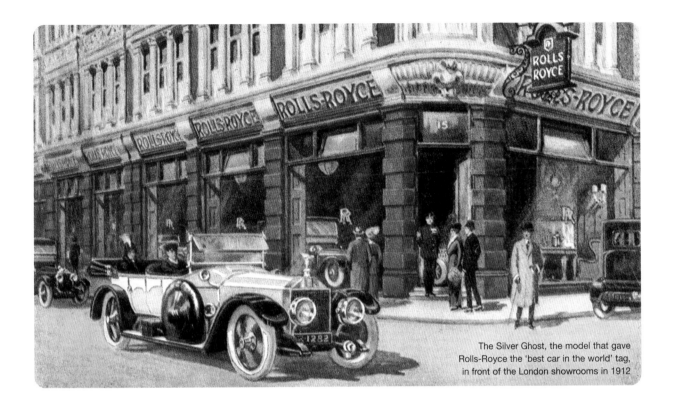

The Silver Ghost, the model that gave
Rolls-Royce the 'best car in the world' tag,
in front of the London showrooms in 1912

conserved for better use in other directions." The
Automobile Engineer in 1911 did not agree with him,
snorting: "The manufacturer who buys finished parts and
puts them together has been generally regarded rather
contemptuously and it is usual to assume that cars made
in this way cannot be really good."

Morris found a low-rent building for his assembly
plant in an old military training school at Cowley, outside
Oxford, and the Morris Oxford, described by Autocar as "a
two-seater torpedo", appeared in 1912 to a generally
enthusiastic reception. It could not compete on price or
space with the four-seater Ford Model T (£180 against
£135), but Morris added extra features usually found on

larger cars, a psychological strategy that worked. His low-
cost base also enabled him to survive the post-war
industrial slump, which killed off less economic
manufacturers.

In general, the proliferation of models and emphasis
on craftsman-building ensured that British-made cars were
uncompetitive against the thrusting American companies
with their standardised mass products. Output was almost
on a cottage-industry level. Until 1914, no UK firm managed
to produce more than one car per worker per year,
whereas as early as 1904, well before mass-production
got going, Ford workers were turning out more than three
per man. Except for Morris, who was adept at both, the

men who ran the industry understood the mechanical side more than the business aspect. Oddly enough, though, the first British car manufacturer to see that limiting its model range would give it more power in the market was the one that would become an icon of technical excellence for the world – Rolls-Royce. Neither Henry Royce, the dour engineer, nor the Hon. Charles Rolls, the sporting old Etonian and champion rally driver, were particularly distinguished by commercial acumen, but when they set up their company in 1906 they had the sense to appoint a business manager who was.

Claude Johnson, a former stalwart of the Automobile Club (later the Royal Automobile Club), was the man who persuaded the partners, after they had initially produced several different Rolls-Royce models, to concentrate on just one, the Silver Ghost. The six-cylinder, 48hp car became a world-beater. Johnson was a marketing genius with a flair for the PR masterstroke; he never put dignity and exclusivity at risk. His idea in 1907 of naming the 40/50 tourer the Silver Ghost, then coating it in aluminium paint and silver-plating its headlamps and radiator was one of the great marketing brainwaves of the century. He hired the artist Charles Sykes to design the Spirit of Ecstasy mascot, for which Sykes used the society belle Eleanor Thornton as model.

After the Ghost covered 14,000 miles without a stop in the Scottish reliability trials, Johnson's biggest PR coup came when a motoring writer, unsolicited, described it as "the best car in the world". Sadly, the dashing figure of Charles Rolls was soon out of the picture. Four years after the company's launch, he was killed in a flying accident at Bournemouth when his Wright biplane broke up in the air, but Royce (and at least until the takeover by BMW, the cars were always called Royces by the people who built them) lived until 1933.

The Rolls-Royce company did not, however, have an easy start. From the profits of his electrical business, Royce had put in £10,000 in cash and the remaining £50,000 capitalisation of Rolls-Royce Ltd. was intended to be raised through a public share offering, but this fell short by £10,000. Only a desperate last-minute appeal to one of its customers, a rich wool manufacturer, saved the company from being strangled at birth. At the beginning, car manufacturers had been able to raise share capital with relative ease, but until 1905 returns to investors were low and there were several bankruptcies. Financial institutions remained sceptical, unable to gauge the industry's true potential, and these years saw the beginning of battle lines being drawn between manufacturing and the City.

Management in the car industry, though, was not impressive. There was a lack of long-term planning, which has been blamed by business historians on latent fears of social revolution in Edwardian England. Shortly before his death, Charles Rolls even proposed building a duplicate production plant in France as a precaution against industrial anarchy. Apart from Morris, Herbert Austin was one of the few to demonstrate both technical and commercial skills, steadily raising his own equity and that of other investors until he was able to float the company in 1914 with 250,000 non-voting preference shares being taken up by the public.

Meanwhile, finance on an international scale was something in which Britain, as now, excelled. The 1900s were in many ways a period of early globalisation, with communications such as the wireless telegraph shrinking the world, the gold sovereign as powerful a global currency as today's greenback dollar and Britain's traders and investors moving easily across borders and financing dams, railways and bridges in countries from Malaya to Mesopotamia. In fact, the surge of investment in overseas projects, particularly railway companies, was proving detrimental to development at home, setting a pattern of chronic under-investment in British railway networks that was to continue degrading the industry up to the present day.

There was widespread fascination with and debate over the geo-politically sensitive Berlin-to-Baghdad railway, launched in 1903 to open up the oilfields of Mesopotamia but truncated by the outbreak of war in 1914. (See panel.) Dividend-hungry investors were also lured by the returns offered by North and South American railroads. Issues from the struggling Great Central, Great Northern and Great Western in Britain, even at four per cent, were spurned in favour of the five per cent promised by the Buenos Aires Central and Southern San Paolo or the four and a half per cent offered by the Kentucky and Indiana. Only ten or 15 years earlier, a home stock yielding three per cent would have satisfied investors. Between 1907 and 1914, more than £600m of UK capital was pumped into foreign and colonial railways at the expense of the domestic companies, and the only technological advance that might have attracted investors – electrification – was as slow to be adopted as other modernisations. A year before the Great War, 82 per cent of issues on the London capital market were for foreign undertakings, and only 18 per cent for domestic ones.

"British money continued to be invested in such nationally irrelevant projects as Argentine tramways while British industrial equipment 50 years old went without replacement," wrote Correlli Barnett in his devastating indictment of the first half of Britain's 20th century, The Collapse of British Power. Brinley Thomas, an economic historian, has also observed that the Edwardian mania for overseas investment hampered British development in a number of industries – just when productivity was being transformed in Germany and the US through the industrial application of electricity. "British investors showed little interest in re-equipping industries at home. They preferred to indulge in an orgy of foreign investment… Britain lost a

The only way to travel: Great Western Railway posters tempt the holiday-maker in 1910

golden opportunity in the early years of this century when the craze for foreign securities led to a failure to take full advantage of contemporary technical innovations… the marginal social cost of the foreign investment undertaken in the years 1900-1913 was very high. In later years, the British economic system was to pay dearly for the neglect of home industry in the period when the technical foundations of modern productivity were being laid."[6]

Complacency about the value of global investing and trading was crystallised in the now-infamous book The Great Illusion, whose author Norman Angell gave a lecture to the Institute of Bankers in January 1912 on his thesis that the intertwined nature of commerce and finance across borders meant that war was now an economic impossibility. (Despite this being monumentally disproved between 1914 and 1918, Angell was still defending his theories in the 1930s.)

The City of London led the pursuit of globalisation. "Most leading members of the Stock Exchange were far more at home in Monte Carlo than in Manchester," the City's historian, David Kynaston, has written. The square mile of banks, finance houses and commodity brokers was in its golden age in the 1900s. It was the centre of international trade in wool, tea, rubber and dozens of other commodities from furs to spices. With the advent of wireless telegraphy, shipping was a huge City business: in 1910, the shipowner Sir John Ellerman was the richest man in Britain. London was where the world came for mining expertise – the future US president Herbert Hoover was honing his professional skills working as a junior partner in a City firm of mining engineers. It was also the world's leading securities market, thanks to its access to short-term credit. By 1910, about one-third of the world's issued securities were quoted in London. (It was kept a deep secret that on the outbreak of war in August 1914, the London Stock Exchange owed the outside world £81m.) More than half of London's 160 banks were foreign or colonial and its merchant banks "for the most part held

the global money man

One man personified the extraordinary world of Edwardian international finance, where grand commercial projects interlocked with grand diplomacy and most of the strings were pulled by socially prominent individuals relying on a network of personal contacts and trust. He was **Sir Ernest Cassel** (right), a close friend of King Edward VII and the Duke of Devonshire, so highly regarded by the Treasury's mandarins that they would introduce every new Chancellor of the Exchequer to him within weeks of taking office.

While still in his twenties and thirties, the German-Jewish Cassel, who was converted to Roman Catholicism at the dying wish of his wife, was involved in financing Mexican railroads, raising government loans for Mexico, Uruguay, Argentina, Brazil and Egypt, investing in Swedish steel mills and facilitating mergers in the arms industry. He was always willing to take on foreign government work at a loss on the principle that it might lead to lucrative commercial opportunities in those countries.

Then, as now, there was an international race to win business in China. Following its military defeat by Japan in 1895, the country was in desperate need of foreign capital. Cassel's achievement in brokering a multinational loan of £33m made him admired in the Foreign Office as well as the Treasury. In Egypt, where Britain had

taken on a direct governing role since the 1880s, Cassel led investment in the Aswan Dam and Assyut Nile barrage, both of which were constructed by a British firm, Aird and Company.

In 1903, the foreign secretary, Lord Lansdowne, initially encouraged British involvement in a German plan to build a railway from Constantinople, the Turkish capital, to Baghdad to open up the oil and mineral resources in Mesopotamia (now Iraq). The idea was eventually to extend the line westwards to Berlin. Cassel and a City colleague arranged a 50-50 partnership with Deutsche Bank, but already there were widespread fears of the Kaiser's military ambitions, and Lansdowne, unnerved by anti-German outbursts in the popular press, withdrew Foreign Office support. Cassel persisted in trying to make British involvement work, helping to establish a Turkish national bank in 1908 to give financial credibility to the region. The partly-built project was abandoned on the outbreak of the Great War.

Even by the standards of his time, Cassel's working methods were remarkable. He had very few staff, was constantly on the move and rarely in his London office, juggling any number of simultaneous major international deals yet always available for meetings where decisions had to be taken. Despite this, he remained the supreme networker, finding time to entertain business and social contacts at his palatial

mansion on London's Park Lane and other homes at Newmarket (for the racing set), Cowes (for the yachting set) and Switzerland. He operated so fluidly and flexibly that he has left an aura of mystery behind, compounded by a lack of papers.

Not content with being a financial fixer, he was actively interested in the day-to-day management of his international ventures, taking a hand in the choice of managers and contractors. He sometimes served as a board director but preferred to act as a trusted adviser, a sort of senior non-executive or eminence grise. Almost alone among City financiers, he did not oppose Lloyd George's "People's Budget" of 1909, which most of Cassel's peers thought dangerously socialistic. But that was undoubtedly for tactical reasons; keeping in with the current government was always his philosophy. Later that year, he quietly shifted a large part of his assets to the US to escape the new Lloyd George taxes.

(Source: Business History, January 1986. Pat Thane: Financiers and the British State: the Case of Sir Ernest Cassel.)

aloof from domestic industry," says Kynaston.[7] A common criticism in industry was that British joint-stock banks lacked entrepreneurial ambition in comparison with their German counterparts, which then, as now, invested directly in their own country's industrial companies.

The City had its scandals in these years. In 1902, an embezzler from the mining company where Herbert Hoover worked went on trial. The following year saw the failure of a Lloyd's syndicate that foreshadowed the bigger crash 90 years later and caused The Economist to thunder that the public needed to be protected in its dealings with Lloyd's underwriters: "That he [the offending member] should have been allowed to go on unchecked… shows how complete a lack of control over individual members exists at Lloyd's."

But the City's leading financiers commanded enormous prestige on the international stage and were prominent in society, even in royal circles. Sir Ernest Cassel, one of Edward VII's intimate circle, exemplified their global reach, raising capital for infrastructure projects, arms deals, railway launches, oil contracts and mining ventures from Egypt to Russia, Turkey to China. He was regarded as the ablest man in the City and together with Sir Edgar Speyer, a backer simultaneously of the London Tube and the Baghdad Railway, represented the business face of imperialism. (See panel.) Such men saw the world as their oyster: when, during the 1906 election, Joseph Chamberlain in his campaign for protective tariffs suggested that holding large foreign investments might not be the best way to help British trade, he was publicly attacked by the City banker Sir Felix Schuster, on the grounds that placing British capital in foreign countries helped British exports to those countries and thus created jobs at home.

But what was also going on was a destructive dependence on imports, especially from Germany, in several key industries, among them machine tools, chemicals and scientific instruments. The British machine tool industry

had led the world in the first half of the 19th century, championed by figures such as Maudslay, who later went into motor cars, and Whitworth, the future armaments king. But US companies took the ascendant as early as 1850, especially with the milling machine, a tool that enabled gears to be cut for greater precision, rather than cast. It was a Vermont firm that supplied the British government with machine tools for arms manufacture in the Crimean War, and by 1865 there was a US distributor in London, Charles Churchill. In the late 1880s, his business was substantial enough to tool up the entire Gatling machine-gun works in Birmingham, which was run by an American manager.

Imports of US machine tools, cheaply produced by automation, boomed in the bicycle craze of the 1890s. They were often of inferior quality, but their manufacturers swept the market by mass-producing one or two models. In contrast, British firms were still offering an ambitious range along with multifarious other products – even torpedoes and turbines in one Manchester company. There was a revival of the British industry in the 1890s, led by Alfred Herbert of Coventry, then a small entrepreneurial start-up whose workforce rose from 12 in 1887 to 930 by 1903. Herbert, the son of a Leicestershire farmer, was alert to American production methods and by 1897 was employing an American engineer to re-organise his plant, which soon established itself as the finest in Europe.[8]

But on the whole, British machine tool makers relied on a few regular engineering clients and made little attempt to seek new markets or produce new designs. Like their compatriots in cars and locomotives, they worked to a craftsman tradition of solidly engineered, durable tools and left innovation to others, chiefly the Germans. Instead of trying to match or outdo the more advanced German and American products, British manufacturers between 1870 and 1914 were content to act as agents for them, leaving Britain dangerously exposed on the eve of the Great War in

Workers putting in the last plates at Bank, during the extension of the Central Line Underground railway, to Bank, London in 1912

an industry that was critical for the production of munitions. Far from living up to its past glories as the Workshop of the World, England by 1914, as Correlli Barnett acidly observed in The Collapse of British Power, "was well on the way to becoming a technological colony of the United States and Germany". Several major engineering contracts in the early 1900s, notably for British city tramways and the London Underground, were won by the American GEC and Westinghouse.

Machine tools were far from being the only key industry in which Britain depended on German imports. The same was true of ball-bearings, scientific and optical instruments and above all, chemicals, pharmaceuticals and dyestuffs. Britain had only one factory making ball-bearings and imported all the rest from Germany. Magnetos, on which all motorised vehicles depended, came almost entirely from the German firm of Bosch, even though the magneto had been jointly developed by Britain's F. R. Simms in partnership with Robert Bosch. In 1901, F. R. Simms had formed the Simms Manufacturing Company, but as one industrial historian has commented, "as happened all too often, he tried several other lines as well – engines, cars, vans, lorries – and did none of them properly. In 1907, Bosch purchased Simms's magneto department and henceforth supplied the British market entirely from Stuttgart."[9]

On and on went the catalogue of dependency,

depressingly chronicled in the 1920s in the government's own history of its ministry of munitions. Ninety per cent of optical glass for scientific instruments came from Germany; nearly all the chemical apparatus in British laboratories was of German manufacture. Most shocking of all was the almost complete lack of a chemical and pharmaceutical industry. Britain relied on German imports for dyestuffs (in which Germany led the world, producing 88 per cent of all synthetic dyes in 1914) and basic drugs such as aspirin, which had been invented by the Bayer company. Even after the outbreak of war the British government was forced to continue importing German drugs via neutral countries.

Britain's almost total dependence on Germany for synthetic dyes was, like the magneto story, the result of failure to follow through an early British invention. The first synthetic dye, the colour mauve, had been extracted from aniline by the chemist W. H. Perkin as early as 1856, and 13 years later Perkin synthesised alizarine, the red colouring of the madder plant, from a by-product of coal. Britain, with its abundant coal resources, looked about to take the world lead in the new aniline dye industry, but no sizeable British company was formed until the 1880s, by which time Perkin's patents had expired and German chemists were cracking the code.

In August 1914, when Britain was importing 75 per cent of its dyestuffs requirements from Germany, there was not enough khaki dye to supply Kitchener's armies. Volunteers trained in scratch uniforms made of surplus blue cloth – which they hated – and a 70-year-old judge, Lord Moulton, was brought out of retirement to weld together a number of domestic dyestuff companies in an early nationalised enterprise, British Dyes. Meanwhile, Germany's flourishing coal-tar industry, from which many of these synthetic products derived, was quickly adapted in August 1914 into the manufacture of high explosives. The bill was about to be presented for Britain's complacent readiness to let other nations catch the tide of innovation.

usiness far
from usual

66 The maxim of the British people is,
'Business as usual'. 99

**Winston Churchill, speech at the Guildhall,
November 9, 1914**

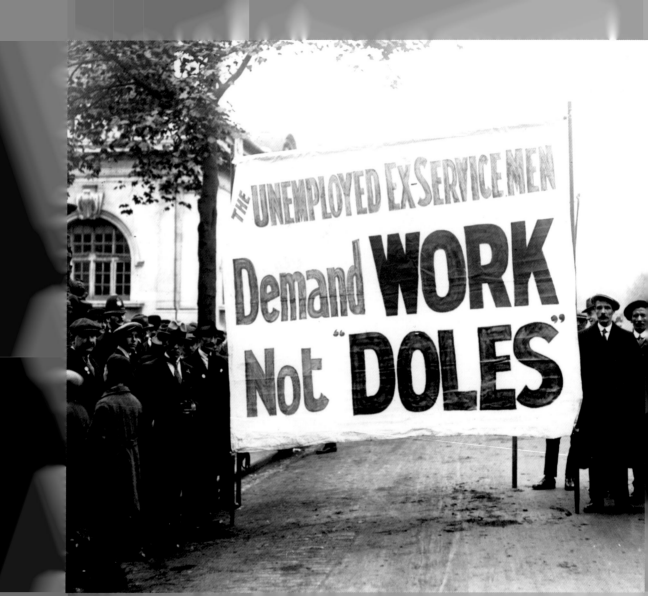

The First World War changed business life far more profoundly than the Second, shattering the trinity of beliefs in free trade, finance and enterprise that had ruled the pre-war world. As the European powers embarked on a conflict of unprecedented destruction, they ripped apart the web of trade and finance that had connected the advanced countries of the world and had led influential thinkers such as Norman Angell to say that a major international war could never happen because it would be against every country's self-interest.

The war brought an acceptance of collectivism and central government control that would never completely leave Britain and would be mightily reinforced in the 1940s. But it also had a galvanic effect on the old complacent attitudes that had for so long let British industry rest on its dusty laurels and held its practices back from innovation. It was, the historian Correlli Barnett vividly writes, "as if a portly and elderly retired gentleman had suddenly leapt from his armchair and embarked on a new career".

Between 1915 and 1918, Britain virtually carried out a second industrial revolution, dragging Victorian practices and attitudes into the 20th century and working flat out to fill the gaps in production and innovation that war had suddenly exposed. More than 200 new model factories were set up with government money, manufacturing everything from precision gauges and ball-bearings (Britain had only one ball-bearing plant in 1914, along with one magneto factory) to reinforced concrete slabs. Wire had to be manufactured to replace German and Belgian imports. "It would be hard to name a basic necessity of advanced industrial technology in which Britain was self-sufficient in 1914," says Barnett scathingly in The Collapse of British Power.

There were few light engineering or precision instrument plants and virtually no pharmaceutical industry: Britain had been heavily dependent on German drug companies, even for basic necessities such as aspirin. A few heavy chemical companies – among them, Tennants and Brunner, Mond – were leading producers of alkali commodities such as soda ash, chlorine and sulphuric acid, while Nobel's Explosives, founded by the Swedish inventor in Glasgow in 1871, led the world in the production of dynamite and gelignite. But Nobel's was linked so closely to sister companies in Germany that as late as June, 1914, just before the assassination of Archduke Franz Ferdinand triggered catastrophe, a conference of British, German and American explosive

Nobel's explosives works at Ardeer, Scotland, in the 1880s

manufacturers was meeting in London to discuss new market-sharing agreements.

In the dyestuffs industry, Hoechst, the German chemical firm, had been producing nearly all of Britain's indigo from a factory in Ellesmere Port. Coal tar, the basic constituent of aniline and anthracene dyes, was a key element in the manufacture of TNT – a fact German chemists had not been slow to exploit. Lord Moulton, the septuagenarian law lord chosen to create Britain's first nationalised industry – he had specialised in patent law as well as being a distinguished scientist knowledgeable in explosives – was one elderly retired gentleman who rose splendidly to the challenge of a new career. He not only created the British Dyestuffs Corporation but devised a formula for using less of the scarce TNT by combining it – in the teeth of brass-hat opposition – with ammonium nitrate, a commodity Brunner, Mond could manufacture in vast quantity.[1]

War on the scale that unfolded in 1914 was initially so unimaginable that for a while, as shockingly demonstrated in the "shell scandal" of spring 1915, supply and demand were grossly mismatched: just one artillery barrage before a big battle, it was found, could use up 1.5 million shells, three times the entire national output in 1914.[2]

Whole industries were created and productive capacity vastly developed during the four years of war. The electricity industry, which had been sluggish before 1914 because of the cheap availability of coal, was urgently modernised to power the new factories. Output of optical and scientific instruments ballooned 20-fold between 1914 and 1918, from £250,000 to £5m. An entire aircraft industry came into being; Sopwith, A. V. Roe and de Havilland would become household names by Armistice Day.

The price for this innovative surge, though, was a massive extension of state powers. The first emergency measures, rushed through as soon as Britain's ultimatum

THE CHANGING CENTURY

Facts from the business archives:

1914: The world's first feature-length colour film, The World, The Flesh and The Devil, opened at the Holborn Empire in London. A 1hr 40min melodrama, it was produced by the Union Jack Co. and shot in Kinemacolor, the two-colour system developed in Brighton by George Albert Smith in 1906

1914: The General Post Office (GPO) took over the privately run Portsmouth telephone system, leaving the City of Hull as the only place in Britain with its own telephone network

1915: A group of businessmen, concerned by the amount of excessive drinking among factory workers, now key to the war effort, asked the government to introduce prohibition.* The government refused but outlawed "treating": from October, anyone caught buying someone else a drink was liable for a £100 fine

1915: The circulation of the Daily Mail fell overnight from 1,386,000 to 238,000 after the paper's proprietor Lord Northcliffe wrote an article savaging Lord Kitchener for failure to equip British soldiers with high-explosive shells

1919: A. V. Roe introduced Britain's first scheduled civil airline service

in Britain. Two-seater biplanes flew holidaymakers between Alexander Park in Manchester to Blackpool and Southport. The return fare? Four guineas. In the same year, the North Sea Navigation Co. started flying businessmen between London (Hounslow) and the North (Hartlepool, Hull, Scarborough and Harrogate)

1919: The first international airline service out of Britain, and the first in the world with a daily schedule, began with Air Transport and Travel's 09.10 flight from Hounslow to Paris. The first passenger paid a single fare of £21 for the two-and-a-half-hour journey

1919: The first regular airmail service began in Britain. It was

inaugurated by Air Transport and Travel and carried letters between Hounslow and Paris

1919: The first Indian restaurants in Britain were opened in London's West End. The proprietor was a company called Indian Restaurants Limited

1920: The first beer mats appeared in Britain's pubs. They promoted Watney's Pale Ale and Reid's stout

*Alcohol abuse by factory workers had been a problem for decades. Attempts to introduce legislative curbs had been opposed by the Conservatives, who had links to the brewing and distilling industries.

Sources: Christopher Lee: This Sceptred Isle, Twentieth Century, BBC and Penguin Books, 1999; Patrick Robertson: The New Shell Book of Firsts, 1994, Headline Book Publishing

to Germany expired at 11pm London time on August 4, banished the pre-war freedoms in trading, finance and business practices. Within hours, 90 per cent of imports were under government control along with all shipping in British waters, all 130 railway companies and key industries such as fuel oil, metals, coal, textiles and, of course, food production, in which the civil servant William Beveridge – later to be the architect of Britain's welfare state – played a key organising role. The Cabinet moved swiftly to buffer any trading panic by imposing a one-month moratorium on debts and extending the August bank holiday to three days. Bank rate was pushed up to eight per cent. The gold sovereign, hitherto the only passport a British traveller needed around the globe, gave way to non-convertible banknotes to stave off a run on the gold reserves. No loans could be made or renewed without government approval.

It was the beginning of the end of London's pre-eminence as the hub of global finance, which soon shifted to New York. "The First World War was the worst thing that ever happened to the City of London," observes David Kynaston in his magisterial history of the City, quoting a merchant banker who said the war burst upon the Square Mile "like a bolt from the blue, and no-one was prepared." (As late as July 29, the Financial Times was reassuring its readers that the Liberal government of Herbert Asquith "may at least be trusted to keep this country out of the area of conflict.") Between 1914 and 1918 Britain had to liquidate 15 per cent of its massive overseas investments in order to pay for the war. These had totalled nearly £4bn on the eve of war, almost one-third of the entire national wealth, most of it invested outside Europe.

Many leading City banks such as Schroders, Kleinworts and Huths were under suspicion as "German houses", while respected City financiers of German background such as Sir Ernest Cassel and Sir Edgar

Entrepreneurs of the air: Thomas Sopwith and his seaplane, 1910, and (below) "Look, no hands" - A.V. Roe in his Avromobile. Both companies played a leading part in World War 1

Speyer (who had raised most of the capital for the London Tube) were hounded out of their business and social networks after the Cunard liner Lusitania was torpedoed in May 1915 and 1,198 people, including hundreds of women and children, were killed. Speyer emigrated to New York. Cassel was the target of an unsuccessful attempt to strip him of Privy Council membership. Both men were deeply embittered at their treatment.

Yet many branches of German firms, of which there were hundreds in Britain in 1914 (153 in Manchester alone, in chemicals, textiles and banking), continued to trade with impunity. British piano manufacturers protested through their trade association about the 32 German piano makers that continued to compete with them. Eventually, in 1916, an amendment to the Trading With the Enemy Act was passed enabling every German-origin business to be investigated, even if the owner had been resident for years, married into a British family and/or changed his name. Hundreds of cases were considered, from Siemens down to a family tailoring company with annual profits of £150, and the majority were wound up. British business benefited

from the forced sale of German assets: the English Electric Company was created by purchasing Siemens' dynamo works, GEC bought the German-owned shareholding in the Osram Lamp Works and the Anglo-Persian Oil Company acquired British Petroleum, a German oil marketing subsidiary in Britain linked with Deutsche Bank, although it would not adopt the BP name until 1954.[3]

Nineteen seventeen was a particular annus horribilis for the City. Baring's Bank was the London agent for the Tsarist government, which was overthrown in the October Revolution. After three years of war and air raids, the City's streets were largely deserted by 3pm. One bombing attack in June 1917, by planes rather than Zeppelins, killed 100 people and hit a train just leaving Liverpool Street station for Cambridge. The raid was witnessed by the poet Siegfried Sassoon, on leave from the trenches, as he cashed a cheque at his bank in Old Broad Street. "In a trench one was acclimatised to the notion of being exterminated and there was a sense of organised retaliation," he wrote. "But here one was helpless; an invisible enemy sent destruction spinning down from a fine

THE CHANGING CENTURY

A snapshot of science and technology:

1914: Middlesex Hospital in London announced that it had successfully used radium in the treatment of malignant tumours

1914-1918: Tanks, submarines, military aircraft, new machine guns and the use of radio signals to target missiles and locate the enemy changed for ever the concept of warfare; this was the dark side of the technological revolution sweeping the developed world

1915: Alexander Graham Bell worked out the technology to make a telephone call between

New York and San Francisco – a breakthrough in long-distance communications

1917: In America, AT&T installed the world's first telex service

1919: Professor Ernest Rutherford of Manchester University "split" the atom

1920: The Marconi company began transmitting speech and music from a 15kw transmitter at its Chelmsford works; British public broadcasting was born. The first "live radio concerts" featured members of Marconi's own engineering staff on piano, oboe and cornet

Listen with the family: wireless was social entertainment in 1922

Sources: Christopher Lee: This Sceptred Isle, Twentieth Century, BBC and Penguin Books, 1999; Patrick Robertson: The New Shell Book of Firsts, 1994, Headline Book Publishing

David Lloyd George and Winston Churchill. Which of them coined the slogan "Business as usual"? It caught on again in 1940

who really said it first?

Was it Lloyd George, Winston Churchill or a long-forgotten executive at W. H. Smith who coined the slogan "business as usual?" The phrase quickly became synonymous with the home front in the Great War and was seen again on many shattered shopfronts in the Blitz of 1940/41.

The association with Churchill, cited most recently in Niall Ferguson's The Pity of War, has little provenance, other than a speech at London's Guildhall on November 9, 1940, although along with other government ministers, he no doubt found it a convenient rallying cry. Historian Gerard J. DeGroot, in his 1996 book Blighty: British Society in the Era of the Great War, and London University lecturer David French, in a paper published in War and the State (1982), both quote David Lloyd George, chancellor of the exchequer, using it in a speech to reassure bankers and traders on August 4, even before war had been declared at 11pm.

An earlier history of the home front, Arthur Marwick's The Deluge: British Society and the First World War (1965), traces its first appearance to August 11, 1914, when Herbert Morgan, controller of printing at W. H. Smith, promoted it as the nation's slogan in a letter to the Daily Chronicle. Marwick was not infallible on dates (his book places the sinking of the Lusitania in April instead of May, 1915), but W. H. Smith's own house journal, The Newsbasket, also gives the credit to Morgan in its issue of July, 1915. (Charles Wilson: First With the News: The Story of W.H. Smith.)

The likeliest answer is that Morgan picked up the slogan at the Lloyd George meeting. He can certainly take the credit for disseminating it among the business community. But it was fairly short-lived. "Business as usual" was abandoned early in 1915 as the grim realities of war began to bite.

weather sky; poor old men bought a railway ticket and were trundled away again dead on a barrow…"[4]

But for the first few months of the war, Britain's financiers and traders subscribed willingly enough to the defiant slogan used by David Lloyd George, chancellor of the exchequer, when he assured a conference of bankers and businessmen on August 4 that the policy of the government was "to enable the traders of this country to carry on business as usual". A week later, an executive of the bookstall chain W. H. Smith took up his theme of

"business as usual" in a letter to the press. Harrods, the fashionable department store, then used the phrase in a prominent newspaper advertisement, a conference of advertisers and traders promoted it and soon it was in shop windows everywhere. (See panel: "Who really said it first?")

The phrase was more than just exhortation, however. Behind Lloyd George's use of it lay years of misplaced contingency planning for a war with Germany in which it was assumed that Britain's principal armed role would be left to the Royal Navy and its famous Dreadnoughts. The British regular army of 100,000 would join the allied armies of Europe to defeat Germany on land, leaving the domestic labour force more or less intact and able to gear up for war supplies. Britain's role, as one historian of the home front has put it, would be chiefly that of "the bank, the larder, the factory and the arsenal of the Entente".[5]

This comforting fantasy was exploded as early as August 5 when the formidable Field Marshal Lord Kitchener of Khartoum, "K of K", was appointed secretary of state for war. Kitchener was more far-sighted than some of his younger colleagues in high command. He predicted, correctly, that the war would last at least three years and he told a dismayed Cabinet, which had been calculating on a duration of nine months, that Britain must be prepared to put an army of "millions" into the field and keep them there. Kitchener's famous recruiting posters were only the beginning: it wasn't long before he called for two million volunteers, which completely scuppered the government's "business as usual" strategy. He did try to ban skilled men from volunteering but was overruled on the principle that this would contravene the labour laws as well as spoil the "spirit" of volunteering.

Soon, labour shortages became starkly evident: among the first volunteers were 10,000 skilled engineers, 145,000 construction workers and 160,000 coal miners. In the first year of war, a quarter of workers in electrical

engineering enlisted, nearly the same proportion from the chemical industry and more than 20 per cent from coal-mining and the metal trades. Old John Lewis, the curmudgeonly founder of the department store group, complained to the recruiting authorities that his staff had been reduced to a collection of "waifs and strays". John Benjamin Sainsbury, son of the grocery chain's founder, tried to persuade his young managers that their job was as important to the war effort as getting into khaki. Despite his efforts, more than a thousand of Sainsbury's male staff volunteered before conscription came in, and a third of those in their early twenties never came home. By Armistice Day, each of the firm's 128 branches on average had lost four men.[6]

Later in the war, an attempt was made to set up a "ministry of national service" to direct and manage the country's diminished labour resources. It was to be headed by Neville Chamberlain, a former mayor of Birmingham who would become the "appeasement" prime minister in the 1930s, but it never got beyond the planning stage. Most of the unions, apart from the miners, agreed to forgo strike action for the duration and take disputes to arbitration, but the price was that their structure grew much more bureaucratic and entrenched. One major strike early in the war, prompted by the Glasgow engineering firm Weir hiring American workers

THE CHANGING CENTURY

A snapshot of Britain:

1914: As the storm gathered in the Balkan states, Britain was almost being brought to a standstill by industrial action. In the summer of 1914, more than two million workers – mainly builders, miners and railwaymen – were on strike

1914: Spring and early summer saw

increased activism from suffragettes, much of it violent in nature. Sylvia Pankhurst (younger daughter of Emmeline) was arrested twice. Fellow suffragette, Mary Richardson, was sentenced to six months after vandalising a painting of Venus in the National Gallery. She was force-fed in prison

1914: The war started on August 4. By November, it was costing

approximately £1m* a day. Britons were asked to help pay the bill in a budget that doubled the rates of income tax and supertax (the surcharge on high earners) and raised the duties on beer and tea. Further tax increases were announced the next year

1914/1915: The number of women in the workforce increased by two million. Thousands of girls aged 14

and over went to work in munitions factories. Many worked 12 hours a day and seven days a week for an average wage of 32 shillings (£1.60)

1916: Conscription was introduced, and the government began a campaign to encourage more women to take up jobs traditionally done by men. It announced equal pay – provided the woman did as good a job as a man

at a higher wage than the local rate, not only caused 5,000 engineers to down tools but for the first time raised the shop steward, previously an unimportant functionary, to a threatening position of power in industrial relations.

The unions grudgingly agreed to the employment of women to fill the gaps in the factories, some stipulating that they should only operate automatic machines, after they had been set up by men. At first their main use was in the munitions factories, which saw a rush of working-class women eager to escape their only alternative form of employment, the drudgery of domestic service. In August 1915, a trade magazine observed patronisingly that women seemed able to perform not only repetitive tasks demanding "little or no manipulative ability" but also work that "taxed the intelligence of the operatives to a high degree". Grudgingly, the writer added that "the work turned out has reached a high pitch of excellence…"

Sir Charles Addis of the Hongkong and Shanghai Bank, otherwise by all accounts a cultured and gentlemanly character, justified the lower wages paid to women on the grounds that they were only two-thirds as efficient as men on account of "the inability of the female sex to stand a prolonged strain, their more frequent absence from work, and their liability to nervous breakdown in the face of

Munitions workers in 1915. A gender revolution took place in World War 1 as some two million women joined the labour force

1916: A proposal to allow women to work in the docks in Liverpool had to be abandoned because of opposition from male workers

1916: Supplies of guns to the front were threatened by striking workers at a munitions factory in Clydeside

1916: A royal commission was set up to investigate the rise in the number of cases of venereal disease. It found that in Britain's largest cities as much

as 10 per cent of the population was infected by syphilis and that even more had gonorrhoea; prostitutes were haunting every army camp

1917: The movement of troops helped spread a flu epidemic, which, by 1919, had claimed millions more lives worldwide than the war**

1918: The number of men killed in action stood, on conservative estimates, at 10 million; Britain and

her colonies had lost 947,000 troops

1918: H. A. L. Fisher's Education Bill was introduced. It raised the school leaving age to 14

1918: Dr Marie Stopes's book, Married Love, came out. Its discussion of sexual habits and contraception shocked the nation

1919: As the war effort was dismantled, women lost their jobs.

By 1920, there were fewer women in work than there had been before the war

*at 1914 prices

**estimates vary between 20 and 70 million

Sources: Christopher Lee: This Sceptred Isle, Twentieth Century, BBC and Penguin Books, 1999; Patrick Robertson: The New Shell Book of Firsts, 1994, Headline Book Publishing

Making light of heavy work: women even worked as railway porters, replacing men away at the war

THE CHANGING CENTURY

Key developments in British politics:

1914: The Irish Home Rule Bill was introduced into the Commons. Opposition from Unionists was fierce; civil war in Ireland looked increasingly likely

1915: Arthur Henderson became the first socialist cabinet minister. He was appointed President of the Board of Trade in Asquith's coalition government

1916: Padraic Pearse, commander of the Irish Republican Brotherhood (the forerunner of the IRA), led 2,000 armed men into the centre of Dublin in what became known as the Easter Rising. Pearse and fellow ringleaders were executed by British soldiers. Their martyrdom greatly aided the Republican cause

1917: The Foreign Secretary, former prime minister Arthur Balfour, declared Britain's support for the "establishment in Palestine of a national home for the Jewish people"

1918: The Representation of the People Act gave women the vote – provided they were at least 30 years of age and either rate-payers or rate-payers' wives

1918: The post-war general election marked a watershed in politics. The Liberal Lloyd George was re-elected but on an essentially right-wing ticket. His coalition Liberals were in alliance with the Conservatives and at odds with the "pacifists" in the Liberal camp who had opposed conscription. The Liberal party, weakened by internal divisions, was receding; the Labour party, which won 57 seats and

sudden emergency".[7] Despite this, the banking and finance sector saw a phenomenal growth in female employment during the war years, from 9,500 in 1914 to 63,700 in 1917.

The coming of conscription in 1916 finally let down the drawbridge. By that summer, women were becoming a familiar sight in the transport infrastructure as tram and bus conductors, ticket collectors, railway guards and van drivers as well as taking on strenuous industrial cleaning, delivery and farm-working jobs previously done by men. Out of sheer necessity, women at last became recognised in professions such as medicine: the first year of war saw the demand for women doctors far outstrip the numbers who had qualified up to that time. Middle-class women flocked to join the Voluntary Aid Detachment of auxiliary nurses, including the writers Agatha Christie and Vera Brittain, the mother of Baroness Shirley Williams. Around 100,000 joined the newly established women's sections of the armed forces.

Historians differ on the total numbers of women who came into the labour force, changing the face of industry and commerce, but nearly 200,000 served in government departments, 500,000 moved into offices to replace male clerical workers and 250,000 worked on the land. Biggest of all were the numbers employed on munitions and in other engineering trades; almost 800,000 in the first year of war. The suffragette leader Christabel Pankhurst had made her point when she led a march of 30,000 down Whitehall in the summer of 1915 under the banner "We demand the right to serve".[8]

Meanwhile, business was encouraged to look on the war as an opportunity to exploit markets that were now closed to enemy countries. Patent laws were relaxed so that British firms could manufacture German products that had been dominant imports, especially toys, clocks and glassware. (One German invention that was quickly copied was the gas-mask.) A Liberal MP with the flamboyant name of Leo Chiozza Money was determined to look upon the bright side. He assured British traders that the war meant they could "confidently count upon several years freedom from German competition".

But many small firms were unable to invest in the production facilities that would have enabled them to tap the new markets, and there were worries that any commercial benefits from the war would not outlast it and therefore not justify radical change. In London, almost one third of companies with fewer than 100 employees reported that trade was suffering because of a shortage of credit. There were no such restraints on their bigger

polled two and a half million votes, was slowly but surely emerging as the new opposition

1918: Sinn Fein, which had won 73 out of 81 seats in Southern Ireland, withdrew from Westminster and set up its own unofficial parliament in Dublin. The Dail was born

1918: Fabian Society founder Sydney Webb wrote the outline for the constitution of the Labour Party. It included clause four, the pledge to nationalise many of Britain's major industries, including banks and other commercial institutions

1918: Sinn Fein's Constance Gore-Booth became the first woman to be elected as an MP but never took her seat: she refused to swear an oath of allegiance to the monarch

1919: Nancy Astor became the first woman to take a seat in Westminster, succeeding her husband as member for the Sutton division of Plymouth

1919: The Irish Republican Army (IRA) was founded, led by Michael Collins

1919: The British army killed 379 demonstrators at Amritsar in India. Gandhi responded with a campaign of civil disobedience; control was slowly slipping away from the Raj

1920: The Communist Party of Great Britain (CPGB) was formed; the MP Lt. Col. Cecil L'Estrange Malone, who had been converted to communism in 1919, was given a six months' prison sentence for sedition

1920: Large parts of Ireland were brought under martial law

Sources: Christopher Lee: This Sceptred Isle, Twentieth Century, BBC and Penguin Books, 1999; Patrick Robertson: The New Shell Book of Firsts, 1994, Headline Book Publishing

Mrs. Emmeline Pankhurst, matriarch of the women's suffrage movement, being forcibly arrested in a 1914 demonstration

brothers, growing fat on war contracts. Traders in scarce supplies could virtually name their own price and obtain contracts by issuing options, without even having the goods in stock. Banks fell over each other to issue credit on War Office contracts. Lord Brand, a director of Lloyds Bank, recalled in 1919 his impression of wartime board meetings as occasions "when we ladled out money… because everybody said they were making and were going to make large profits".[9]

The war was barely eight months old when a new term of business abuse – "profiteering" – came into everyday use, though it would not enter the dictionaries for another 20 years. Shipowners in particular were well placed to inflate their already substantial personal wealth. Although some 40 per cent of the merchant fleet was lost, German ships were acquired in return and handsome profits made. The upright Andrew Bonar Law, chancellor of the exchequer in 1917, was driven to tell the House of Commons how shocked he was at the size of his shipping dividends. Profits in the industry were running at a third higher even after payment of the excess profits tax, introduced in 1916 but acknowledged just a year later to have failed as a moral restraint.[10]

It was not always a case of deliberate greed. Demand for essential supplies and services such as shipping was so intense that profits could not help but rocket. Although the government had the power to requisition, it persisted in the early years in buying on the open market. One newcomer to the woollen trade made £150,000 in six months simply through buying and selling yarn. Businessmen bargained with the government over prices, and were not compelled to reveal their costs until 1916. Many genuinely feared that having prices held down would hamper their ability to compete after the war.

Greed was there, nevertheless. Some exporters were shameless in demanding their right to continue supplying German markets so long as the products were non-military. In this they found surprising support from The Economist, which argued speciously that one-way trade with Germany would deplete Berlin of its foreign exchange.[11] Although trading with the enemy had been outlawed within a month of the outbreak of war, there were ambiguous loopholes that were not closed until 1916. For goods shipped to neutral countries, the government left it to exporters to determine their ultimate destination and, as with Iraq and other dictatorships in our own time, many did not inquire too deeply.

Lloyd George was forced to admit as early as January 1915 that the government turned a blind eye to many cases of profiteering in order to ensure continuation of supplies. The first requisition order of the war, however, was imposed as a result of one bare-faced piece of profiteering: a Dundee jute merchant had tried to charge the War Office three times the regular price of sandbags.[12] Later, the government admitted that profiteering had seriously damaged the national unity shown early in the war.

Nowhere was this more evident than in public outrage at the way food prices were soaring to the benefit of producers. Helplessly, the government's first food controller, Lord Devonport, told Lloyd George that "profiteering is rife in every commodity: bread, meat, tea, butter". The masses, he said, were being "exploited right and left".[13] A Welsh flour-milling company, Spillers and Bakers, was exposed in May 1915 as having paid dividends to its shareholders swollen by an additional 54 per cent.[14] In October 1916, a major Commons debate on profiteering revealed many similar cases, and in the following year a tougher food controller was appointed, the Welsh coal-owner and shipowner D. A. Thomas, Lord Rhondda, who attacked food profiteers as "blackmailers". Eventually a Profiteering Act was introduced, under which many small shopkeepers were prosecuted.

Biscuit manufacturers were some of the few food producers to emerge with an unsullied reputation, and Huntley and Palmer enjoyed a deserved boom in sales. Other exemplars of public-spiritedness were Dunlop, which held the commercial price of tyres steady despite having to supply the government at controlled prices, and Shell, which hired out its tankers to the government at pre-war rates and even tried to reduce the price of petrol. The latter was, sadly, ill-rewarded for its efforts: it suffered a damaging run on supplies when its competitors failed to follow its lead and unfairly took the rap when every oil company's prices rose.[15]

While many industrialists were admired for a willingness to think about the greater good – Herbert Austin and William Morris, for example, switched their car plants to government use for little or no financial benefit – on others, the verdict was mixed. Pilkingtons saw huge growth from the shutdown of glass imports from the Continent, especially occupied Belgium, but still substantially increased prices. Yet no-one could accuse this family-owned business of unpatriotism: on the declaration of war, three family directors had volunteered for the army, two of them winning the DSO. The third, Austin Pilkington, joined up in 1916 well over age at 45. Pilkingtons also donated to charity its wartime revenue from shell production.[16] The drug industry, meanwhile, gained a bad reputation: a parliamentary committee found that hugely excessive prices were charged for aspirin, in which the German patent lead, held by Bayer before the war, was now open to all-comers.

Legitimately, of course, any industry supplying war needs was bound to prosper. By 1916, profits in coal, shipbuilding, iron and steel and engineering had risen by a third. Cammell Laird, the shipbuilder, recorded a rise of 74 per cent.[17] Motor vehicle production boomed, ratcheting up demand for flat glass, tyres and petroleum with consequent benefits to Pilkingtons, Dunlop and the fast-growing Shell and Anglo-Persian Oil. By the end of 1918, the last was a massively bigger and more powerful company than it had been in 1914.[18] Rolls-Royce switched to producing armoured cars (the Silver Ghost proved a reliable staff car, and T. E. Lawrence had one in the desert), while William Morris's plant with its American-style assembly techniques proved ideal for the production of a new mine-laying mechanism.[19] Brunner, Mond and Nobel's, the two main companies supplying explosives, were natural beneficiaries, the latter increasing its profits by 150 per cent – on conservative estimates. By 1918, the UK chemical industry as a whole had narrowed the pre-war gap with Germany.

Even products not directly connected with the war did well, thanks to increasing consumer demand generated by higher pay and wage-earning women. Lever Brothers, which became the UK's second largest manufacturing company by 1919, captured the lucrative market for margarine when Dutch exports dried up. It also saw a big rise in soap consumption. Courtaulds enjoyed greatly increased sales of its artificial silk – rayon – at premium prices as women's earning power made itself felt. There was a longing for glamorous fabrics after days spent in drab overalls at a factory bench filling shells or fitting fuses. By 1920, Courtaulds was the world's largest producer of rayon, and its market capitalisation had risen to £12m – from just £2m in 1914.

Women were also taking to cigarettes in a big way, and Imperial Tobacco grew fat on the huge wartime rise in smoking among both sexes: by 1920 it controlled 72 per cent of the UK cigarette and tobacco market. Massive increases in excise duty early in the war proved no deterrent: an advertisement for a pipe tobacco called Murray's Mellow Mixture pleaded "Don't stop smoking because tax on tobacco has increased. It is your duty to the State to keep on smoking".[20] Patriotism was a popular card for advertisers to play, even in the most unlikely contexts. In

October 1914, the Wolsey underwear company warned women readers of the Daily Mail to take care what they were buying because "there is a great deal of unmarked German-made underwear about".[21]

Britain's business landscape changed in the war, its predominantly small-scale companies giving way to larger units through amalgamation. In 1915, the five main London transport companies merged, as did the city's principal milk distributors, which became United Dairies. Steel companies such as Dorman Long, GKN and Stewarts and Lloyds moved into the top 50 companies through acquisition and merger. By the end of the war, 43 banks had become the Big Five, and by 1921, 130 railway companies – among the biggest businesses in the land – would be grouped into just four.

In 1916, the Federation of British Industries (later the Confederation, the CBI), came into being to promote the interests of manufacturers "in a manner commensurate with their strength and importance".[22] Business and the trade unions were pulled into a closer relationship by the national emergency, and many companies acknowledged for the first time the right of their workers to join a union. The board of one that did, Imperial Tobacco, was persuaded by the advantages of standardised wage-setting and union discipline keeping difficult workers in line. [23]

Businessmen were drafted into government in unprecedented numbers. The all-important ministry of munitions, formed in June, 1915, in response to the government's shambolic and wasteful procurement methods, which had led to the shell shortage, was entirely staffed and run by businessmen.[24] They soon became used to the idea of state intervention, which would once have been regarded as threatening and socialistic. Some managed to combine official work with running their companies, though government demands depleted a number of boardrooms; three directors at John Brown, the

Clydeside shipbuilder, were seconded during 1916-17.

Working in Whitehall was said to be draining in other ways. Sir Alfred Mond, of whom Lloyd George said "no better business brain has ever been placed at the disposal of the state in high office" (he was first commissioner of works in Lloyd George's wartime administration), observed with commendable frankness that "a curiously paralysing influence seems to come over everybody as soon as they begin to work for the state".[25]

Those over military age or protected by reserved occupation status are generally agreed, with a minority of profit-seeking exceptions, to have served the country well in the four-year crisis. Correlli Barnett's metaphor about old gentlemen leaping out of their armchairs came close to literal truth: retired managers did leave their gardens and golf courses to return to the fray. Many gave up holidays and put in long working hours. (Dudley Docker, an ebullient Midlands industrialist given to colourful over-statement, said that managers were suffering as much stress as soldiers on the battlefield.) Several wealthy businessmen, including Sir Alfred Mond, Marcus Samuel and William Lever, later Lord Leverhulme, gave generously to the Red Cross and other war charities.

But if business served the nation well in war, how much had it learned for the peace? Structurally, businesses had

Sir Alfred Mond, Britain's most influential businessman after World War 1, outside 10 Downing Street in 1922. In 1926 his chemicals company Brunner, Mond would become one of the four founding firms in the new ICI

been shaken up and loosened, in many cases, from the rigid bonds of family ownership through amalgamations; they had been spurred into new products and markets and taken the leap into some new technologies, but there was still a failure to take full advantage of change, or to realise that a temporary effort would not be enough to sustain success. Short-term horizons, as ever, bounded their vision, and as one commentator observed, the "gentlemen v. players" culture in British industry survived the war unscathed.[26]

Like most comfortably off Britons, perhaps, businessmen assumed that peace would automatically restore the status quo in which they had been accustomed to operate. After all, Britain had emerged victorious, with a little help from its friends across the pond. "Wartime profits and the defeat of Germany lulled the senses and led to the belief that somehow peace would deliver to Britain the kind of economic ascendancy she had enjoyed in late Victorian years…"[27] In 1919, imports were back to within 12 per cent of their 1913 levels and the balance of payments was in surplus again.

Historians agree that on the whole British businessmen in a range of major industries failed to exploit the benefits and opportunities that wartime conditions provided. This could also be said of the post-war government: for example, medical science had blossomed during the war through

All out! Even the police go on strike in 1919 amid fears of red revolution in Britain

Association, crystallised the two cultures when, arguing for nationalisation of the coal mines, he said that left to themselves businessmen simply produced "slums and millionaires".[28]

For a year or two after the euphoric celebrations of November 11, 1918, Britain seemed to have survived the economic trauma – if not the long lists of the "lost generation" and bereaved families in every street – surprisingly well. As controls fell away (though rationing continued for years, lasting in the case of sugar until the end of November 1920) industry enjoyed a boom period.

However, wages and prices were rising fast and inflation was waiting in the wings. Strikes returned with a vengeance, affecting the cotton and iron industries, the London police and the national railway network. Things turned nasty in Glasgow in January 1919 over demands for a 40-hour week, culminating in the government ordering in troops, tanks and machine-guns in "the battle of George Square". There was real fear of a British revolution, and indeed Willie Gallacher, an activist on "Red Clydeside", admitted years later: "We were carrying on a strike when we ought to have been making a revolution".[29]

The brief boom ended in late 1920 and was followed by a long and deep depression. It was not going to be easy – and perhaps not even possible – for Britain to return to business as usual.

the Medical Research Committee, producing valuable work on antiseptics and infectious diseases such as dysentery and typhoid. After the Armistice, this impetus fell apart for lack of funds, although the Committee did stay in being, and was renamed the Medical Research Council in 1920. (Its North London centre, the National Institute for Medical Research, has been responsible for five Nobel Prizes as well as identifying the influenza virus in 1933.)

Scientific advances tended to remain within the orbit of state control and there was little meeting of minds between top scientists and the business community. Sir Charles Parsons, the esteemed inventor of the steam turbine who by 1919 was president of the British

in never-
never land

66 This was the England of arterial and
by-pass roads, of filling stations and factories
that look like exhibition buildings, of giant
cinemas and dance-halls and cafes,
bungalows with tiny garages, cocktail bars,
Woolworths, motor-coaches, wireless,
hiking, factory girls looking like actresses,
greyhound racing and dirt tracks, swimming
pools, and everything given away for
cigarette coupons. 99

J.B. Priestley, English Journey, 1934

3

The defining image of the Depression, as unemployed men march from Tyneside to London

S urveying the serried ranks of businessmen around him in the new Conservative-Liberal coalition parliament of December 1918, Stanley Baldwin famously observed that they were "a lot of hard-faced men who look as if they had done very well out of the war". A political enemy might have said the same of Baldwin himself, a former industrialist whose family iron and steel business in Worcestershire had made fat profits out of government war contracts. But Baldwin was a man of principle, much under-rated in the decades since his three premierships. He gave £120,000 of his war profits to the Treasury as a contribution to the national debt, which had soared frighteningly to pay for the war, from £620m in 1914 to nearly £8bn in 1920.

Of the three great economic shocks that hit British industry in the first third of the 20th century, the Great War was to have by far the worst and longest-lasting impact, despite the modernising impetus it gave to many sectors. Neither Britain's ill-judged return to the gold standard in 1925, which immediately made British exports uncompetitive and sent unemployment through the roof, nor the 1929 Wall Street crash and subsequent international slump had anything like the same dislocating effect. Industrial production was not to return to its 1914 levels until fuelled by rearmament in 1937, while the inflated profits and prices of 1914-18 created unrealistic expectations of Britain's ability to compete in the resumption of global trading.[1]

Industry had also been changed utterly during the war years by the scale of central government control. To some extent this was beneficial, resulting among other things in the creation of a sizeable chemical industry, the consolidation of 130 railway companies into four and an effective machine-tool trade association that helped its members complement rather than compete wastefully with each other in international markets. But there was also an

enervating aspect. Business leaders acquiesced in centralisation to such an extent that some business historians today think nationalisation could just as well have occurred after 1918 as after 1945. David Lloyd George, prime minister for the last two years of the war, told a delegation of the fledgling Labour Party in 1917 that society was so "molten" that Labour could imprint almost anything on it, "so long as you do it with firmness and determination".[2]

In fact, the top priority of all three governments in the decade after the war (coalition 1918-22, Conservative 1922-24 and Labour 1924-29) was to restore business to its freebooting status of 1914 or "normalcy", as the new US president, Warren Harding, chose to call it. "Home rule for industry" was the watchword in Whitehall and Westminster.

At first, there seemed a good chance of this happening. The wild celebrations of Armistice Day, November 11, 1918, were followed by a euphoric two-year industrial and speculative boom, fuelled by such government pump-priming as the short-lived "homes for heroes" housing programme. This collapsed in 1921 when the Treasury, fearing that the economy was overheating, pulled the plug on its subsidies to local authorities for house-building.[3] On a wider front, business optimism for the post-war world was to prove wildly unrealistic.

The dominance of Britain's old commodity industries such as steel, coal and cotton was on the wane, but no-one could see it, cushioned as they had been by government war contracts. Overseas markets that had closed down as a result of the war found other suppliers or built up their own producers, and Britain was left with her low-margin imperial markets, some of which would soon begin to undercut British exports themselves. Britain's unbalanced imperial role, in which she failed lamentably to exploit the empire's business benefits, was a drain on the post-war economy: Malaya produced 56 per cent of the world's rubber and 31 per cent of the world's tin, for example, yet

Britain bought 20 per cent of her rubber elsewhere and took only 10 per cent of Malayan tin exports.[4]

The empire for its part never hesitated to wage its own protectionism, as in the Ottawa Agreement of 1932, which defeated Britain's attempt to impose import duties as a way of regulating her balance of payments after abandoning the gold standard. Britain ended by agreeing to take more imports from imperial markets and to export less to them. The only benefit – but one that became a near-fatal stranglehold after the Second World War – was the emergence of a "sterling area" in which Empire or Commonwealth countries traded in sterling, thus helping to stabilise the British currency after its break with gold.

Coal and cotton were the two staple industries hardest hit by economic conditions after 1918. The war had caused a massive fuel switch from coal to oil, especially in shipping, and oil exploration was booming in the newly discovered Persian oilfields and in the US. Cruelly, the cotton industry enjoyed its best-ever year of productivity in 1920, furnishing a third of all British exports – even higher than in 1913. The cotton owners ploughed money into new mills and machinery. Then depression struck in 1921. Export markets fell away, the victim of lower-cost producers – notably in India. Many of those shiny new mills never went into production; workers all over Lancashire were thrown out of their jobs.

Meanwhile, the war had sent the cost of living soaring: by 1920 it was 125 per cent higher than in 1914. Unit costs in industry were rising steeply, as organised labour flexed its newly discovered muscle. The pre-war working week of 56 hours was now down to 48, and unions were clamouring for 40. Employment patterns had changed as a result of around two million women coming into the workforce during the war, nearly all of them members of trade unions. "Lady

THE CHANGING CENTURY

A snapshot of science and technology:

1922: Insulin was isolated by Dr Frederick Banting at the University of Toronto Medical School

1925: A medical team at Guy's Hospital in London used insulin to treat a six-year-old diabetic girl

1926: In America, space travel pioneer Robert H. Goddard produced the first rocket to be powered by liquid fuel

1926: John Logie Baird demonstrated television to the public

1926: Marconi in Britain and RCA in America introduced the world's first

transatlantic facsimile transmission service, designed for sending news photos, facsimile signatures, plans and documents etc. to and from New York

1927: Charles Lindbergh made the world's first non-stop solo transatlantic flight, covering the 3,600 miles between New York and Paris in 33½ hours

1928: Dr Alexander Fleming of St Mary's Hospital, London, discovered penicillin

1930: The world's first general purpose analogue computer was built by Vannevar Bush at MIT, Boston

1935: Britain's first general purpose analogue computer was built by

Douglas Hartree and Arthur Porter of Manchester University

1936: The BBC inaugurated the first public high-definition television service. Broadcast from Alexandra Palace, it marked the arrival of television as an entertainment medium. Transmission, though, stopped when war began

1935: The government built Britain's first air-defence radar (radio detection and ranging) stations. By 1939, a chain of 20 stations, stretching from Ventnor to the Firth of Tay, was on continuous watch

1939: John Logie Baird (above right) received colour television, transmitted from Crystal Palace to his home in Sydenham

1939: Professor Otto Hahn published his work on nuclear fission. He won the Nobel Prize for chemistry in 1944 but was unable to attend the awards ceremony: he was then being held prisoner by the British

Sources: Christopher Lee: This Sceptred Isle, Twentieth Century, BBC and Penguin Books, 1999; Patrick Robertson: The New Shell Book of Firsts, 1994, Headline Book Publishing

typewriters", as the operators of those new-fangled machines were known, were now a common sight in offices across the land, and women at last had the vote – although only if they were over 30 and either householders or the wives of householders.

Wages, which had risen to ensure non-stop war production, were at an uneconomic level, but any move by the employers to reduce them ran up against fierce union opposition. The TUC contained a powerful "triple alliance" between miners, dockers and railwaymen, wielding a threat of national shutdown that eventually happened in 1926. Government tried to recognise the new realities by setting up "trade boards" to regulate minimum wages in different industries, but these were only partially effective, and the Treasury didn't like them. It would be another 70 years before a national minimum wage was written into law.

The early 1920s were riven with labour unrest: in 1921, around 90 million days were lost to strike action, second only to 1926 with 162 million days. The ill-advised return to the pre-war gold standard in 1925, coupled with higher interest rates, had the effect of hitting British exports and skewing the balance of payments, squeezing manufacturers' profits and throwing people out of jobs. Unemployment rose to around 10 per cent and became the dominant political issue. Between 1931 and 1933, when the world was gripped by depression, one in five were out of work.

It is hard now to understand why the Treasury and the Bank of England persuaded the chancellor of the exchequer, Winston Churchill, to return to gold. The decision, which was to sully Churchill's reputation, pegged sterling to the US dollar at a wildly overvalued $4.86 all the way through the Wall Street crash of 1929 and the global fall-out that followed. The British economy only began to recover after the National Government, the all-party coalition of 1931, ended the experiment. At the time,

'Lady typewriters' at work: by 1920, the typing pool was a feature of big company offices throughout Britain

however, Lord Bradbury, a former head of the Treasury, believed the return to gold was the only "knave-proof" way of removing monetary policy from political manipulation, while Montagu Norman, governor of the Bank of England, called it the best "governor" of a stable currency.

Among industrialists who tried to counter their soaring costs by cutting wages were the pit owners, who were feeling the effects of resumed German coal production in the Ruhr. There had already been one bitter coal strike in 1921, and in the summer of 1925 there was another when the employers unilaterally ended an agreement on wages and hours from the previous year. The miners immediately rejected this with the slogan, "Not a penny off the pay, not a minute on the day". Nearly a year later on May 4, 1926, their allies in the docks and on the railways joined them and the general strike began. Transport was all but halted across the country; the printing trades joined in, so did the iron and steel and engineering unions and those in construction, metals, heavy chemicals and the electricity and gas utilities. The only union members to continue working were journalists, firemen and electrical engineers.

Popular myth portrays the nine-day strike as an amiable, Ealing-comedy class skirmish, with Oxford and Cambridge undergraduates driving London buses under the eye of benevolent bobbies. This was far from the whole truth, especially in the depressed northern towns where violence broke out, though no lives were lost. But it is extremely difficult to find any figures for the financial cost of the general strike, which suggests that it was not easy to quantify. Major manufacturing firms such as Pilkingtons do not seem to have suffered directly, though their half-year profits fell from March to September because of the continuing coal strike, which is on record as costing the economy £150m.

When the general strike was settled by the lawyer Sir

Herbert Samuel, the miners rejected his proposals for a resumption of negotiations and for disputes to be referred to a national wages board. Embittered, they dragged out their strike for another seven months before being forced to return for no gain. The Baldwin government then swiftly brought in the Trade Disputes Act of 1927, which banned sympathetic strikes and made intimidation illegal.

Deeper-rooted problems within British management also contributed to the collapse of post-war business hopes. As early as 1916, the steel and engineering industries had expected to profit from a big post-war export trade to the US, yet none of their leaders seemed to show any awareness of the technical advances happening across the Atlantic. In 1925, the director of the British Engineers' Association, representing 440 firms, was asked by a government committee when he had last visited the US to acquaint himself with the latest technical developments. His answer was 1899.

Years of drama: left to right, in the 1926 General Strike, Oxford students volunteer to keep services going; food deliveries are protected by convoy;

The Balfour Committee on Trade and Industry in 1929 delivered a harsh verdict on the conservatism that encrusted both management and labour, and made Britain so different from the US. Employers were reluctant to scrap old plant that was still usable, while trade unions clung to obsolete habits that prevented them getting the best out of machinery at the lowest cost. In particular, the Balfour Report attacked the "artificial hard and fast lines of demarcation between different skilled crafts, or between workers of different grades of skill" that impeded the ability to adapt to rapid economic change.

Industries still stuck in the past "threw away the financial advantages which the war gave them", one business historian, writing in the 1990s, has observed. All kinds of modern business practices were ignored. Cost accounting was virtually unknown in Britain; "even the depreciation of fixed assets was handled in a hit and miss way". And, as would be seen again and again throughout

the century, British business leaders simply did not understand the importance of marketing.[5] War profits were often not invested wisely, and there always seemed to be more money at the turn of a tap, to the extent that easy credit from the clearing banks has been blamed for the eruption of serious post-war inflation. Throughout the 1920s, indeed, the banks behaved as irresponsibly – technically "lending short" on inadequate collateral – as they would in the housing bubble of the late 1980s.

For some leading companies, however, this period of easy credit would be a key stage in their expansion, enabling them to raise new capital and lay sound foundations for a long future. Among these firms were: Courtaulds, which doubled its share capital to £4m in 1919 and trebled it to £12m in the following year; Pilkingtons, which benefited by providing window-glass for the brief post-war housing boom; and Lever Brothers, which prospered on a national upsurge in demand for soap.[6] Lever Brothers would soon

a strike-breaking bus is armoured in barbed wire; a City commuter turns train guard. Far right: the Wall Street Crash, 1929

Soap production at Lever Brothers, 1929 meets a rising demand for household goods

grow even faster through amalgamation, in a period that would not be matched for ambitious mergers until the 1960s.

The biggest of the inter-war amalgamations were Unilever, formed in 1930 by the joining of Lever Bros to its Dutch margarine partner, and Imperial Chemical Industries in 1926, a four-way tie-up between Brunner Mond, Nobel Industries, United Alkali and British Dyestuffs Corporation, the state-controlled business set up by Lord Moulton in 1915 to fill the gap left by the loss of German imported dyes. The government was keen to see BDC taken under the wing of

THE CHANGING CENTURY

Facts from the business archives:

1920: The Automobile Association (AA) opened Britain's first bulk-storage petrol filling station, the Aldermaston garage in Berkshire

1921: Coco Chanel brought out the world's first designer perfume, Chanel No. 5

1922: The British Broadcasting Company, forerunner of the BBC, was established by Marconi and other radio manufacturers. Its first programme was a news and weather report

1922: Sausage maker Thomas Wall, concerned by the cost of having to run his Acton-based factory during the summer off-season, diversified into ice-cream. A Wall's employee sold cheap, wrapped ice-cream "brickettes" direct to the public from his tricycle

1922: An ex-Coldstream Guards officer, John Jervis Barnard, founded

the world's first football pool company. A year later, his idea was being copied by John Moores, whose coupons were printed under a pseudonym – Littlewood. Before the decade was out, Moores was a millionaire

1924: Kellogg's Cornflakes came on to the British market

1924: The first neon advertising sign appeared in Britain. Erected on a 35ft by 20ft display in Piccadilly Circus, it advertised Army Club, a popular brand of cigarettes

1924: In Massachusetts, one Clarence Birdseye set up the General Seafoods Corp. for the commercial development of preserving food by deep-freezing

1925: The American company 3M invented self-adhesive tape as a masking tape for automobile paint-sprayers. Originally, only the edges of the tape were self-adhesive. Thinking this a cost-cutting move by 3M, the paint sprayers dubbed the product "Scotch tape"

1926: The first British-made sound-on-film talkies went on general release. They were shot in Clapham by the de Forest Phonofilm Company and were "shorts" featuring vocalists and musicians

1925: Champney's, the world's first health farm, opened its doors in Hertfordshire

1927: The British Broadcasting Company became the British Broadcasting Corporation, a public body set up under royal charter

1927: The Southern Railway Company became the first business in Britain to set up an employee share ownership scheme

1928: William Wallace of York became the first Briton to graduate in business studies; he was awarded a Master of Commerce degree by London University

1928: Billy Butlin unveiled a new attraction at his Jungle Amusement Park in Skegness: the dodgem car

1928: Arsenal broke the record for

football transfer fees, paying Bolton Wanderers more than £10,000 for David Jack

1929: Alfred Hitchcock's Blackmail premiered at the Regal, Marble Arch. It was the first talking feature film made in Britain

1929: Fry's of Bristol launched the Crunchie bar

1929: Peter Jackson Ltd. introduced Britain's first brand of tipped cigarettes. It was called Du Maurier, after the actor-manager Sir Gerald du Maurier (father of Daphne)

1929: Frozen food pioneer Clarence Birdseye sold his company to the Postum Co for $22m. It was agreed that his name should be split into two and used for brand identification

1930: The Odeon cinema chain was founded by Birmingham-born Oscar Deutsch, son of immigrants from Eastern Europe. By 1941, there were 258 Odeons throughout Britain. The acronym stood for "Oscar Deutsch Entertains our Nation"

private enterprise, and early in 1926 a former chancellor of the exchequer, Reginald McKenna, suggested over a lunch with Sir Harry McGowan, chairman of Nobel Industries, that Nobels might like to acquire it. McGowan, a canny Glaswegian who would become one of the giants of inter-war British business, replied that it wasn't their "line of country", but urged McKenna to think more ambitiously and form "a British IG."

At this time, I. G. Farben, the mighty German chemical combine that had been growing by a series of mergers since 1904, commanded an alarmingly unchallengeable position in the international marketplace, and the autumn of 1926 saw a frenzied series of meetings in New York between the leaders of UK and US chemical companies, seeking to defuse the German threat either through alliances with "the IG" or by defensive mergers against it. Just as McGowan had suggested to McKenna earlier in the year, the four British companies agreed to amalgamate. McGowan got on particularly well with Sir Alfred Mond, the chairman of Brunner Mond, despite the two men being very different in personality. McGowan was a big, assertive, cigar-chomping man once described as looking like the model for a

1930: London printers Norman & Hill started marketing the Filofax, Britain's answer to America's Lefax. The name Filofax was thought of by typist Grace Scurr, who eventually rose to become chairman of the company. She lived to see the Filofax become a symbol of Yuppiedom in Thatcher's Britain

1931: The first unit trust, the M & G General trust as it is now known, was launched in Britain. It included shares in Anglo Persian Oil, Harrods, Boots, Commercial Union and Shell

1932: The GPO introduced Britain's first business reply-paid envelopes

1932: The Polytechnic Touring Association of London flew wealthy Britons to Basle for a seven-night stay. The British air charter holiday had been born; by 1938, Thomas Cook and Pickford's were among those offering inclusive air holidays to Continental destinations

1932: Mars Bar was launched in Britain by American confectioner Forrest Mars. It was manufactured at a plant in Slough that then employed just 12 people

1932: The London, Midland and Scottish Railway Company introduced Britain's first buffet car

1933: Polythene was invented at ICI's laboratories in Northwich, Cheshire

1934: Meccano started making Dinky Toys

1934: Monopoly was brought to market in America by its inventor, Charles Darrow. Unable to get a games company interested in his idea, Darrow had had 5,000 sets privately printed. The product hit Britain in 1936 and went on to become the biggest selling board game of all time

1935: Rowntree brought out Chocolate Crisp, the forerunner of the best-selling brand, Kit Kat

1935: The paperback revolution began when the first Penguin books went on sale. The books, marketed by Sir Allen Lane as a "whole book for the equivalent of 10 cigarettes", were mainly sold in Woolworths

1936: Stanley Tools of Sheffield introduced the Stanley Knife, originally designed for cutting through fibreboard

1936: Air Dispatch became the first British airline to appoint an air hostess. The 19-year-old Daphne Kearley flew on the "dawn express" Avro (A. V. Roe) 642 from Croydon to Paris. One of her duties was to type letters dictated in flight by business passengers. Press reports claimed she received 299 airborne proposals of marriage in 10 months

1936: Maltesers were introduced by Mars

1936: J. Arthur Rank opened Pinewood Studios in Buckinghamshire; Hollywood-style film-making had come to Britain

1937: The American chemical company E. I. du Pont de Nemours developed and patented nylon, under the direction of one Dr Wallace Carothers. The next year, du Pont manufactured the first commercial nylon product, toothbrush bristles

1937: A. Hormel & Co. of Minnesota started to make a new meat product. The product's name was a contraction of Spiced Ham – Spam

1937: Rowntree launched Smarties and Rolo

1937: Nestlé launched Milky Bar

1937: Bristol company H. W. Carter & Co. developed Ribena. The name came from the Latin for blackcurrant, Ribes Nigra

1939: ICI put polythene into regular production. Most of the war-time output was used for cable insulation and for components for airborne radar systems

Source: Patrick Robertson: The New Shell Book of Firsts, 1994, Headline Book Publishing

Victorian painting called 'Success', while Mond was a shy intellectual with a habit of lowering his chin as he spoke. He was still painfully conscious of the heavy German accent that neither an English public school education nor Cambridge University had been able to disguise.

Leaving New York together on the Cunard liner Aquitania, Mond and McGowan spent the six-day voyage locked in negotiations with their advisers over an exchange of shareholdings in the four companies and over who was to be No. 1 and No. 2 of the new Imperial Chemical Industries. (McGowan ceded the chairmanship to Mond but the pair effectively ran the company in tandem.) By the time the ship reached Southampton the deal was done, typed out on four sheets of Cunard Line stationery. The document was ever after known as the "Aquitania Agreement" and created a company of 5,000 product lines and nearly £100m in assets.[7]

The organisational model of Imperial Chemical Industries was a decentralised corporation with a strategic and financial core sitting above otherwise largely autonomous silos for different functions of the business. Other, looser, models of this period with less central control included AEI, Tube Investments, Imperial Tobacco (Britain's third biggest company in 1935 after the Post Office and the London Midland and Scottish Railway Co.), Tootal, Hawker Siddeley, GKN and EMI.[8]

The mosaic of thousands of small family companies that had made up British business was already becoming history. In 1907, a mere eight companies had been capitalised at more than £8m; by 1924, the number was 25. As the trend grew, reaching 61 by 1939, there was much debate about the problems of managing large-scale businesses. In 1931, a government committee was told by a banker that the most difficult problem in business was finding "a man who can control 10 million spindles". Even Sir Alfred Mond told the House of Commons: "I have

THE CHANGING CENTURY

A snapshot of Britain:

1921: Prime Minister David Lloyd George made a peace with Sinn Fein leaders, the Anglo-Irish treaty

1921: Strike action forced the government to declare a state of emergency; coal rationing began

1922: In accordance with the Anglo-Irish treaty, an Irish Free State, consisting of the 26 counties of Southern Ireland, was formed. Only the six Protestant counties in the North remained part of the UK. Unionists were not happy. Neither were Irish Nationalists: Southern Ireland was now self-governing –

but as a dominion of the British Commonwealth. Michael Collins, who had signed the treaty, was murdered in an ambush by Republicans

1925: Plaid Cymru was founded in Wales

1928: The Commons passed the Equal Franchise Bill; the age at which women could vote was lowered from 30 to 21

1928: The National Party of Scotland was founded

1928: Neville Chamberlain, health minister, handed more responsibility – and more money – to local authorities. His reforms were the

beginnings of the local government system still in place today

1929: Margaret Bondfield became the first female cabinet minister, appointed minister of labour in Ramsay MacDonald's second government

1929: The government opposed plans put forward by the French prime minister, Aristide Briand, for a United States of Europe. The Conservatives gave Briand qualified support, saying Britain's future really lay with her Empire

1929: Lloyd George in opposition proposed public road-building and construction programmes to provide jobs; his plan was backed not only

by the economist John Maynard Keynes but also by Oswald Mosley, then a Labour junior minister

1929: As the economic crisis deepened and ministers struggled to deal with the consequences of the Wall Street crash, the following exchange took place between the King and J. H. Thomas, the Lord Privy Seal.

George V: "Tell me, Mr Thomas. What state is my country in?"

Thomas: "If I were you, I'd put it in your wife's name."

1930: The Simon Commission on the future of India published its report. It proposed the creation of a

come to the conclusion that it is impossible for any human being efficiently to control any industry beyond a certain magnitude…" Just six months later, he was helping to put together Britain's biggest industrial merger, ICI.[9]

Courtaulds shied away from acquisition, and it was not until 1957 that it bought its main competitor, British Celanese. But other market leaders had no such inhibitions. ICI, Reckitt and Colman, Fisons, Metal Box, Distillers, Tube Investments, Allied Newspapers and Wiggins Teape, the paper maker, all grew fast through takeover deals between the wars, the 71 leading acquirers each swallowing an average 20 firms over the two decades.[10]

Yet even before the formation of ICI, Britain's two biggest employers were proving that large enterprises could be well managed. The Post Office and the London Midland and Scottish Railway Company, each with over 200,000 on its payroll, were both efficiently run organisations throughout the inter-war years. As late as 1935 the "Big Four" railway companies – the others were the London and North Eastern Railway (LNER), which boasted the world's fastest steam locomotive, the Mallard, the Great Western Railway (GWR), and the Southern Railway (SR) – ranked second, third, fourth and sixth respectively among the UK's biggest employers. When formed out of the 130 pre-war companies in 1921, they had a combined share capital of £1.25bn at 1913 prices.

Nothing in Britain's business landscape between the wars was bigger than the railway companies, most of whose revenue came from freight and mail – immortalised in W. H. Auden's wonderfully evocative poem 'Night Mail' on the soundtrack of the famous documentary film ("This is the Night Mail crossing the Border, bringing the cheque and the postal order…"). The Post Office meshed seamlessly with the mail trains to provide a service that postal users in the 21st century can only dream of: even in the trenches of the Great War, soldiers had received their letters from home within two days.

federation of self-governing provinces

1933: The Liberal paper The News Chronicle declared that Hitler's appointment as German chancellor was "a good and necessary thing". Few in Britain saw its real significance

1934: Four areas – Tyneside, West Cumberland, Scotland and South Wales – were officially recognised as economically depressed. The average wage was then about £2 a week; four pounds short of the £6 needed to keep a family of four above the poverty line

1935: Eight hundred strikes and stoppages meant more than two million working days were lost

1936: Marchers from Jarrow converged on Hyde Park in a rally organised by the Communist Party of Great Britain (CPGB)

1936: Baldwin and Cosmo Lang, Archbishop of Canterbury, advised the King not to marry the twice-divorced American Wallis Simpson; Baldwin said that the Cabinet would resign if the King went against their advice. Edward VIII ignored it and abdicated on December 10

1936: About 2,000 Britons, among them W. H. Auden, George Orwell and Laurie Lee, joined the International Brigade to help the Republican cause in Spain. They were fighting General Franco and, by extension, the Italian and German fascists who supported him. Five hundred of them died

1936: In the East End of London anti-fascist demonstrators and members of the CPGB repelled the Black Shirts in what was to become known as the Battle of Cable Street

1937: As the rearmament programme got fully under way, the jobless total fell

1937: The Irish Free State was renamed Eire

1939: The IRA began a bombing campaign in London, Manchester and Birmingham. The government in Eire began a series of measures to try restrict the movements and activities of the IRA

1939: Around one and a half million Anderson shelters (named after Sir John Anderson who was in charge of Air Raid Precautions) were distributed to people living in areas expected to be Luftwaffe targets. The first were erected by residents in Islington

Sources: Christopher Lee: This Sceptred Isle, Twentieth Century, BBC and Penguin Books, 1999; Kenneth O. Morgan: Twentieth Century Britain, Oxford University Press, 2000

For more on industrial unrest and poverty and unemployment, see the statistical appendix

Don't mess with me: press baron Lord Northcliffe wielded immense media power in the 1920s

The swift and reliable steam trains were also responsible for the growth of Britain's national newspaper industry, which was spreading the products of London's Fleet Street into every corner of the provinces, mowing down the once sturdy local press. The number of provincial newspapers fell from 40 at the end of the First World War to 25 by 1937. Mass circulation took off between the wars and, boosted by competitive stunts and promotions, it hugely enriched newspaper barons such as Northcliffe, Beaverbrook and Rothermere. The Berry family, proprietors of the Daily Telegraph and the Sunday Times, collected no fewer than three peerages between them: Camrose, Kemsley and Hartwell.

As the size of business organisations grew, technology made the job of managing them easier. The number of telephone subscribers trebled between 1922 and 1938 to three million, a third of them corporate users, while innovations such as the Hollerith accounting

THE CHANGING CENTURY

Two years, four prime ministers:

October 1922: Lloyd George, prime minister since the end of 1916, was now on thin ice. His appeasement policy in Ireland had angered hardline Conservatives and put the coalition, which had held power since 1915, under strain. His foreign policy, which had brought Britain to the brink of a war with Turkey, was being denounced as reckless. The Conservatives decided to fight the forthcoming election independently; Lloyd George resigned

November 1922: The Conservatives were returned to power; Andrew Bonar Law became prime minister

May 1923: Bonar Law, who was suffering from cancer, resigned. Stanley Baldwin, the businessman cousin of Rudyard Kipling, took over

December 1923: Baldwin, seeking support for the Conservative trade policy of protectionism, went to the country. He lost 107 seats to Labour and the Liberals, making his grip on power tenuous

January 1924: The Conservative government was defeated in Parliament. Control passed to the political leader who had won the second highest number of seats at the election: Labour's Ramsay MacDonald. Without a working majority his position, however, was as weak as Baldwin's

November 1924: Stanley Baldwin, having abandoned his campaign for protectionism, was re-elected. The Conservatives had 419 seats; Labour 151, the Liberals were down to 40. Winston Churchill, a fierce supporter of free trade, who had not sat on the Conservative benches since 1904, was now back in the Tory fold, as Chancellor of the Exchequer

FOOTNOTE: MACDONALD'S 1924 ELECTION DEFEAT

The following were among factors in Labour's fall:

☐ A plan to lend the Russians money

☐ The decision not to prosecute the British communist, J. R. Campbell, for inciting mutiny among British soldiers in Ulster

☐ The infamous Zinoviev letter. Shortly before the election, a letter ostensibly written and signed by Grigori Zinoviev, the chairman of Russia's Comintern, was made public. In it, Zinoviev instructed British communists to prepare for revolution and to set up cells within the armed forces. The letter turned out to be a fake but stoked British fears of violent revolution. In this climate, Britons were more easily persuaded that they needed the firm old hand of the Conservatives.

Source: Christopher Lee: This Sceptred Isle, Twentieth Century, BBC and Penguin Books, 1999

machine enabled big decentralised corporations to control their financial data. Accountancy as a profession was beginning its long ascent to the boardrooms of Britain: Dunlop and Unilever were among the first companies to appoint accountants to board positions. By 1939, more than half of all the qualified accountants in Britain were employed within commerce and industry.

Large organisations did have difficulties recruiting talent to their boardrooms, but the problems were largely of their own making. There was, after all, proven management skill in the railway companies which, curiously enough, were hardly ever trawled by other industries. The civil service was a popular hunting ground, especially the Inland Revenue, which supplied ICI with three senior board members in the 1930s including Paul Chambers, who became a long-serving chairman. Vickers, the shipbuilder and armaments manufacturer, was one of many to choose retired military and naval officers as directors, a practice that would become widespread after the Second World War.

The move from private businesses with family management and shareholders to publicly floated companies was already well established by the early 1920s. In

Hello, central: switchboard girls at work as telephone usage booms

Northcliffe's rival Lord Beaverbrook used his Daily Express to pursue political campaigns

Operating Hollerith accounting machines, forerunners of office computers

corporate scandal, 1920s-style:

the chairman who went to Wormwood Scrubs...

Seventy years before Enron's financial misdeeds destroyed confidence in the probity of big corporations and their accountants, the scandal of the Royal Mail Steam Packet Company and the jailing of its 68-year-old chairman, Lord Kylsant, (right) shook the City of London to its foundations.

Royal Mail was founded by Royal Charter in 1839. One of its ships, the Trent, had sparked a major diplomatic row between London and Washington during the American Civil War, when a Federal warship stopped it and arrested two Confederate diplomats.

From 1909, Kylsant built the business into the world's largest shipping company, winning scores of mail contracts for the UK and other governments. However, his imposing presence – he was six foot five and dressed with Edwardian formality, always wearing a top hat in London – belied a sharp way with a balance sheet. His system of pyramidal gearing to finance his many acquisitions, laced with cross-shareholdings, meant that by 1930 he controlled a third of RMSP's £5m voting share capital for a relatively small outlay. What brought him down was the issue in 1928 of a £2m debenture stock, largely to finance Royal Mail's elaborate new headquarters building in the City. The prospectus claimed: "During the past ten years, the average annual balance available has been sufficient to pay the interest on the present issue more than five times over."

Royal Mail's published figures confirmed that the company had been earning average annual profits of more than £500,000 over that period, but Kylsant had massaged these every year

from 1921 to 1929 by including money from the reserves such as surpluses from the sale of ships and tax provisions that had proved unneeded. Far from the £6m profits claimed in a period of severe recession in the global shipping industry, Royal Mail had lost nearly £1m.

The whistle was effectively blown by Kylsant's elder brother, Viscount St. Davids, a trustee of the debenture issue, who circulated holders of the stock in July 1929, saying that it had been issued without his knowledge, and announced his resignation in the autumn. Investors began to query the true value of the company's assets and the share price dived. By the autumn of 1929, the company was unable to repay a £2.5m loan. The annual report for that year revealed a loss, and that Kylsant had used £300,000 from the insurance fund as carry-forward. The auditors, Price Waterhouse, now changed the way they presented the accounts, showing the actual depreciation value of the fleet instead of an unnamed allocation, and revealing that the company had gone from a profit of £490,000 in 1927 to a loss of nearly £80,000 in 1929. They also pointed out that the group's investments were recorded at "considerably in excess of present values".

Kylsant was forced to hand control to a triumvirate of City grandees in exchange for bank support. But he now seemed bent on self-destruction, still maintaining to the Treasury and the company's bankers that profits over the preceding four years had averaged more than £500,000 annually. After a searching article in the Economist and a series of angry shareholder meetings, the jig was up. In June 1931, Kylsant and Harold Morland, the Price Waterhouse auditor, were charged with issuing misleading accounts in 1926 and 1927. Kylsant was additionally charged with publishing a fraudulent

prospectus for the 1928 debenture issue.

In his defence at the Old Bailey, Kylsant boldly claimed that it was standard practice to use reserves to even out profit fluctuations from year to year; otherwise, he said, investors would panic every time profits were down. Ironically, if the 1929 Companies Act had come a year earlier, Kylsant would not have been able to deceive his investors: the new legislation required every prospectus to contain a statement by the auditors confirming profits earned in the preceding three years.

The Price Waterhouse man was acquitted but Kylsant was sent to Wormwood Scrubs for 12 months. Coming so soon after the scandal surrounding financier Clarence Hatry (see opposite) – but involving a far more prestigious company – the Royal Mail affair seemed a fitting curtain-raiser to the Depression, which began to bite in 1931.

Kylsant served nine months of his sentence. When he was released in August 1932, he was given a feudal welcome home to his Welsh country seat, his car hand-drawn by 40 estate workers. His London clubs welcomed him back with open arms, as did the House of Lords. It was as if the establishment were acknowledging that Kylsant was not alone in his financial manipulations – just the one who got caught.

(Sources: Anthony Vice: Financier at Sea, 1985, and Business History, 1972, Davies and Bourn: Lord Kylsant and the Royal Mail.)

1924, there were 726 quoted companies in manufacturing and distribution on the London Stock Exchange, and nearly 60 per cent of profits were generated by public companies. But many founders were reluctant to sell out or go public and those that did usually retained a family grip and/or voting control through large shareholdings. Today, some 40 per cent of the stock of the grocery firm Sainsbury, which has had six family chairmen over 130 years of its history, remains in the founding family's hands.

Contested or hostile acquisitions were rare in these years, partly for reasons of family resistance and partly because of the unreliable nature of company information available to prospective bidders or even shareholders. The Royal Mail Steamship scandal (see panel) of 1931 was only the tip of an extremely large unseen iceberg. Thanks to the laxity of company law on the need to furnish true and fair accounts, there were probably scores of chairmen like Lord Kylsant of Royal Mail, found guilty of falsifying a share prospectus. Kylsant spent 12 months in Wormwood Scrubs prison but others went undetected. There was, says business historian Leslie Hannah, "significant, yet legally permitted, deception by directors".

Governments were reluctant to intervene in corporate affairs, holding that boards had the right to privacy in conducting their business. Hannah quotes an unnamed chairman as saying: "We bring into our accounts just as much… as will enable us to pay dividends we recommend and to place to general reserves, or add or carry forward just as much as will make a pretty balance sheet."[11] Directors had virtually unlimited discretion over what information to hold back or release to the marketplace, and the Institute of Directors, far from being the guiding mentor of corporate governance that it is today, was a sleepy club of 200-300 members, many of whom failed even to pay their annual subscriptions.

Directors were not only able to be highly selective

…and the matinee-idol fraudster

Clarence Charles Hatry (below right) became a byword for 1920s corporate wrongdoing. Some historians even blame him for helping to trigger the Wall Street crash through stock-market reverberations from the collapse of his own empire. Rakishly bow-tied and moustached, he looked like a screen matinee idol of the period and his personal vanity was legendary: a secretary noticed that he even had the soles of his shoes polished.

Hatry was a company promoter with a long history of launches that went belly-up, though he had enough successes to persuade banks to keep lending him money. One of these was the merger of most of London's private bus companies before their sale to the London General Omnibus Company, the forerunner of London Transport.

Hatry's downfall came when he attempted to wrest control of a large section of the British steel industry and found that the banks were beginning to cold-shoulder him. To raise loan collateral, he turned to forging scrip certificates for the corporations of Gloucester, Swindon and Wakefield (having long been involved in the municipal loans business, more or less respectably).

The scheme set City alarm bells ringing and by mid-September 1929 shares in Hatry's empire were collapsing. He was arrested for fraud and put on trial in January

1930. The judge handed down a savage sentence of 14 years' penal servitude, condemning his activities as "the most appalling frauds that have ever disfigured the commercial reputation of this country", though in the light of some later doings, that seems over the top. David Kynaston, the City's historian, says it was certainly fraud, "but not the most heinous fraud ever committed".

Hatry was eventually released after nine years and, during World War II, borrowed enough money to buy Hatchards of Piccadilly, London's most upmarket bookshop, to the horror of the City establishment. He made a last comeback in the 1950s, buying up newly fashionable coffee bars in the West End, and died in 1965 at the age of 77.

(Source: Kynaston: The City of London, Volume III, Illusions of Gold, 1914-1945.)

over the information they released, but also free to profit from what would now be condemned as insider dealing. What is more, they enjoyed the right to "compensation" for agreeing to mergers – usually either a place on the new board or cash for loss of office, which could amount to as much as one-tenth of the price of the acquisition. Dudley Docker, a Birmingham motor and cycle manufacturer whose son Bernard and his wife would become gossip-column fodder in the 1950s for their flamboyant lifestyle (most famously symbolised by Lady Docker's gold-plated Daimler), made a fortune out of suggesting various mergers and disposals to Vickers, on whose board he sat. He had acquired his Vickers directorship in 1919 through negotiating the over-valued, £12m sale of the rolling-stock company he then chaired, the Metropolitan Carriage, Wagon and Finance Co. When Vickers sold off its

electrical businesses to AEI in the late 1920s, Docker pocketed as much as £50,000, worth between £2m and £3m of today's money.

One company that indubitably defined British success in the inter-war years, prospering on the century's fastest growing new industry, was Morris Motors, which had gone public in 1926. It is still regarded as one of the first examples of modern management, despite its founder's eccentric habit of spending months each year out of touch in Australia (see panel). William Morris, later to be Viscount Nuffield, had managed the firm brilliantly as a private company, introducing mass-production and single-handedly changing the British automobile from a costly plaything for the few to everyday transport for the many. He visited the US and learned from their assembly lines – but some of his automated techniques were even ahead of Detroit.

Morris survived the 1921 slump by cutting his prices dramatically, reviving a dormant market and making profits through volume rather than margin. He did it by rigorous cost-cutting, by increasing borrowing and by arm-twisting suppliers to accept deferred terms of payment. It was a strategy that paid off within months, and by 1926 Morris was making 41 per cent of all the cars produced in Britain. "One of my dreams… is to put England on top industrially again," he wrote in 1927. As a result of his mass-production revolution, output in the British car industry trebled between 1922 and 1929, while the average price of a car halved over a decade, from £259 in 1924 to £130 in 1935-36.[12]

The success of Morris carried with it the fortunes of two other famous names in the car component industry, Lucas and Wilmot Breeden (founded by a former Lucas representative), both of which supplied his large-volume production lines. Morris was one of those rare individuals in the car industry who combined the skills of a mechanic with the hard nose of a businessman. One of his coups was to lever Triplex, the safety-glass manufacturer, out of

Assembling Morris cars in 1930: the company pioneered mass production in Britain

leadership lessons, 1930s:
how Morris lost the plot

William Morris, later Viscount Nuffield, brought mass production to British industry and enabled car manufacturing to survive the 1930s depression. One of Britain's greatest philanthropists, he was progressive in many ways. He effectively created Britain's first modern industrial management structure in 1923, decentralising it under a board with himself as chairman and "governing director".

Like many brilliant founder-entrepreneurs, however, he became too emotionally involved in the business, and this caused a dangerous break with one of his deputies, Leonard Lord, who would become the deliberate instrument of his business decline. Another fine manager he lost through inability to delegate was Miles Thomas, who eventually became chairman of BOAC.

He also developed a fatal tendency to appoint cronies as senior managers without considering how they would fit into the organisation. This led to a culture where the business was managed erratically by informal contact among the chairman's coterie instead of through defined reporting channels. In the end, Morris simply took his eye off the ball, regularly spending winters abroad – a common practice among successful British industrialists of the period.

The rot set in when he appointed E. H. Blake of Dunlop, one of his business acquaintances, as managing director and deputy chairman in 1927. That same year, Morris began his

practice of travelling by slow boat to Australia as part of his personal export drive; later, he developed a liaison with an Australian woman that kept him away for months at a time.

In the late 1920s, Morris was Britain's most admired businessman, never more so than when he won two court cases against the Inland Revenue, which claimed that his practice of ploughing the public company's profits back into the reserves (including his personal dividends) was a tax dodge. Morris was acquitted in the first case, and the second was personally thrown out by the Attorney-General, Sir William Jowitt, who had been impressed by Morris's attempts to fight Ford in the global marketplace. Afterwards, Jowitt and Morris walked away from the court arm in arm.

The year 1927 was the high point for Morris Motors, when the newly floated firm made 61,632 out of the 164,000 cars produced in Britain. Between then and 1935, British car production doubled, but Morris only once bettered its 1927 output. Its pre-tax 1928 profits, £1.59m, would not be exceeded until 1936. When the market bounced back after the depression, Morris had a much smaller share. (Morris and Austin together had taken 60 per cent in 1928.)

The once-unerring instinct that Morris and his first managers had for the right products – simple, affordable cars for the mass market – was straying. The company moved upmarket to large cars just as the government of the day slapped punitive tax differentials on them. It went into

Cars ready for despatch at Morris Motors, 1937

aero-engine manufacture after acquiring Wolseley but concentrated on the civilian market instead of defence and failed to gain government contracts.

In the 1930s Morris, by now Viscount Nuffield, did appoint a brilliant deputy in Leonard Lord. He saved the company but his prickly insistence on autonomy irritated his equally autocratic boss. When his strategy paid off, Lord demanded a performance-related bonus. Morris blew up and the pair parted acrimoniously. Lord nursed a grudge, vowing to "screw Nuffield into the ground" and take his business apart "brick by bloody brick".

He took his grudge off to Austin, undercutting the Morris prices ruthlessly, and in 1952 finally achieved a pyrrhic revenge when the drifting Nuffield Organisation was subsumed with Austin into British Motor Corporation (BMC). The British motor industry was never the same again.

(Sources: Martin Adeney: Nuffield, a Biography, and Economic History Review, 1996. Roy Church: Deconstructing Nuffield: the evolution of managerial culture in the British motor industry.)

its agreement with Austin by purchasing Triplex shares through nominees until he controlled the company.[13]

Motor manufacturing was one of the outstanding successes of British industry between the wars and was

described as such by a Cabinet committee planning for reconstruction after the Second World War. In 1920, there were 550,000 motor vehicles on the roads of Britain; by 1922, there were nearly a million and by 1930 over 2,200,000.

Radio days: domestic luxuries such as radiograms tempted 1930s buyers through the new hire-purchase schemes

But the Second World War blocked this upward progress; then came post-war shortages of raw materials and the desperate need to export all new cars for dollars. Sadly, Morris's successors lacked his vision and business skills, and from the 1950s on, the road for British car manufacturing was all downhill.

The motor industry probably would never have thrived as it did in the high unemployment of the 1930s, however, without the introduction of the financial tool that went on to underpin many new consumer industries of the time – hire purchase. Paying for goods "on the never-never", as it was popularly known, fuelled an upsurge of consumer demand for previously unheard-of luxuries – not only the family car, but electric cookers, vacuum cleaners, radios, radiograms and even pianos. These shiny new appliances and instruments graced the new affordable homes that were being built along the by-passes around London – "Metroland", as Sir John Betjeman was to call the area in his verse – and other big cities.

The first company to enter the consumer-credit market in a big way, encouraged by the Bank of England, was United Dominions Trust, a leading credit operator with annual turnover of £5.5m and a 10-year track record of helping to

THE CHANGING CENTURY

New Britain:

1921: The GPO introduced a standardised design for telephone kiosks: the red public call box was born

1921: Dr Marie Stopes opened the first family-planning centre, the Mothers' Clinic on London's Holloway Road

1925: The South Wales Power Company erected the first electric pylons

1926: The first electric traffic lights appeared. A manually operated set of red, green and amber lights was installed at the junction of St. James's Street and Piccadilly in London's West End. An automatic set was installed in Wolverhampton the next year

1930: Television receivers became available to the public. The market, though, was small: the receivers were priced at 25 guineas each

1931: The Ministry of Transport published the Highway Code

1932: The GPO started a telex service

1932: The Lancashire Constabulary became the first British police force to equip patrol cars with radio. Two years later, the Met introduced a 24-hour a day radio patrol system

1934: Belisha beacons, yellow signs to mark crossings, were introduced by the Minister of Transport, Sir Leslie Hore-Belisha

1935: The MoT made driving tests compulsory

1937: The emergency telephone number, 999, was introduced

1939: Two hundred Citizens' Advice Bureaux were opened

Source: Christopher Lee: This Sceptred Isle, Twentieth Century, BBC and Penguin Books, 1999

finance the purchase of motor vehicles – principally those used for professional or business purposes such as doctors' cars and tradesmen's delivery vans. Montagu Norman, governor of the Bank, liked UDT's probity and knew that its managing director, J. Gibson Jarvie, was an entrepreneurial businessman who was looking for new markets. The Bank had been under criticism for not doing more to help domestic industry and saw this as an opportunity to give a shot in the arm to Britain's small manufacturers. Finance was to be provided to retailers and wholesalers, not the final customer, thus ensuring that the trader was responsible for his customers' credit-worthiness. The scheme was launched by the Treasury buying an initial £250,000 worth of UDT shares with as much again held in reserve.[14]

The electricity supply industry, which was already gaining over gas for cost reasons, introduced its own hire-purchase schemes for big-ticket products that would consume the most electricity such as cookers and boilers. Manufacturers also set up their own deferred payment systems: in 1938, three-quarters of all vacuum cleaner sales were on h. p., as were three-quarters of radio sales. The establishment of the British Broadcasting Company in 1922 had created (and was at first financed by) a huge market for "the wireless" – initially the cumbersome crystal set or "cat's whisker", and subsequently the valve radio in its Art Deco wood or Bakelite casing. Broadcasting was effectively nationalised in 1926 when the BBC – by now the Corporation – was given its charter to raise finance

through a licence fee. In the same year, the distribution of electricity was also nationalised under the Central Electricity Generating Board, and the face of the English countryside was soon covered by marching lines of pylons.

Sales of radios and radiograms quadrupled in seven years, from half a million in 1930 to two million in 1937. A third category of h. p. schemes was set up by finance houses on behalf of manufacturers, particularly those of radios and pianos.[15] In 1936, more than 20 per cent of the business of one hire-purchase company, Bowmaker, came from advances for radios and musical instruments, incidentally proving those wrong who predicted that the coming of radio and the gramophone would kill live music.

Without hire purchase, both the economy and the quality of life of Britain in the 1930s would have suffered. Late in the decade, vacuum cleaners cost between £7 and £8. With the average weekly wage still less than £5, few working-class households could have afforded to buy one outright. Similarly, refrigerators cost up to a quarter of a year's manufacturing wage (and would not become widespread in working-class homes until the 1960s), cookers up to 15 per cent and even a humble electric bar fire nearly one per cent.

Retailers – in particular, the big department stores – were supercharged by the "never-never" culture. Advertising and marketing became more important and the whole business of selling to the domestic consumer moved up several gears in the 1930s.

In a period that is generally remembered for images such as the Jarrow March of unemployed men from the north in 1936, cars and consumer goods were visible

Rayon, a synthetic silk, was one of the new growth industries of the 1930s, creating further employment for women

industrial successes. In fact, as historians now acknowledge, productivity was surprisingly high, aided by the modernisation forced into British factories by the Great War. Although full economic recovery would only be provided by rearmament after 1935, there were five big growth areas through the inter-war decades – motor vehicles, chemicals, electrical

products, rayon or artificial silk and paper. The slump that followed Wall Street's catastrophic collapse in October, 1929, principally affected Britain's old staple industries: the new ones bounced back to pre-crash levels as early as 1933.[16] For those in work, wages in 1933 were actually 10 per cent higher than in 1929.

Whole towns were revolutionised by the new industries. Dagenham, home of the British Ford company, had the highest population growth, followed by Dover, Slough and Welwyn Garden City. Already the economy was shifting towards the service sector and away from heavy manufacturing, thanks in part to a sizeable incursion of US companies. The town of Harrow had the Kodak camera company; Slough was home to the Mars confectionery business and numerous light industries; clean, modern factories in Welwyn made popular cereals such as Shredded Wheat. Leicester's biggest employer was the Imperial Typewriter Company. In 1933 there were an estimated 30 firms in Birmingham less than 10 years old making plastic products – not yet polythene, which would be accidentally discovered in an ICI laboratory late in 1933, but Bakelite and similar cellulose compounds.

The new light industries in midlands and southern towns were helping to create two Englands; one of clean, bright factories on busy by-passes, staffed predominantly by young women, and the other of empty streets and derelict industrial plant in the north and in the mining valleys of Wales. Steelworks, pitheads and shipyards lay silent and deserted. In Glasgow, where the half-built hull of the Queen Mary lay on the stocks of Clydeside for a year until rescued in 1934 by a Parliamentary bill providing finance, half the population was out of work. The impact varied even within industries; in the textile towns, more jobs were lost in Oldham spinning factories than in Bolton weaving mills.

With bitter irony, while so many had enforced leisure thrust upon them, the burgeoning service sector in the south displayed a new emphasis on leisure and entertainment. Grand Art Deco buildings went up to house Odeon cinemas and dance-halls. Billy Butlin, an energetic Canadian entrepreneur, created a whole new type of leisure business, opening his first holiday camp at Skegness in 1936. Two years later, there were more than 100 holiday camps in Britain, capable of accommodating 500,000 people in high season. Football pools became a national weekly passion, turning the Moores family of Liverpool, who founded Littlewoods, into multi-millionaires. On a more elevated note, Penguin paperback books, launched by Allen Lane in 1935, revolutionised publishing and released a huge new public for book-buying at six old pence a time.

One glamorous new industry that did not take off to its full promise until the rearmament programme was aviation. Just 11 years after the Wright brothers' clumsy biplane made the first powered flight in 1903, the First World War had brought the development of aircraft dramatically forward. Companies such as A. V. Roe, Sopwith and Handley Page were household names, thanks to the daring wartime exploits of the Royal Flying Corps. By 1918, when 30,000 aircraft were produced, there was an established British industry. British aero engines led the world in quality and quantity. But without the spur of war, production soon tailed off, and in 1924 only 503 planes came out of British factories.

Private enterprise was doing its best to get civil aviation off the ground: as early as 1919, when Alcock and Brown flew the Atlantic from Newfoundland to Ireland, a company called Holt Thomas started up the first daily air service between London's Croydon aerodrome and Paris. It was mainly a freight operation, with just two or three passengers carried on each trip. By January 1920, three British companies were competing with regular cross-channel services, but it soon became clear that airlines were not going to be a profit-making business. When

Billy Butlin, the holiday camp king, plays bowls with some of his campers

Imperial Airways was founded in 1924, it was on the back of a government subsidy and with several government appointees on the board.

Lack of international routes was one obvious handicap, and Britain failed here, as in so many other areas of commerce, to make the most of the opportunities offered by her global empire for passenger travel and mail transport by air. Despite the huge public interest in the exploits of such British pioneer flyers as Sir Alan Cobham (first to make the round trip to Australia) and Amy Johnson, who flew solo to Australia and South Africa, imperial air routes in 1930 totalled a mere 23,000 miles, not much more than the rail network in Britain. France had a much smaller empire but served it with 19,400 miles of air routes. Where US airlines in 1930 carried nearly 400,000 passengers and Germany 93,126, air services in the British Empire carried only 58,261.[17]

Domestically, however, Britain was extraordinarily well served by air. By the mid-1930s every major town had an aerodrome, and islands from the Channel to the Highlands and Orkney were linked to the mainland. Seaside resorts like Blackpool were a target for new start-ups, and a company called Hillman Airways (no known connection with the car manufacturer) operated, improbably enough, between Romford and Clacton in the summer. In 1935 there were nearly 20 independent companies operating 76 services, none of which made money, and soon there was an inevitable move towards consolidation. Hillman Airways merged with three others to become British Airways, competing with Imperial on continental routes. (It was Imperial, later transformed into British Overseas Airways Corporation and British European Airways, though, that was

to inherit the British Airways name in the 1970s). In all, around 40 airline companies were set up between 1933 and 1939, but only just over half survived the coming of war.

The number of domestic air services is surprising in view of the then comprehensive, cheap and reliable rail network – 20,000 miles of track, serving everything from the big cities to tiny halts in rural Cornwall. Rail travel was in general more efficient and certainly more comfortable than early air travel. It cost just over a penny a mile whereas air fares averaged three to 10 times as much. The railway companies were quick to defuse the novel competition by acquiring powers to operate their own aircraft, but they were never profitable.

Rearmament, starting in the mid-1930s, gave a huge boost to the economy at large. As early as 1935, when a

THE CHANGING CENTURY

Labour premiership, Tory power:

May 1929: Ramsay MacDonald and Labour were re-elected, but not with an overall majority. Labour had 288 seats, the Conservatives 260, the Liberals 59. MacDonald depended on Liberal support

1930: The Liberals started to campaign for electoral reform. MacDonald considered the idea of proportional representation but made no firm promises. In May, therefore, Lloyd George therefore withdrew his support for Labour in the Commons

August 1931: Lacking Liberal support, the Labour government fell. It was replaced by an all-party National

Government, set up to deal with the national emergency – the economy. MacDonald presided over a Cabinet of four Labour, four Conservative and two Liberal ministers

October 1931: A general election returned the National Government but the balance of power looked much different: the Conservatives now had 473 seats in the Commons. Ramsay MacDonald, the first Labour prime minister in British history, was presiding over a cabinet in which the Tory party was the dominant force. Baldwin, the real centre of power, was made Lord President of the Council

June 1935: In poor health, Ramsay MacDonald stood down as prime minister; Baldwin was back. In October, he called an election. The

result confirmed that this was in effect a Tory government: the Conservatives had 432 seats, to Labour's 154 and the Liberals' 20. Churchill, who had fallen out with mainstream Tories over India, did not make it into the Cabinet. He was, however, appointed to the Air Research Committee

FOOTNOTE: POLITICS ON THE FRINGES

1930: The newspaper baron Lord Beaverbrook formed the United Empire Party. Frustrated by Baldwin's consensual-style of politics, Beaverbrook wanted to go back to the Tory "good old days" of protectionism. The party did not last, but its sentiments remained, for the next 40 or so years, a

recurring theme in the pages of Beaverbrook's big seller, the Daily Express

1932: Much more disturbing than Beaverbrook's activities was the emergence of the British Union of Fascists, led by Oswald Mosley. Something of a political gadfly, Mosley had left his post as a junior minister in MacDonald's second government and gone his own way. He now started to lead the Black Shirts in marches against London's Jews. His activities were curbed by the 1936 Public Order Act, which outlawed political uniforms and gave the government powers to ban marches if it believed they would lead to incitement.

Source: Christopher Lee: This Sceptred Isle, Twentieth Century, BBC and Penguin Books, 1999

When flying was fun: an Imperial
Airways plane prepares to take off
at night from Croydon aerodrome

key by-election campaign was lost on the issue, propelling Baldwin's government into action, The Economist said: "Britain's rearmament programme is the greatest public works programme ever devised in time of formal peace". In getting the unemployed back to work, it was the UK equivalent of President Franklin D. Roosevelt's New Deal programme of dam-building and other great infrastructure projects. The number of new jobs more than trebled between 1935 and 1938: altogether nearly 1.5m were created in the principal industries stimulated by rearmament – aircraft, shipbuilding, construction and mechanical engineering – though more than two million were still out of work. Income tax rose steeply in the late 1930s to pay for the programme, from 4s.6d in the pound in 1934 to 7s. in the pound in September 1939.[18]

Until the threat from Nazi Germany galvanised it into life, the British aircraft industry resembled motor-car manufacture before the Great War; small-scale, fragmented and with much of the work still done by hand. The companies were run by designers rather than industrialists. As historian Correlli Barnett notes, they had "an almost total lack of production engineers and managers of the kind now common in American and German industry, and able to organise and manage assembly-line production. Except for its stock-in-trade… the British aircraft industry in the early 1930s presented the classic picture of British industry 100 years earlier".[19] Even design failed to move with the times until the demands of war intervened. While Germany and the US were turning out streamlined, fast monoplanes built of metal, British manufacturers were still making biplanes, lumbering constructions of wood and fabric. Production was often a shambles. The needs of the RAF eventually inspired brilliant conceptualists such as R. J. Mitchell to design the Vickers-Supermarine Spitfire, and Sydney Camm of Hawker to produce the Hurricane, but companies struggled to cope with the expansion caused

by rearmament, and the Air Ministry constantly complained of delays. The only aircraft builder rated by the government as well-organised in production was Handley-Page.

By 1938, the government had poured nearly £10m into creating a modern, high-production aircraft industry, setting up airframe and engine manufacture in "shadow" factories operated by the car firms. This in turn made enormous demands on industries such as construction, steel, machine-tools and precision instruments as well as on skilled manpower; until the Munich attempt at appeasing Hitler in September 1938 was seen to have failed, no diversion of resources was allowed from normal peacetime production to help the rearmament push.[20] Incredibly, Hitler's Germany was allowed to dominate half the world's machine-tool production between 1933 and 1937. The US had another third of the market, and the UK, seemingly oblivious to the lessons of 1914, just seven per cent.[21]

The consequence was serious delays in turning out the fighters and bombers required by the RAF. Sometimes it was sheer managerial incompetence. One key component that was chronically late was the Rolls-Royce Merlin engine that powered the Spitfire and Hurricane. In 1937, when only 260 out of 3,350 on order had been delivered, the government discovered that Rolls-Royce had made "insufficient allowance for the effect of holidays when estimating deliveries".

It was not until August and September, 1939, that British combat aircraft production equalled that of Nazi Germany, but because of shortfalls in the domestic machine-tool industry, many of the aircraft that would defend homeland skies in the Battle of Britain were only there by courtesy of German, Swiss and American machine tools.[22]

The eleventh-hour nature of British industrial ingenuity was about to be put to the test for the second time in a generation.

the crucible
of war

66 Give us the tools and we
will finish the job. 99

**Winston Churchill, addressing
President Franklin D. Roosevelt in a
radio broadcast, February 9, 1941**

4

Make do and mend: a seamstress carries on working behind her bombed-out window

In 1914 the British Expeditionary Force had been obliged to go to war wearing uniforms dyed khaki with German-made chemicals. In 1939 British industry was in a much stronger position to meet wartime demands, in spite of letting Nazi Germany scoop a global market share in advanced machine tools. The chemical industry was in good shape, boasting a world competitor in ICI. Over the next six years it would innovate and diversify into many new pharmaceutical drugs, plastics, synthetic fabrics and key agricultural products such as DDT and weedkillers. The petro-chemical industry that would play such a key role in the post-war world was born around 1942 when Shell developed the first synthetic detergents.[1]

Prime Minister Neville Chamberlain tells Britain it is at war again, September 3, 1939

What a later age would call "sunrise" industries were also thriving, particularly radio and TV. When prime minister Neville Chamberlain's dry tones came over the radio on the sunny Sunday of September 3, 1939, declaring that Britain was once again at war with Germany, there were nine million wireless sets in the country, the fruit of a flourishing new light industry and greater spending power as Britain came out of the Depression. On September 1, the BBC's fledgling television service had been shut down for the coming war in the middle of a Mickey Mouse cartoon: when it was resumed on June 7, 1946, the same cartoon came on screen with the same announcer, Jasmine Bligh, saying: "remember me?"

The motor industry had also matured into mass production for a mass market on the back of increasing prosperity, and by 1939 the modern plants of Austin, Morris, Ford and the Rootes group were well placed to switch quickly

to the government's "shadow factory" scheme whereby aircraft jigs and other wartime production equipment were set up. This arrangement between the Chamberlain government and private industry had been made gradually since rearmament got under way in 1936, and by the end of the war there were more than 260 shadow factories, controlled by three different defence departments – the ministries of supply and aircraft production and the Admiralty.

ICI alone constructed 18 between 1937 and 1939, ending up with 25, and became the government's biggest single industrial agent. All the shadow factories were owned and funded by government and the "agent" company on whose premises they stood received a management fee. Workers were employed under that company's usual conditions and wage scales, but were paid from government funds.

Ammunition was made separately in Royal Ordnance factories (ROFs), of which 40 new ones were hastily built in addition to the three pre-war sites at Woolwich and elsewhere. At their peak in 1942 the ROFs employed some 300,000 men and women.[2] A variety of other outside firms agreed to provide additional production space for the war effort, among them Cadbury, which in May 1940 turned over part of its Bournville site to manufacturing munitions and war materials ranging from rockets to gas masks. The department that formerly made moulds for pouring chocolate was fitted out with 53 vertical milling machines for rifle manufacture. Joseph Lucas, the Birmingham motor and aero parts manufacturer, set up on the site to make parts for Lancasters and Spitfires, and the Austin Motor Company and two government departments also moved in.

These activities were disguised under a management company called Bournville Utilities, run by Cadbury's managing director Laurence Cadbury. Nothing of its true nature was revealed until May 1945, except for a passing reference in the Bournville works magazine to products being made "other than cocoa and chocolate". The site was painstakingly camouflaged with brown and green hessian attached to wire netting, but the Cadburys discovered after the war that the plant was identified in alarming detail on a Luftwaffe map, though it was never targeted.

The Cadbury family directors, most of them practising Quakers, were divided over the issue of making munitions – individual Cadburys in both world wars served in the Friends' Ambulance Unit – and the filling of anti-aircraft rockets was only taken on after a great deal of discussion, though later it was said jokingly at the works that it was "just the packing of a new kind of assortment box". Ultimately, Quaker consciences were eased by the knowledge that most of the war production was defensive in nature.[3]

The all-important aircraft industry, though beefed up since rearmament, was still on a fairly small scale. In the mid-1930s it employed only 35,000 workers: the Vickers plant at Weybridge in Surrey was one of the biggest, with 1,700 employees. At the outbreak of war, 16 aircraft manufacturers and four engine makers got the bulk of Air Ministry contracts but they could barely cope with the volume of wartime demand. Fighter production rose to meet the challenge of the Battle of Britain and was above target by 1942, though the output of heavy bombers was still short by more than 25 per cent.

There were hundreds of sub-contractors to firms such as A. V. Roe, which made the Lancaster bomber at

THE CHANGING CENTURY

Facts from the business archives:

1940: The first brands of nylon stockings were launched in the US

1941: Nylon went into production in Britain; British Nylon Spinners set up in Coventry and later, in Stowmarket. Wartime output was confined to government and services needs, particularly parachute fabric

1941: In Accrington, Lancashire, Terylene was developed by J. R. Whinfield and J. T. Dickson of Calico Printers Association

1942: Kemball, Bishop & Co. of Bromley-by-Bow became the first commercial company to make penicillin. During the war years, most of its consignments were for military use

1942: The Co-operative Society introduced Britain's first self-service grocery – a screened-off section in its Romford branch

1942: "October 17" was stamped on packs of Lyons Coffee – the first recorded sell-by date in Britain

1942: The US started to supply sailors with a new piece of kit – a knitted cotton shirt with short sleeves set at right angles to front and back panels. The "T-Type", said the Navy, "meant greater sweat absorption under arms". It passed into civilian use as the T-Shirt

1943: In Britain, the pay-as-you-earn taxation scheme was introduced. From now on, the nation would be taxed at source. Every employee would have a personal tax code, applied to their wages

1943: A Briton, Henry Martin, acquired the rights to Laszlo Biro's ball-point pen. The following year, he began producing ball-points for the RAF in a disused aircraft hangar near Reading. (Biro's invention, he had found, was unaffected by changes in air pressure or atmosphere.) His staff of 17 girls produced 30,000 finished pens the first year

1943: BOAC recruited its first stewardesses, calling for young ladies with poise and an educated voice. "Glamour girls," added the airline, "are definitely not required"

1945: Decca introduced the world's first hi-fi record player, the Piccadilly

1945: The American chemist Earl W. Tupper, formerly of Du Pont, started to develop a range of airtight plastic boxes and containers. Twenty years later, he was marketing his products through Tupperware parties, held by housewives

1946: BOAC inaugurated Britain's first commercial North Atlantic passenger service, flying between London and New York. Scheduled flight time was 19hr 45min

1946: A new board game, Lexico, was brought to market by its inventor, Alfred Mosher Butts. Two years later, the company Selchow and Righter bought the rights and began to mass-produce sets under a new name, Scrabble

1946: The first British-made nylon products hit the shops: stockings

Making Spitfires for the Battle of Britain

Manchester, Vickers Supermarine, which built Spitfires at Castle Bromwich, and Rolls-Royce, which made the Spitfire's Merlin engine. The Halifax bomber was produced by Handley Page with help from English Electric, Fairey Aviation, Rootes motor group and even the London Passenger Transport Board. Littlewoods, the Liverpool football pools firm, which had a particularly good reputation for managing its young female workers, made floors for the Halifax, fuselages for the Lancaster and even entire Wellington bombers. The Ford plant at Trafford Park, which had pioneered mass-production in Britain with the Model T, broke down Rolls-Royce's craftsman-built Merlin engine to simple assembly methods and trained thousands of workers to put it together without previous aerospace experience.

Some of the sub-contractors were worthy of an Ealing comedy: components for De Havilland's Mosquito fighter-

1947: Britain's 1,500 collieries were nationalised

1947: In an effort to increase productivity and decrease absenteeism from work, the British government banned mid-week sporting fixtures

1947: The state of the post-war British economy demanded new austerity measures. Newspapers were once again restricted to four pages; businessmen were allowed no more than £8 a day to spend on overseas trips; in some areas, industrial and domestic power supplies were turned off for one day every week

1947: In Yeovil, Somerset, a company called Westland Aircraft started series production of a helicopter under licence from the

American firm Sikorsky. Some 40 years later, the future of the company would spark a Cabinet crisis (see chapter 8)

1947: In Woking, Surrey, Kenneth Wood came up with the design for a new domestic appliance, the all-slicing, all-shredding, all-mincing, all-mixing, Kenwood Chef

1948: The first household articles made from polythene, washing-up bowls, came on to the British market

1948: At the Amsterdam Motor Show of April 30, Rover unveiled the first British jeep-style vehicle specifically designed for civilian use. The Land-Rover was born

1948: Britain's railways and electricity industry were nationalised

1948: At Manor Park, the London

Co-operative Society opened the first full-sized self-service grocery shop in Britain. (It would, however, be another 10 years or so before supermarkets entered the mainstream – see chapter 5)

1948: In California, the first McDonald's burger joint opened, promising fast service and low-cost food

1948: Rowntree brought out Polo Mints

1948/49: The British iron and steel industries were nationalised

1949: Bendix Home Appliances opened the first self-service

launderette in Europe – at 184 Queensway, west London. It was equipped with coin-operated Bendix washing machines

1949: The sugar king Lord Lyle mounted an anti-nationalisation campaign (below), railing against the champions of state ownership as "long-haired boys from Bloomsbury". (Lord Lyle was a Conservative supporter)

Sources: Patrick Robertson: The New Shell Book of Firsts, 1994, Headline Book Publishing; Christopher Lee: This Sceptred Isle, Twentieth Century, BBC and Penguin Books, 1999

Jet genius: Frank Whittle (right) with the engine that changed aviation history

bomber, which was fabricated in wood, were made by a hotch-potch army that included furniture makers, church pew carvers, piano makers and a housewife named Mrs. Hale from Welwyn Garden City who made Mosquito parts in her home with a group of neighbours.[4]

Most of the 120,000 aircraft built in Britain during the war were based on 1930s technology. The big technical breakthrough was the Gloster Meteor jet fighter in 1944, based on Frank Whittle's epochal technology, which was later to give Britain a leading, if short-lived, edge in post-war aviation with the de Havilland Comet airliner. One major lesson that had been learned from the disastrous technological shortfalls of 1914, leaving large areas of key industry to German dominance, was the necessity of government-backed industrial research programmes. The work of the Department of Scientific and Industrial Research, set up in 1915, had been continued between the wars, though that did not prevent the eminent scientists Solly Zuckerman and J. D. Bernal from criticising the failure to mobilise the country's scientific talent in an anonymous but influential Penguin special called Science in War.

Yet British scientists did come up with the two most significant scientific developments of the Second World War – radar and the atom bomb. The process of locating objects in space through the use of short radio waves – Radio Direction and Range-finding – had been perfected for military purposes in 1935 by Robert Watson-Watt, and a coastal chain of radar masts, put in place before September 1939, was the determinant factor in winning the Battle of Britain, although the public was fed the propaganda story of "night vision" among the fighter aces, aided by Vitamin A. Countless children were encouraged to eat up their carrots as a result of the exploits of John "Cat's-eyes" Cunningham and his fellow pilots, though in private Cunningham himself attributed all but one of his 20 enemy kills to radar.

But the masts were highly vulnerable to air attack and it was another British scientific breakthrough in the first winter of the war that enabled radar to be installed in aircraft and warships and become a major, mobile secret weapon. This was the cavity magnetron, discovered by J. T. Randall and H. A. H. Boot, which could reduce to 10 centimetres or less the wavelengths that acted as "mirrors" for the signals being bounced back from the target.

One more invention was needed, however, to make mobile radar workable – a lightweight insulating material – and it was found in a compound called polythene. This had been discovered through a laboratory

'Cat's eyes' Cunningham: ace fighter pilots were rumoured to have 'night vision' aided by Vitamin A

accident at ICI in 1933 and had languished ever since while the company wondered what commercial use could be found for it. Neither of the two existing insulating materials, rubber and gutta-percha, was effective or light enough to make centimetric radar practical, but polythene had the ideal properties. After the war, though sadly no longer under British patents, it would become one of the 20th century's most versatile products – the ubiquitous material of household goods ranging from cling-film to kitchen buckets.

The first ton of polythene for experimental radar cables was delivered by ICI soon after the outbreak of war and although polythene-insulated sets were not ready for the Battle of Britain in 1940, they came into their own at the end of the Blitz on London that autumn when RAF night fighters equipped with the lightweight installations were able to locate and shoot down German bombers with accuracy. Installed in battleships of the Mediterranean Fleet, they accounted for a decisive victory against the Italians at the Battle of Cape Matapan in March, 1941, and later guided Allied bombers in the night raids on Hamburg and Berlin.

ICI was also intimately involved with Britain's pioneering work on an atomic weapon, to the extent that it even presented Churchill and his scientific advisers with an official tender to manufacture a bomb. British, French, German and Italian scientists had been working on nuclear fission since the end of the 19th century, and research papers were well in the public domain by 1939. Experiments had begun at Birmingham University that spring on weapons' use of uranium, and just two days before the outbreak of war Sir Henry Tizard's Committee for the Scientific Survey of Air Warfare was presented with a paper by two brilliant emigré physicists at Birmingham University, Professor Rudolf Peierls and O. R. Frisch. Peierls was a refugee from the Third Reich and Frisch an Austrian who had worked with the nuclear physicist Niels Bohr in Copenhagen and was on a holiday visit to Britain when war broke out. Their paper contained a

virtual blueprint for a bomb based on uranium 235. It sparked off a series of feasibility studies under the aegis of the top-secret Maud Committee, the government body responsible for work on an atomic weapon (Maud was the first name of the English nanny to Bohr's children). Intensive work took place within ICI on separating the U235 element from natural uranium, and by July 1941 the company had submitted a formal proposal to produce a 5kg bomb by the end of 1943 at a capital cost of £5m. ICI declared itself willing to execute this work "for the British Empire".

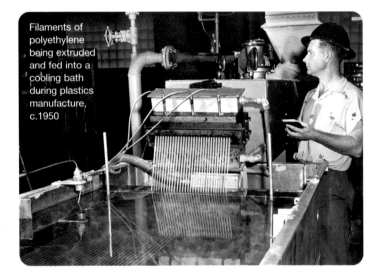

Filaments of polyethylene being extruded and fed into a cooling bath during plastics manufacture, c.1950

Churchill's personal science adviser, Professor Frederick Lindemann, later Lord Cherwell, recommended that British work on the bomb should go ahead – though no-one seriously considered it being undertaken by a commercial organisation. The project was given the vaguely industrial but innocuous title of Tube Alloys, on the grounds that, as its director Sir John Anderson (of Anderson shelter fame) explained: "I think you can assume that there will always be a tube in anything… It's quite meaningless but it sounds as if it's got some kind of importance." In the end, of course, the task of developing a nuclear weapon went to the US, where similar research was leaping ahead with greater resources, and the Manhattan Project was established in the Arizona desert under Professor Robert Oppenheimer. This would give birth to the bombs that destroyed Hiroshima and Nagasaki in August 1945, ending the Pacific war.[5]

Other key British technologies had earlier crossed the Atlantic in the autumn of 1940 to be more fully developed with the resources of the US military – famously those of radar and Whittle's jet engine. Churchill was at first reluctant but was persuaded by Sir Henry Tizard that Britain's dire war situation demanded it. Tizard took full documentation of the radar and jet technologies and a sample of the first resonant magnetron to Washington in his so-called "black box" – literally a black metal deeds box. A US scientific historian later described it as "the most valuable cargo ever brought to our shores". Another critical British innovation lost to the US because of lack of resources and a shortage of trained micro-biologists was penicillin, discovered by Alexander Fleming at St. Mary's Hospital in west London in 1928 and developed as an anti-bacterial agent by Howard Florey and Ernst Chain in 1940. The result was that Britain had to pay royalties to the US for supplies to treat its war wounded.

THE CHANGING CENTURY

A snapshot of science and technology:

1941: At the Radcliffe Infirmary in Oxford doctors used purified penicillin to treat a policeman suffering from blood poisoning. It was the first clinical use of the drug in the world. In the same year, the first large-scale penicillin production plant was built. The Oxford-based plant was set up under the direction of Professor Ernst Chain who, together with Alexander Fleming and Howard Florey, was awarded a Nobel Prize in 1943

1941: Flight Lieutenant P. E .G. Sayer made a test flight in the Gloster-Whittle E.28/39, Britain's first turbojet aircraft. The Gloster-Whittle, designed by Frank Whittle, attained speeds of up to 466mph

1943: At Bletchley Park in Hertfordshire, under the direction of Professor Max Newman, the world's first electronic computer, Colossus, was built. The invention, which enabled the British to crack the German Enigma code, was the work of tragic genius Alan Turing. (The Apple Computer logo is widely believed to be a homage to Turing, who killed himself by biting an apple laced with cyanide)

1943: In Switzerland, Buhrle & Co. designed the first telephone answering machine capable of giving and receiving messages. The machine, marketed as the Ipsophone, even allowed the subscriber to access his or her messages remotely. It hit Britain in 1952, and was used mainly by businesses

1944: Decca issued the first high-fidelity (hi-fi) recordings

1944: The word "antibiotic" was coined by the American Selman Waksman, who developed Streptomycin to treat throat infections

1945: For the first time, the atomic bomb was used, dropped on Hiroshima from the US bomber Enola Gay on August 6. Three days later, another atomic bomb devastated Nagasaki

1948: The hormone cortisone was developed for clinical use by Philip S. Hench and Edward C. Kendall of the Mayo Foundation, Minnesota and used to treat a 20-year-old arthritic. The patient, who had been incapacitated by his condition, was active four days later

1948: At Manchester University, Professor Tom Kilburn and (Sir) Freddy Williams built the first computer with a memory. The computer, the Small-Scale Experimental Machine (SSEM) or "Baby", could store not only data but any short user programme in electronic memory. The next year, the Baby was used as the basis for a larger model, the Manchester Mark 1, which included a high-speed magnetic drum, the forerunner of today's disc. The Manchester Mark 1 became a prototype for the first electronic computer to be made commercially in Britain, the Ferranti Mark 1

1948: For the first time in Britain, closed-circuit TV was installed. EMI supplied a system for Guy's Hospital, London

1949: Wing Commander R. P. Beaumont test-piloted the first British-designed jet bomber, the English Electric Canberra B Mk 1 (below), powered by Rolls-Royce engines

Main sources: Patrick Robertson: The New Shell Book of Firsts, 1994, Headline Book Publishing; Christopher Lee: This Sceptred Isle, Twentieth Century, BBC and Penguin Books, 1999

Despite being undertaken on shoestring budgets and often in rickety laboratory conditions, drug development advanced enormously during World War II, including the sulphonamide group for treating infection and the anti-malarial compound Paludrine that was discovered by an ICI team in Blackley, Manchester, in 1942. The ICI scientists worked in such a polluted area that the team leader, Dr. Frank Rose, recalled smuts coming in every time a laboratory window was opened. Paludrine had the advantage over previous anti-malarials of not turning the patients yellow. It was clinically proven just in time to be flown out to British troops in the Burmese jungle.[6]

Paint technology, electrical engineering, aeronautics, valve technology, chemical engineering and plastics were all industries that benefited hugely from the spur of war. Another was the US discovery of nylon, which had been launched by Du Pont at the New York World's Fair in 1938. Nylon stockings became the GI's tactical weapon of choice when dating British girls. They were not widely available in Britain until the 1950s, and the phenomenon of the post-war "spiv" with his suitcase full of black-market nylons became a familiar sight in city streets.

In the meantime another, even more versatile synthetic fibre – polyester – had been discovered in a back-street Manchester laboratory by two chemists working for the Calico Printers Association (CPA). Wallace Carothers, the tragically unstable Du Pont scientist who successfully developed nylon but later took his own life, had attempted but failed to isolate the molecular make-up of polyester, derived from terephthalic acid. The CPA patented it as Terylene and brought it to ICI to develop. It introduced the era of the drip-dry shirt and became a huge post-war success in women's clothing from 1946 – though its success was to ram another nail in the coffin of "King Cotton".

Wartime working conditions were stressful for both employers and employees, especially during bombing raids.

ICI scientists Frank Curd and Frank Rose, discoverers of the anti-malaria drug Paludrine

Half of Marks and Spencer's 234 stores were damaged, the main premises in Birmingham being completely destroyed. Many of the company's undamaged shops were requisitioned for government food storage, and it was not until 1953 that its selling space reverted to pre-war levels. The firm's Baker Street headquarters, meanwhile, played a key part in some of the most secret aspects of the war in Europe, housing Combined Operations and the Special Operations Executive that trained and sent agents into occupied France to aid the Resistance.[7]

Industrialists were plagued with petty bureaucracy. In a scheme to release some 4,000 employees from the soft drinks industry for war work, it was decreed that all brand names should be abolished, prices standardised and lemonade bottles distinguished by numbers. Trade unions agreed to let their members work for up to 56 hours a week for the duration but at the height of demand for munitions in 1942 many ordnance factories worked their employees for up to 71 hours. Health hazards were ignored: TB was rife in the boot and shoe industry, and after the war a number of premature deaths among factory workers was attributed to blackout fabric covering up ventilation shafts.[8]

Women aged between 18 and 40 formed a much higher proportion of both the armed forces and the home front workers in World War II than in 1914-18, when their role in society was still restricted. By 1943, eight out of 10 married women and nine out of 10 single women were estimated to be in the forces, in industry or in public-service occupations such as studio engineers at the BBC. Some physically strong women even worked as railway porters, to the embarrassment of many male passengers.

One progressive idea in combating the them-and-us atmosphere of British industry was the Joint Production Committee, the legacy of a similar effort in the Great War. Some 4,500 such committees were set up and did good work in, for example, accepting ideas for improvement from the shopfloor. But the impetus did not last and by 1948 only 550 survived.[9]

More team-work in industrial relations and the emergence of "sunrise" industries of the future ought to have positioned Britain well to seize markets in the post-war world, although so many patents and licences had been abandoned to US development. Some historians consider that at the end of the war Britain still ranked among the richest nations of the world, despite the cost of the war being twice that of 1914-1918, wiping out overseas assets by March 1941 and leaving a debt of £3bn to the sterling area. Britain was rescued from imminent bankruptcy by $27bn worth of supplies sent from the US under Lend Lease, though after the programme was abruptly terminated in 1945 Lord Keynes was forced to go cap in hand to Washington for more loans. In technology, however, Britain ended the war among world leaders, especially in such industries of the future as aircraft and electronics.

Meanwhile, old economic staples such as cotton were living on borrowed time, given a temporary blood transfusion by wartime demand. Shipbuilding prospered in wartime conditions and for about 10 years afterwards, and Pilkington, the family-run glass business in Lancashire, reckoned to have re-glazed London twice over as a result of bomb damage. In 1941, its sales were 50 per cent up over those of 1938 in spite of car manufacture being suspended.[10]

But full order books masked antique machinery in many industries – notably textiles – and even more antique working practices such as the demarcation arrangements in shipbuilding that enabled men from four different unions to share out one simple task. This – like the issue of working hours – had been put aside by the unions for the duration, but would immediately be re-imposed in 1945.

Keynes, the apostle of demand management who acted as the Labour government's negotiator for the $3.75bn post-war US loan, felt that shipbuilding alone of all Britain's old traditional industries could hold its own against the world. He had no time for the inefficient textile industry where the mill-owners had been content to work old machinery into the ground and ignore modern automated practice. In a 1945 paper on Britain's economic future, he wrote scathingly that if every factory on the north-east coast and in Lancashire could be destroyed, "when the directors were sitting there and no-one else, we should have nothing to fear". Keynes distinguished between the old, inefficient industries and the new, world-changing ones such as aircraft and radar technology where, he wrote, "we have the rest of the world licked on cost".[11]

Bombs blast the suburbs: few places were safe from air raids

Bletchley Park, the country house where the Enigma code was cracked

Even more of a foothold on the future was promised by technology that would bring about the third industrial revolution, based on electronics and computing. It evolved from the highly secret code-breaking activities at Bletchley Park, the country house in Buckinghamshire where the Nazis' Enigma machine was finally defeated. The "Colossus" calculating machine, developed there in February 1944 by the brilliant mathematician Alan Turing and others, was effectively the world's first programmable digital computer, though it had no memory and was powered by thermionic valves, not transistors or chips. Working with young University of Manchester scientists after the war, Ferranti made the world's first commercial production computer in 1951, and it was sold to the Lyons catering empire, of "Corner House" fame.

Lyons, an innovative and forward-looking business dating from the 19th century and run by the Salmon and Gluckstein families, was already among the world's leading companies in office management systems. It had an enormous number of transactions to process each week: apart from the payroll for its 30,000 staff, there were all the waitresses' receipts from the teashop business, its frozen food manufacturing side, and exhibition catering, among other activities. It had recruited a Cambridge mathematician called John Simmons to create a complete management accounting system. Simmons kept abreast of the infant

computing field, in which a Cambridge team was already building a stored-data calculator, the EDSAC, and in October 1947 proposed to the Lyons board that the company take an active part in promoting the commercial development of computers. Simmons told the directors that for the first time, "there is a possibility of a machine which will be able to cope, at almost incredible speed, with any variation of clerical procedure, provided the conditions which govern the variations can be pre-determined... the possible saving from such a machine should be at least £50,000 a year. The capital cost would be of the order of £100,000."

No-one else had yet contemplated applying computing to business use – the technology was considered to be primarily of value to scientists – but Lyons' board decided to go ahead. Standard Telephones and Cables were commissioned to provide the technology, but this was soon replaced by superior equipment from Ferranti, and in February 1951 the LEO central computer (for Lyons Electronic Office) was able to perform a ceremonial test programme for Princess Elizabeth, the heir to the throne. Later that year, Lyons began accepting contract computing for, among other bodies, the Meteorological Office, the Inland Revenue, the Institute of Actuaries and Ford Motor Company at Dagenham. Lyons eventually sold off its computer business in 1962 to English Electric for more than £1.8m, covering all its costs on the venture.[12]

As in computing, British inventiveness in the aviation industry had also been burnished by war, and this time round the War Cabinet was determined not to let the advances in technology run into the sand in peacetime markets. In 1945, Britain had 22 aircraft companies, nine engine manufacturers and a support network of government R&D laboratories. The pioneer pilot Lord Brabazon, who had been minister of aircraft production in 1941-42, was recruited to plan the post-war industry, a central point of which was to develop a British challenger to the Lockheed Constellation airliner, which had commanded the pre-war North Atlantic route.

Several prototypes for different markets were developed at Bristol, all codenamed Brabazon. The first, a massive propeller-driven airliner designed to carry 50 passengers in the luxury of dining-rooms and sleeping cabins, flew its trials but never went into service. Brabazon 2 became the four-engined, medium-haul turbo-prop Vickers Viscount, a best-selling and long-lived triumph for the British aerospace industry. Brabazon 3 was the Bristol Britannia, a long-haul turbo-jet known as "The Whispering Giant".

Lord Brabazon, mastermind of Britain's postwar aerospace industry

THE CHANGING CENTURY

A snapshot of Britain:

1940: Ration books (right), last seen in British households in 1918, were re-introduced

1940: The IRA campaign continued; two Irish terrorists were hanged in Birmingham

1940: The Home Guard, parodied in the 1970s comedy Dad's Army, was set up. Its membership was to reach a peak of 1.7 million; it would be disbanded following D-Day in 1944

1940: The Ministry of War began a national public awareness campaign, "Careless talk costs lives", warning the nation that what they said could be used against them by enemy sympathisers. Many of the posters were designed by the Punch cartoonist Fougasse and had a humorous touch. Memorable copylines included "Be like Dad, keep Mum"

1940: In May, 80 Conservatives rebelled against the leadership of Neville Chamberlain. Two days later he resigned, and Winston Churchill emerged as the wartime leader. Labour and Liberal MPs joined his government

1940: By the end of May, the British Expeditionary Force had retreated from Dunkirk. Churchill gave orders for the evacuation of British troops. Operation Dynamo, in which 600 so-called "little ships" were requisitioned to aid the Navy, was hailed as a triumph. Churchill had somehow managed to seize a victory from the jaws of a humiliating defeat

1940: The pressure on Britain intensified in June as France finally fell to Germany

1940: In September, Londoners began sleeping in tube stations as the blitz on the capital began. Luftwaffe strikes on Coventry, Plymouth, Liverpool, Hull, Swansea and other major cities and ports followed. For the first time, civilians were the targets of enemy fire and, by 1945, some 60,000 would have been killed. (The human cost did not end with the casualty list: the evacuation of some 827,000 children to the seaside and countryside

severely disrupted family life. Many years later, some evacuees spoke of the hardship they had endured at the hands of the adults who took them in)

1941: The US offered 50 destroyers to help the British war effort. But there was a controversial quid pro quo: 99-year leases on bases on the West Indies. Any tension in the Anglo-American relationship, however, was swept aside by events in December: Japanese aircraft attacked Pearl Harbor. To the relief of Churchill, the US joined the war

1942: A reluctant Churchill agreed to hold talks on the future of India, whose campaign for independence was being supported by Roosevelt. Sir Stafford Cripps was sent to renew the offer of dominion status once the war was over. Gandhi, however, rejected the offer. In August, the All-India Congress passed a resolution that Britain should leave India, and another campaign of civil disobedience began

1942: For the first time in two years, church bells rang out: Rommel had been forced back by Field Marshal Montgomery in the Battle of El Alamein and the British had recaptured the Libyan port of Tobruk

1942: More than 80,000 British and empire troops in Singapore surrendered to the Japanese. The inability of Britain to repel the Japanese advance – Malaya and Hong Kong had also fallen – put severe strains on the imperial system

1943: Plans were laid for the Allied invasion of Normandy

1944: Britain met with America, China and Russia at Dumbarton Oaks, a mansion in Washington DC, to work out a system for guiding the future of world security. The United Nations was born

1944: It was decided that half a million prefabricated homes were to be built to help plug the housing gap created by the destruction of war. Prefabs – single-storey dwellings of around 600 square feet– were meant to be temporary; in fact, many survived into the 1980s

1944: A new Education Act, brainchild of the reformist Conservative, R. A. Butler, was passed. It raised the school leaving age to 15 by 1947 and promised state provision of three forms of secondary education – secondary modern, technical and grammar. In the same year, female teachers were at last given pay parity with their male counterparts

It was popular with passengers in the late 1950s on transatlantic and Africa-UK routes, though on the latter it had to make several refuelling stops. Brabazon 4, however, was the focus of Britain's aviation ambitions. This became the Comet jetliner, a beautiful but doomed plane built by De Havilland. For a brief, proud moment in the late 1940s, it appeared to have a three-year lead over Boeing in the passenger jet market, with the prospect of earning millions of those much-needed dollars.[13]

British Overseas Airways Corporation, as Imperial Airways and the smaller British Airways of the 1930s had become under state ownership in 1939, had such confidence in the Comet that it ordered 14 off the drawing-board without a prototype. Construction began in 1946 and three years

1944: Nearly 90 per cent of Welsh miners went on strike for more pay; only 44 of the 200 pits in South Wales were working. Since coal was vital for the war effort, the government intervened and agreed to the miners' demands

1945: Air Chief Marshal Sir Arthur "Bomber" Harris ordered 800 Lancasters to attack the town of Dresden. More than 400 American B17s continued the onslaught, in which an estimated 130,000 civilians died. Harris's rationale was to make sure that the German spirit was crushed utterly and that there would be no further attempts to prolong the war

1945: On May 23, Churchill resigned as wartime prime minister but formed a caretaker government to run the country until elections were held. With the war all but over, the coalition was beginning to disintegrate. Clement Attlee and Labour began to prepare for power; the electorate wanted something better than they had before the war and the Beveridge Report (see welfare state box) offered it. In the July election, Labour won 393 seats, the Conservatives only 213

1945: The Potsdam Conference, a gathering of the three major allies, the Soviet Union, the US and Britain, was held to decide the future of territories that had been overrun by Germany. The outcome was Soviet domination of eastern Europe

1946: In Missouri, Churchill delivered a speech that was to resonate for decades to come. It included the words: "From Stettin in the Baltic to Trieste in the Adriatic, an Iron Curtain has descended across the Continent". The curtain, of course, was Stalin's

1946: The government realised that the post-war reconstruction scheme had to include the building of new towns. Shortages of labour and materials and the worsening economic climate meant, however, that by the end of the 1940s most designated sites were still fields of mud and rubble

1946: As food shortages continued, the government was forced to re-issue wartime make-do menus. Included on the recommended-recipe list: squirrel pie

1946: The divorce laws were relaxed; the six-month wait between decree nisi and decree absolute was reduced to six weeks. Thirty-eight thousand divorce petitions were heard; many thousands of them came from soldiers, sailors and airmen whose domestic lives had been wrecked by war

1946: The Muslim leader Muhammad Ali Jinnah proposed that India be divided. The Muslim territory in the north would be known as Pakistan

1947: An agreement was signed in London giving Burma self-government; the post-war decolonisation of the empire had begun

1947: Britons experienced another black-out: coal shortages led to power cuts. Homes, businesses, courts, government offices and surgeries were all lit by candles. In a winter in which temperatures fell to -17 degrees fahrenheit, gas and coal fires were banned

1947: In June, the US secretary of state George C. Marshall devised a plan whereby the war-devastated economies of Western Europe would be offered $15bn in aid. The Marshall Plan became effective the following year

1947: Britain transferred power in India; the Indian Constituent Assembly was convened, led by Jawaharlal Nehru

1948: The British mandate in Palestine, which had been granted by the League of Nations in the post-war carve-up of 1920, and which helped give Britain control over the Suez canal, ended; Israel was declared a state. Both Jews and Arabs refused to withdraw to the agreed lines in the Negev Desert; war in the Middle East seemed inevitable

1949: Southern Ireland, previously a dominion of the Commonwealth owing allegiance to the crown, became a republic

1949: The North Atlantic Treaty Organisation (NATO) was created. It would become the basis of western opposition to Soviet military power for the rest of the century. Its principal architect was the British foreign secretary, Ernest Bevin. NATO's first achievement was to help to bring about an end to the Soviet blockade of Berlin and the birth of the German Federal Republic

1949: In September, the pound was devalued against the dollar by 30.5 per cent

Sources: Christopher Lee: This Sceptred Isle, Twentieth Century, BBC and Penguin Books; Kenneth O. Morgan: Twentieth Century Britain: A Very Short Introduction, Oxford University Press, 2000; Juliet Gardiner: From the Bomb to the Beatles: the changing face of post-war Britain, 1945-1965, Collins and Brown, 1999

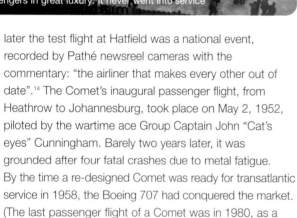
The Bristol Brabazon, an eight-engined giant that carried
50 passengers in great luxury: it never went into service

Inaugural flight for
the Vickers Viscount,
a world-beater for British aviation

later the test flight at Hatfield was a national event, recorded by Pathé newsreel cameras with the commentary: "the airliner that makes every other out of date".[14] The Comet's inaugural passenger flight, from Heathrow to Johannesburg, took place on May 2, 1952, piloted by the wartime ace Group Captain John "Cat's eyes" Cunningham. Barely two years later, it was grounded after four fatal crashes due to metal fatigue. By the time a re-designed Comet was ready for transatlantic service in 1958, the Boeing 707 had conquered the market. (The last passenger flight of a Comet was in 1980, as a Dan-Air charter.)

More bright but illusory promise was held out by the motor industry, whose production lines had been modernised under shadow factory funding. Clement Attlee's Labour government, which had deposed Winston Churchill with a landslide in July 1945, was committed to a massive programme of social reform, nationalising "the commanding heights of the economy" and installing the Welfare State as outlined in the 1942 Beveridge Report. But those commanding heights – iron and steel, coal, gas, the railways and docks – did not include motor vehicles,

and Sir Stafford Cripps, post-war president of the board of trade, was determined to make that industry the star of Britain's export drive for dollars.

For all his austere, killjoy image, Cripps was an enthusiast for innovation, and the only one of Attlee's ministers to have experience in industry. A chemist by training, he had managed an explosives factory in the Great War. Now he tried to galvanise the motor trade into designing for new markets rather than resting on its pre-war domestic laurels. He had the knack himself of spotting winners, backing the development of the Land Rover and persuading the Treasury to exempt it from purchase tax. But he met a hostile reception when he addressed the Society of Motor Manufacturers in November 1945. "We must provide a cheap, tough, good-looking car of decent size – not the sort of car we have hitherto produced for smooth roads and short journeys in this country – and we must produce them in sufficient quantities to get the benefits of mass production," he told the assembled motor magnates. Cries of "No!" and "Tripe!" came from his audience when he added that they should export at least 50 per cent of their output instead of relying on a protected home market.

Apart from the Land Rover (of which not enough were made to capitalise on an eager market) and one or two models such as the rugged Standard Vanguard, no serious attempt was made to come up with new designs. Indeed, at one Standard factory they unpacked all the equipment dismantled in 1940, set it up again and started producing the same models.[15]

Worse blindness was to come. The supremely efficient plant that manufactured the Volkswagen Beetle at Wolfsburg lay in the British Zone of post-war Germany and in August 1946 a British Army colonel wrote to the Board of Trade recommending that the plant be acquired for Britain. It would, he suggested, make a "splendid investment" and the VW itself, then known as the Kdf-Wagen or People's Car, would be an ideal low-cost model for both home and overseas markets. The Board of Trade was not impressed, taking the view that North America, its prime export target, would not be interested in a small car once sponsored by Hitler. Several British manufacturers including Lord Nuffield and Billy Rootes came to inspect the Wolfsburg plant and simply recommended that its advanced machine tools be stripped out for British use. The Board of Trade concluded that the VW "is not considered to have a long-term civilian application by our producers".[16]

By 1956, West Germany had overtaken the UK as the world's leading car exporter, and the VW went on to be the best-selling car in history – in the US as everywhere else. As Peter Hennessy writes in his masterly history of the 1945-51 Labour government, Never Again: "The world market was ours for the taking in the early post-war years. Despite the strictures of ministers and officials in Whitehall, the industry preferred protected, easy and ultimately ruinous business-

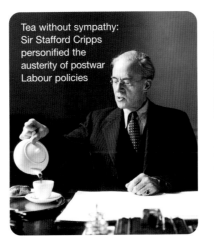

Tea without sympathy: Sir Stafford Cripps personified the austerity of postwar Labour policies

The Standard Vanguard shows its curves: a postwar car intended to appeal to export markets

as-usual." Elsewhere in the same book, he concludes: "In 1945, Britain's sunrise industries outshone its sunsets and its twilights; add in the City of London, the country's financial capabilities that accumulated such a rich heap of 'invisible' exports, and it is plain that we possessed an industrial and monetary base that should have sustained a nation of 46 million people with relative ease…"

On top of that, and it still comes as a surprise to many who assume that defeated Germany got the lion's share of Marshall Aid – on which it proceeded to build its economic miracle – Britain was in fact the major recipient of US largesse. She received a third more Marshall Aid than West Germany – $2.7bn net to Germany's $1.7bn according to one official account, $3.1bn to $1.5bn according to another. Whichever is the true figure, it was the largest slice given to any European nation. In the historian Corelli Barnett's view – and it is hard not to agree – what happened next resembled a sort of ant and grasshopper fable, with Germany using the money to re-build and re-tool its bombed-out industrial base while Britain spent much of it on propping up an unsustainable role as banker to the imperial "sterling area" and funding the infant Welfare State. Certainly by 1948 – in three years

the man who warned of war:
key dates in the life of John Maynard Keynes

1918/1919: Keynes (right), then working for the Treasury, was sent as a delegate to the Paris peace conference

1919: On his return from Versailles, he wrote The Economic Consequences of the Peace. The book warned that the Allies' demands for punitive reparations from Germany were dangerous folly. To reduce the German economy to rubble would, Keynes argued, be to kill the German market for British goods. Worse, it would create the kind of conditions in which nationalism would rise to threaten the rest of Europe. As the Russians had done, the Germans would, said Keynes, come to "listen to whatever instruction of hope, illusion or revenge" was brought to them. (The Economic Consequences of the Peace, chapter 6)

1920: The first signs that Keynes was right started to emerge. The German Workers' Party (soon to be called the National Socialist German Workers' Party) began demonstrating in Bavaria against capitalism and Jews. One Adolf Schicklgruber, now going by the name Adolf Hitler, was its spokesman. Meanwhile, the Allies demanded the Germans pay £12.5m

1921: Keynes counselled the prime minister, David Lloyd George, that British prosperity was dependent on a fundamental policy change – a concentrated effort to make Germany prosperous. Whatever Lloyd George thought of Keynes' views, France was in no mood to listen. Bitterness towards the Germans ran

high. (In 1923, the French and Belgian governments would send 100,000 soldiers to seize goods in kind from the mines, forests and industrial heartland in Germany's Ruhr Valley; at the Krupp steel works in Essen nine German workers would be shot)

1925: Keynes warned against the return to the gold standard; again, he was to be proved right (see chapter 3)

1936: Keynes published his great work, "The General Theory of Employment, Interest and Money". This was an antidote to the Depression and promoted beliefs Keynes had long held. Essentially, the thesis was that employment was tied to demand levels and that demand levels could be raised by cutting interest rates and increasing spending. (Governments would simply have to abandon their obsession with balancing budgets.) Keynes' ideas were embraced by Lloyd George, who, in opposition, proposed public-spending schemes to create jobs, and eventually by F. D. Roosevelt, under the famous New Deal. They would continue to influence political and economic thought for decades to come, meeting their antithesis in 1980s monetarism

1943: Keynes (now Lord Keynes) developed a plan for a world bank and a global monetary fund, which would bail out countries whose economies could not recover by themselves. The fund would lend money in return for the debtor nation accepting its guidelines for independent recovery

1944: Together with Harry Dexter White of the US Treasury, Lord Keynes persuaded delegates at a conference in Bretton Woods, New Hampshire, not to repeat the mistakes of Versailles. At Bretton Woods, a system for fixing currency rates against the dollar was agreed. This helped industrial and world trade and, therefore, promoted international economic stability – a prerequisite, according to Keynes, for peace

1945: In the year before his death, Keynes saw his plans come to fruition. Two agencies of the United Nations were set up: the International Bank for Reconstruction and Development (later the World Bank) and the International Monetary Fund (IMF). They stand as monuments to a man who was heeded too late

Sources: Christopher Lee: This Sceptred Isle, Twentieth Century, BBC and Penguin Books, 1999; Time magazine: The Most Important People of the 20th Century

from a zero base – West German industrial capacity had recovered to 90 per cent of the Third Reich's 1936 level.[17]

Britain's industrial priorities for Marshall Aid were not to advance the forward-looking sectors of motor vehicles, aircraft and electrical products, but to underpin old staples such as coal, steel and agriculture, textiles, bulk chemicals and mechanical engineering, and to meet the cost of US imports such as wheat, cotton, petrol, Virginia tobacco and – a necessary morale-booster in those grey days – Hollywood films. Moreover, using US gold to plug the holes in British financial reserves was a clear failure by 1949, when the pound was steeply devalued against the dollar, from $4.03 to $2.80. By the following spring, the chancellor of the exchequer was forced to admit that the reserves were "still at a lower level than when Marshall Aid began…"[18]

Correlli Barnett's series of books on Britain's 20th-century decline takes a robustly right-wing view of the failure to get to grips with post-war recovery, noting that Attlee's government diverted 7.7 per cent of GDP into defence around the empire, and 11 per cent into what Barnett calls the "New Jerusalem" – setting up the cradle-to-grave NHS and other social services, providing new housing and so on. But other commentators point out that the Labour manifesto had been built on pledges of social reform and that the nation had been so damaged by the war – psychologically as well as physically – that this time round it was going to demand "homes fit for heroes" and the measures planned by Beveridge against destitution and other evils of the past.

Ultimately, however, the funding had never been properly worked out, especially for the National Health Service, and the grand Labour project of nationalisation within a mixed economy did not work as planned. Steel

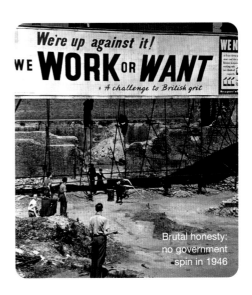

Brutal honesty: no government spin in 1946

was originally the linchpin of those "commanding heights" but proved the last and most difficult of the nationalisations because of the number and variety of companies involved. The nationalisation lasted less than a year before the Churchill government reversed it, and the industry became a political football for decades, being nationalised again under Harold Wilson in 1967 and finally privatised under Margaret Thatcher in 1982.

The string of nationalisations, for which the government compensated shareholders with public stock and sometimes took direct shares in the companies involved, cost the Treasury some £2bn by 1951. Private industry, meanwhile, was being strangled by red tape. The early decision by the Attlee Cabinet to maintain wartime controls for five years so as to manage the risk of boom and slump brought chronic obstructions and bottlenecks to industry. Licences had to be issued for the most trivial matters, even the manufacture of a cricket ball. Bureaucracy worked against the government's exhortations to increase output. Posters plastered the country bearing the bleak slogan: "We Work or Want".

As soon as the war was over Stafford Cripps had launched the idea of the upbeat "Britain Can Make It" exhibition, which opened at the Victoria and Albert Museum in 1946 under the auspices of the Council for Industrial Design. It featured some 6,000 products from 1,300 firms,

The people's coal: the mines come under state ownership, 1947

Not for sale: colourful new textiles in the 'Britain Can Make It' exhibition of 1946 were for overseas customers only

For the first couple of years of peace, the Attlee programme commanded a fair measure of co-operation from private industry. As in the 1914-18 war, central planning had become an accepted fact of life during six years of concerted national effort. Steel distribution had been rigidly controlled during wartime by the Board of Trade; at least one major

On your bike: a streamlined new export model is admired at the 'Britain Can Make It' show

large numbers of which tantalised visitors by not being available for the home market. Cripps also arranged for teams of workers and managers from a number of British industries to visit the US to study productivity techniques: the first, from the Steel Foundry Association, went over in style on the Queen Mary.[19]

utility – electricity – had been effectively nationalised in the 1930s, and public ownership of coal had been widely supported since the General Strike of 1926. Nationalisation

THE CHANGING CENTURY

The British welfare state: a very brief history, 1900-1948

1901: The businessman-philanthropist Seebohm Rowntree (son of Joseph) published a report, Poverty, A Study of Town Life. In it, he called for action to combat the problems of unemployment, old-age and ill-health

1908: Influenced partly by Rowntree, now a close friend of David Lloyd George, the Liberal government introduced the Old Age Pensions Bill. (When chancellor, Herbert Asquith had earmarked £1.2m for pensions)

1909: The first old-age pensions were paid. The non-contributory

scheme gave people who were 70 years old or more and lived on less than £21 a year, five shillings a week. Despite its obvious limitations (average life expectancy was then around 48), the scheme was greeted with national jubilation

1909: The lawyer and economist William Beveridge, an expert on unemployment insurance, joined the Board of Trade and helped set up a national system of labour exchanges

1911: The chancellor, Lloyd George, taking his cue from Beveridge, introduced legislation to set up the National Insurance scheme. The scheme would be modelled on the German system. Contributions from

government (2d), employees (4d) and employers (3d) would be recorded as stamps in National Insurance cards

1912: To the chagrin of Conservative Unionists and Lord Northcliffe's right-wing press, the National Insurance Act was passed. The following year, maternity benefit, sickness benefit and unemployment benefit were introduced

1925: Neville Chamberlain's Widows, Orphans and Old Age Contributory Pensions Act was passed. Pensions were to be paid from the age of 65; widow's benefit was to be introduced

1934: The Unemployment Act set up the Unemployment Assistance Board. Eligibility for relief was widened, but means-testing continued

1940: Supplementary benefits were introduced under the Old Age and Widows' Pensions Act

1943: The Report on Social Insurance and Allied Services came before the government. Its author was Beveridge, and its central premise was the comprehensive cradle-to-grave welfare state*. Perhaps predictably, it got a mixed reception from the coalition Cabinet. After a backbench revolt by Labour's Emmanuel Shinwell and Aneurin Bevan it was eventually accepted

of the gas industry was even advocated in 1945 by the chairman of Unilever.

Whitehall planners had their outstanding successes such as the Town and Country Planning Act, which devised the Green Belt around London, and the first 14 new towns built after 1946 had a generally favourable reception. Seven were built around historic villages or market towns to accommodate London's overspill – Crawley, Bracknell, Hemel Hempstead, Hatfield, Stevenage, Harlow and Basildon – and Welwyn Garden City was extended. The remaining six were in the northeast, Wales and Scotland: Corby, Peterlee and Newton Aycliffe, Cwmbran, East Kilbride and Glenrothes. But for the business community and the populace at large, frequent planning gridlocks and failures caused major daily frustrations.

Bread rationing, something that Britain had managed to avoid even in the worst depths of the war, was introduced in 1946 when people had the right to expect things to be improving, not getting worse. "Austerity Britain" was a dire reality in this writer's childhood, from the power cuts of the

Let them eat cake: queueing for bread, rationed in 1946

apocalyptic winter of 1947, when snow and ice blocked trains from moving coal to the power stations, to the appearance on dinner-tables of such disgusting food supplements as whalemeat, which had the texture of tough venison and an oily, fishy aftertaste. There was not much to buy in the way of consumer goods, and the drive for export dollars meant that even such a modest luxury as

as the basis for Britain's social security programme

1944: The government published a White Paper promising the setting up of a National Health Service

1945: The Family Allowances Act was passed. Under it, every family got a weekly allowance for every child after the first-born. Crucially, the allowances would not be means-tested; the principle of welfare was now extending to all

1946: Aneurin Bevan, minister of health and housing, introduced the first National Health Service Bill, proposing the nationalisation of hospitals and doctors' surgeries. Like Lloyd George's National Insurance

Bill, it was robustly opposed by the British Medical Association

1946: A new National Insurance Act was passed. Every woman between the ages of 16 and 60 and every man between 16 and 65 would be insured in sickness and in health and in old age

1948: In July, nearly 1,000 National Insurance offices were opened and more than 2,500 hospitals came under the control of health boards. To pacify the medical consultants, Bevan allowed them to keep NHS beds in hospitals for their private practices. By the end of the year, about 90 per cent of the population had put their names on GP lists,

and 90 per cent of doctors were members of the NHS

1948: A widows' pension for all was introduced

FOOTNOTE:

The term welfare state had been coined in 1934 by the Oxford professor of International Relations, Alfred Zimmermann

The Attlee government's welfare campaign also included a new drive for state-subsidised housing. It was the dream of Aneurin Bevan that council houses, built to high standards, would form the bulk of "homes for heroes". The programme

fell foul, however, of shortages of money and labour, and bureaucratic delays: in London in the late 1940s, the average waiting time for a council house was seven to eight years

(The first council estate, Totterdown Fields in Tooting, London, had been built in 1901, and provision for local-authority housing had been significantly extended under the Addison Act of 1919.)

Sources: Christopher Lee: This Sceptred Isle, Twentieth Century, BBC and Penguin Books, 1999; Patrick Robertson: The New Shell Book of Firsts, 1994, Headline Book Publishing; Juliet Gardiner: From the Bomb to the Beatles, Collins and Brown, 1999; An Introduction to Social Policy, Professor Paul Spicker of Robert Gordon University (published on the World Wide Web); BBCi

Winston Churchill, with wife Clementine, confidently expects victory in the 1945 election. The voters decided otherwise

patterned chinaware was reserved for overseas customers: only plain white plates, dishes and teacups were on sale for the domestic market.

Under these circumstances, there could not have been a more attractive election slogan than that of Winston Churchill's victorious Conservatives in 1951: "Set the people free". Yet miraculously, despite all the restraints and privations, British industry had done pretty well since 1945. By 1951, industrial production was 50 per cent higher than in 1946, and exports had risen by 67 per cent over the same period. Full employment had been maintained; the arrival of the prefab (a surprisingly popular and long-lived innovation) had eased the lot of families who had lost their homes in the bombing, and shipbuilding was enjoying a post-war boom as it had after 1918.

The British economic recovery compared well with other nations in western Europe, though this would not last out the 1950s – the Korean war and the crippling £4.7bn rearmament programme Britain accepted under US pressure saw to that. But home markets were about to have their reward. Masked by the continual "dollar gap" crises of the late 1940s, the basis was in fact being laid for the consumer society of a decade hence, celebrated by Harold Macmillan in the often-misquoted words he uttered in 1957: "Most of our people have never had it so good".

a fateful dinner at The Ivy

If there were touches of Ealing comedy in some of Britain's war efforts – such as the fighter-bomber parts "factory" set up by housewives in a sitting room in Welwyn Garden City – so there was an element of farce in Britain's first fateful decision to stay aloof from the fledgling European common market, whose prototype was at that time embodied in the European Coal and Steel Community.

On June 1, 1950, the Community issued an invitation to Britain, with the overtones of an ultimatum, to join it under the Schuman Plan, which proposed a European supra-national authority over the coal and steel industries. Prime Minister Attlee and Sir Stafford Cripps, president of the board of trade, were both abroad on holiday and Ernest Bevin, the foreign secretary, was undergoing treatment in the London Clinic. The Foreign Office tracked down Attlee's deputy, Herbert Morrison, to a back room in London's fashionable Ivy restaurant, where he had been having dinner after the theatre.

Pressed for a decision, Morrison (whose grandson, Peter Mandelson, is an arch-Europhile) grunted: "It's no good, we cannot do it. The Durham miners won't wear it". As Peter Hennessy points out in his fascinating history of the Attlee government, Never Again, the Durham miners were also associated with the celebrated Durham Light Infantry, which had just been involved in defeating two members of the nascent European union, Germany and Italy. Suspicion of Franco-German plans to run Europe in tandem continued under governments of both stripes. When an offer to Britain came again, in 1955, the Conservatives under Anthony Eden also rejected it.

Britain's ambivalent mating dance with Continental Europe continues to this day as the debate intensifies on joining the euro-zone currency and signing up to an EU constitution. There could yet be more repetitions of Morrison's late-night dyspepsia at The Ivy.

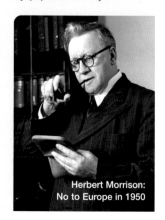

Herbert Morrison: No to Europe in 1950

hings can only et better

66 Let us be frank about it,
most of our people have never
had it so good. 99

**Prime minister Harold Macmillan,
Bedford, July 1957**

5

The 1950s opened with a real sense that the grey, drab years of war and austerity were at last behind the British people, and that consumer heaven was not far off. The return of a Conservative government under Winston Churchill in 1951 was confidently expected to set business – if not the people – free from the heavy hand of state controls, but there was no immediate dramatic change. Only the iron and steel industry was to be denationalised, and a hard winter in 1951/52 brought more crisis in the coal industry and a repeat of the fuel cuts associated with 1947.

Rationing of bacon and meat would persist until 1954, though sugar and confectionery came off the previous year, giving children a Coronation treat. But scientific exploits were in the air – literally, with the development of world-beating planes such as the Comet – and, as Winston Churchill had said a bit prematurely in 1945, there was "an invincible confidence in the genius of Britain".

Even officialdom decided it was time for a bit of light relief. The Festival of Britain had been in the planning by the Labour government since 1947, first as a centenary successor to Prince Albert's Great Exhibition of 1851, worthily showcasing the best of British products, but turning in the end into a more light-hearted celebration that would focus on the arts and sciences. It was Herbert Morrison who had persuaded the Cabinet that "we ought to do something jolly… we need something to give Britain a lift".[1] As Gerald Barry, the Festival's director-general, told a press conference in 1948: "1951 should be a year of fun, fantasy and colour, a year in which we can, while soberly surveying our great past and our promising future, for once let ourselves go…"

The main exhibition site, between County Hall and Waterloo Bridge where the London Eye now stands, certainly provided colour. Its pavilions contained a feast of reds, yellows, blues and greens and were flanked by stunning futuristic buildings such as the slim, aluminium Skylon and the Dome of Discovery, a much better conceived and executed design than its billion-pound white elephant successor the Millennium Dome. Upstream at Battersea Park, there was fun to be had in the Festival Pleasure Gardens (left), with an eccentric model railway, firework displays, a Mississippi-style showboat and a huge circular dance-hall. And the British did let themselves go, even dancing in the open air in their overcoats when the weather cooled.

Michael Frayn, the playwright, who was 18 at the time, remembered the Festival as "a rainbow – a brilliant sign riding the tail of the storm and promising fairer weather".[2] But there were the inevitable critics; those who thought the modest £8m of government money that the Festival cost should have been spent on more deserving projects, and the acid wits who said the Skylon, which was tapered at both ends and seemed from a distance to hover in the air, resembled Britain – being "without visible means of support".

How much the Festival actually boosted British industry is unquantifiable. The exhibits numbered around 10,000 objects from 3,500 firms, and, unlike "Britain Can Make It" five years earlier, much of the furniture, pottery and fabrics on show could actually be bought, even if from a waiting list. However, Marguerite Patten, the veteran cookery writer,

an entrepreneur for all seasons

Sir Terence Conran is still such a power in the business world that it comes as a shock to think of him making his mark a full half-century ago.

Unlike any other British entrepreneur, he has stamped an image on every decade since the mid-20th century, and in doing so has changed the way many Britons live, especially the so-called London "chattering classes". In the early 1950s his impact was in furniture and design, and the first ventures into ground-breaking restaurants with the cheap but wholesome French provender of The Soup Kitchen; in the 1960s, it was in his revolutionary home-furnishings shop Habitat; in the 1970s, the Conran Shop and the Neal Street Restaurant; in the 1980s, the ambitious Storehouse combine (his only major failure); since then, the opening of big, buzzy brasseries such as Pont de la Tour, Mezzo and Quaglino's.

Rather like Ellen Wilkinson, the post-war Labour education minister whose ambition was said to be for British schools to deliver a quality equal to the BBC's unashamedly highbrow Third Programme[22], Conran has always wanted the best to be available to the mass market, whether in crockery, furniture, food or interior decor. Unlike Wilkinson, he succeeded in providing it. Jonathan Meades, the food critic and writer on architecture, says Conran has changed British taste since the 1960s. Another food critic, Matthew Fort of The Guardian, says he has "made eating out part of a theatrical entertainment, like going to a Cameron Mackintosh musical".

Habitat was a completely new concept when it opened in 1964 on a then-scruffy stretch of the Fulham Road. Its distinctive products – Sabatier kitchen knives, duvets, bean bags and the novel Chinese cooking utensil known as a wok – mixed stylish sophistication with student informality. It set new aspirations in home decor and the basement shop itself became a fashionable haunt for celebrities such as the models Twiggy and Jean Shrimpton, singer Sandie Shaw, composer Lionel Bart, comedian Peter Sellers and the up-and-coming actor Michael Caine.

Part of Conran's success is that he is much more than a design or ideas man: he has made furniture with his own hands and still runs his businesses in a hands-on fashion. A graduate of London's Central School of Art, where he studied textile design, he went straight into his first job, aged 20, as assistant to Dennis Lennon, designer of the 1951 Festival of Britain. Soon afterwards, he opened a furniture workshop in an East End studio shared with the artist Eduardo Paolozzi. He set up the Soup Kitchen student-style bistros with a group of friends and sold out his interest after a couple of years for £2,500. Conran Holdings is now worth over £120m, of which Sir Terence (knighted by Margaret Thatcher in 1983) owns 62 per cent.

The only major setback in his Teflon-coated career was the over-ambitious 1980s merger of Habitat, the Conran Shop, Mothercare, Heal's, the old British Home Stores (Bhs) and Richard Shops. The businesses did not hang together, and Conran was unable to add value in the ways for which he had been famous. When he quit Storehouse as chairman in 1990, Conran

Shirley and Terence Conran in 1955, building a restaurant empire

lost Habitat – it is now owned by Ikea, which he praises for "bringing good design to the mass market" – but he retains his flagship Conran Shops.

In 1989, the Conran Foundation invested £4.5m in Britain's first Design Museum, to display the best international design, fashion and architecture of the 20th and 21st centuries. The chosen site was a derelict 1950s warehouse on the south bank of the Thames near Tower Bridge, and the finished museum was praised by the Architects' Journal in August 1989 for its "spirit of quiet ordinariness and light". As of 2001, the group owned 44 restaurants, bars and cafes, 12 Conran shops and London's Great Eastern Hotel, a grand old relic of the railway age.[23]

Now 72, the four-times-married Conran retains an irrepressible zest for new ventures and new ideas. Few would bet on him not being around to change British shopping or eating or some other habits in another decade's time.

has recalled how difficult it still was to buy domestic appliances – refrigerators, cookers or one of the labour-saving new washing machines. "We had to export them because if we didn't export, as a country we would go under. It was a shattering message to give to the people, that we had to wait and wait for all the new equipment of the time."[3]

The consumer society was still half a decade away, but there were harbingers. The Festival's architect, Dennis Lennon, had a 20-year-old assistant fresh out of London's Central School of Arts and Crafts. His name was Terence Conran (see panel), and within a year he would be starting his own furniture company and in two years opening a novel kind of basic restaurant called The Soup Kitchen. The first of three Soup Kitchens in central London opened behind St. Martin-in-the-Fields in 1953 and immediately became a magnet for impecunious students. It dispensed a filling, cheap and delicious meal of home-made soup, French bread and cheeses and set Conran on the road to restaurant fame. The year after that, still aged only 24, Conran opened his first upmarket eatery, the Orrery in the King's Road, Chelsea, which in the next decade would become the main artery of fashionable London. In 1956, Conran set up his own design group, laying the foundation for the revolution in domestic furnishings he would unleash with Habitat in 1964.

The Festival of Britain had been all about design, and to that extent influenced a generation, from the strange spiky chairs of the 1950s to the whole light-coloured, streamlined "contemporary" look that finally swept away the fumed oak, mock-Tudor windows and fusty three-piece suites of the typical pre-war British home.

But while the Festival's eight million visitors between May and October 1951 revelled in its promise of a new feel-better world, Britain's actual economic situation was undergoing a tragic reversal. After five years of privation and sacrifice, the nation's balance of payments had finally moved into a £307m surplus in 1950. A year later it was in deficit to the tune of £369m, and would not return to a surplus until 1958. The reason was the Korean war, which had broken out on June 25, 1950. In the context of the cold war, the Soviet Union's possession of atomic weapons and Britain's supplicant status in relation to the US, it was inevitable that Washington should feel the need

Dennis Lennon, architect of the Festival of Britain, demonstrates a new design

to deal with a Communist military threat wherever it happened and that it would expect Britain to join in.

In his meticulously sourced history of the Attlee government, Never Again: Britain 1945-51, the constitutional historian Peter Hennessy quotes the recollections of Lord Franks, who as Sir Oliver Franks was UK ambassador in Washington at the time. For anyone reading it in 2003, amid the controversy over the rationale for the Iraq war, Franks's 1990 interview with Hennessy has eerie overtones. Recalling his reply to foreign secretary Ernest Bevin, who had asked the ambassador for his view on Britain sending troops to Korea, Franks told Hennessy: "I said two things, really. The first one was that the Americans regarded us as their dependable ally. They would not understand it if we didn't stand with them on the ground in Korea, and I thought that the damage would be deep and long-lasting. Secondly, I said something quite different – that there's something in the psychological make-up of the American nation which makes them like to have company when they're in trouble and, from this point of view, they wanted, under the United Nations flag, allies to help them and they turned to Britain as the key. If we helped them, others would also. This went back, and the Cabinet decided to send the Gloucesters. That's how it happened."

Sending the "Glorious Gloucesters," as they became known for their heroic exploits in Korea, was only the beginning, of course. Britain was sucked into a crippling

defence programme, estimated at £4.7bn between 1952 and 1954, 10 per cent of GNP at the time and around 30 per cent of all government expenditure. This was aimed principally at heading off any Soviet threat in Western Europe – still perceived as very real four years after the Berlin airlift. But it carried a high price. Domestically, income tax went up to 47.5 per cent, with a crushing top rate (surtax and

THE CHANGING CENTURY

Facts from the business archives:

1950: In New York, Diners Club issued the world's first credit cards. (The idea was exported to Britain the next year)

1950: Decca released Europe's first 33 1/3rpm LPs, hammering a nail in the coffin of the 78

1950: The British ad business, which was to benefit from the launch of the commercial break five years later (see below), got its first female supremo. Olive Hirst was appointed managing director of the London agency, Sells. She had started as a secretary in the agency's overseas department

1950: Otis installed the world's first passenger elevator with self-opening doors – at the Atlantic Refining Building, Dallas, Texas

1950: Horizon, the world's first air charter holiday company, was born in London

1950: The Association of British Travel Agents (ABTA) was founded; its membership was to grow from 106 in 1951 to 406 in 1959

1950: In South Carolina, Du Pont started to manufacture acrylic fibre

1950: In Majorca, the Antwerp diamond cutter and water polo player Gerard Blitz created a "holiday village", using US Army surplus tents and cooking equipment. From such humble beginnings, Club Med was built

1951: Premier, Britain's first supermarket chain, went into business, opening a branch in Earls Court*

1951: The age of "drip dry" began; the first products made of Terylene – dresses, lingerie, shirts – came on to the British market

1951: Remington Rand of Philadelphia and Ferranti of Lancashire became the first companies to manufacture electronic computers, bringing out their Univac I and Ferranti Mark I models at the same time. The former was the first computer with input from magnetic tape

1952: Tetley Tea Co. of Bletchley, Buckinghamshire, put tea bags into Britain's shops. (Previously, British-made tea bags had been produced exclusively for export markets)

1952: BOAC inaugurated the first jet (turbo) airline service; a De Havilland

Comet made it from London to Johannesburg (6,724 miles) in 23hr 34minutes. (It stopped en route at Rome, Beirut, Khartoum, Entebbe and Livingstone)

1952: The journal New Musical Express was launched, publishing Britain's first "top ten" record sales chart

1953: The government denationalised the steel industry. In Britain's first privatisation share issue, millions of shares in United Steel Companies were offered for sale at 25 shillings each

1953: Remington Rand brought out the first high-speed computer printer, for use with the Univac. It was capable of printing 600 lines of 120 characters a minute

1953: In France, Bic brought out the first disposable ballpoint pen. It retailed at 50 centimes

1954: At Cadby Hall in London, the headquarters of the food and catering company J. Lyons, LEO, the first electronic

computer in business use, became fully operational (below)

1954: Bill Russell and Peter Hobbs introduced Britain's first automatic electric kettle, the Russell Hobbs K1

1954: Spear & Sons of Enfield, Middlesex, began to produce the British version of Scrabble

1955: British workers were introduced to luncheon vouchers by Luncheon Vouchers Ltd

1955: J. Lyons opened the first Wimpy Bar (see main text)

1955: In California, the curtain went up on the world's first theme park – a 160-acre, $17m Disneyland, complete with Sleeping Beauty's castle and five adventure lands

1955: Commercial television came to Britain with the launch of ITV (see main text). Within a few years, it was gaining audience shares of up to 70 per cent. Among the big ITV hits of the 1950s were Double Your Money, a game show hosted by Hughie Green, and Sunday Night at the London Palladium, a variety show hosted from 1958 by Bruce Forsyth

income tax combined) of 97.5 per cent. Ironically, it would be Britain's embrace of the nuclear deterrent, so controversial in the late 1950s and early 1960s, that reduced the defence budget by 1957, allowing the Macmillan government to leave more defence money in taxpayers' pockets.[4]

Hennessy believes that between 1950 and 1951 Britain had a "golden opportunity" to create its own economic miracle before West Germany recovered its full industrial muscle. He acknowledges that influential officials at the time held other views on reasons for Britain's failure: as the Whitehall mandarin Lord Plowden expressed it, "a national resistance to change, poor management in much of industry, reactionary trade unions, the poor education and training of much of the workforce and too great a concentration on

1955: Bird's Eye started to test market fish fingers in Britain

1955: A former carpenter, Ole Kirk Christiansen of Billund, Denmark, started to make what he called "the automatic building brick". Marketed under the brand name Lego, derived from the Danish words leg godt, meaning "to play well", it was to become one of the world's most popular, most enduring toys

1955: In Coventry, the upper precinct of Europe's first shopping centre opened for business. The centre was built on a bomb-damaged site in the heart of the city

1956: In North London, Polycell Products began to manufacture what no home decorator/DIY enthusiast can now do without, Polyfilla

1956: Tarmac Civil Engineering Ltd. of Wolverhampton began work on a special stretch of road: Britain's first motorway, the eight-and-a-half-mile Preston bypass. The bypass, part of the Birmingham-Carlisle M6, was opened by Prime Minister Harold Macmillan on December 5, 1958. It had taken two years and three months to complete, at a cost of £3.75m. The following year, the first section of the M1 was opened

1956: In Dallas, Bette Nesmith Graham, a secretary at Texas Bank & Trust, invented a typewriter correction fluid, Mistake Out. She was ably assisted by her son, Michael Nesmith, who helped her bottle the tempera waterbase paint in her garage and sell it to friends. The idea, renamed Liquid Paper in 1957, made Mrs Graham $50m. As for Michael, he went on to find fame with pop group, The Monkees. (Probably best remembered as "the one in the hat")

1956: The first Teflon-coated non-stick frying pan was marketed in the south of France by Tefal Co

1957: Transport Ferry Services introduced the first roll-on roll off continental service, carrying passengers between Tilbury and Antwerp

1957: At Aubonne, Switzerland, the first Velcro fasteners went into production. (Velcro was the brainchild of Swiss aristocrat George de Mestral of St-Saphorin-Sur-Morges. De Mestral got the idea in the early 1940s from observing how burrs from burdock weed stuck to the ears of his dog. Examining the burrs under a microscope, he found that they bristled with tiny hooks. It

took him 14 or so years to replicate the effect in textiles)

1958: The last steam locomotive was built in Britain

1958: Qantas launched the first round-the-world passenger service, flying eastbound from Sydney to London via the US in five and a half days and westbound from Sydney to London via India and the Middle East in six and a half days

1958: The West Indian Gazette, Britain's first paper for blacks, was launched. Its first editor was Claudia Jones, the founder of the Notting Hill Carnival

1958: In America, RCA Victor introduced the first cassette tape recorder

1959: The American toy company Mattel brought out the first Barbie doll. Based on a German novelty doll, Lilli, to which Mattel had acquired the US rights, Barbie was designed by Jack Ryan, a future husband of Zsa Zsa Gabor. Barbie and her boyfriend Ken were named after the children of Mattel's founder

1959: The Xerox 914 was unveiled in New York. A breakthrough in photocopier design, it was to

achieve sales of $1bn in eight years and revolutionise office life. Fortune magazine was to call it "the most successful product ever marketed in America"

1959: Du Pont announced the invention of Lycra

1959: At Prestwick Airport, Scotland, Britain's first airport duty-free shop opened

1959: BOAC inaugurated the first jet airline service between London and Sydney

1959: In North Carolina, Allen Gant of Glen Raven Mills developed the first fine-denier tights. The product was inspired by Gant's wife, who wanted something comfortable to wear during pregnancy. It came into its own with the popularisation of the mini skirt in the 1960s

*Supermarkets, still rare in the early 1950s, grew slowly but steadily in popularity. By the end of the decade, there were a few hundred of them in Britain; by 1965, there were around 2,000. (By the new millennium, there were about 4,500).

Sources: Patrick Robertson: The New Shell Book of Firsts, 1994, Headline Book Publishing; Miriam Akhtar and Steve Humphries: The Fifties and Sixties: A Lifestyle Revolution, Boxtree, 2001; The Competition Commission, report on UK supermarkets, 2000; ABTA

old and declining industries". But Hennessy writes: "There are powerful reasons for supposing our best hope for the kind of post-war economic miracle enjoyed by so many western European countries was scattered in fragments in the committee rooms of Whitehall, on the hills above the Imjin in Korea and along the Rhine in Germany as British occupation forces were rearmed in readiness for a Stalinist assault."

And, even if Britain did secure US goodwill through shouldering this defence burden, it counted for little six years later when the fiasco of the Anglo-French action at Suez all but destroyed the "special relationship" forged by Churchill and Roosevelt and cost the UK another $450m of its precious reserves.[5]

On the home front, although Korea and Suez left their very different impacts – and in the case of Suez, bitter national divisions over the Eden government's action – a gloss of prosperity and progress was making business and consumers more confident. Many staple industrial products for the peacetime economy were made in Britain. The pages of The Director, which had been revived by the Institute of Directors in 1947 after a 40-year gap, were filled in 1950 with manufacturing ads – for dumper trucks, mechanical handling equipment, bearings, castings, steel office furniture, calculating machines and Bentley cars. Detergents were not yet dominated by multinationals such as Procter and Gamble or Unilever. Dreft, the first soap-substitute to be marketed in 1948, was made by the British firm of Thomas Hedley, as was Tide. Since soap rationing was still in force, demand for these products was heavy. Package holidays still lay in the future, but a travel ad promised alluringly: "Madeira in 9¾ hours by Flying Boat".

Flying boats were one of Britain's less successful post-war

Geoffrey de Havilland, founder of the aircraft company

The De Havilland Comet, the world's first jet airliner, attracts crowds at the Farnborough Air Show
Below: Comet designer, R. E. Bishop

aviation products, their markets restricted by geography and, ultimately, by faster and more versatile passenger planes. The Vickers Viscount, on the other hand, designed by Sir George Edwards, was in demand around the world – even in the US – and huge national pride was invested in the De Havilland Comet, which was confidently expected to give Britain a three-to-five year world lead in jet passenger aircraft. The industry gained added glamour by attempts to break the "sound barrier" – first achieved in the US. In 1956, a British pilot named Peter Twiss flew at an astonishing 1,132mph in a Fairey Delta 2 above the Sussex coast. In the global defence market, British jet warplanes were unrivalled from the Hawker Hunter to the Canberra, made by English Electric. Vertical take-off technology was also just beginning, though its first ungainly product was lampooned as "the Flying Bedstead". Ultimately, it would lead to the world-beating Harrier jump-jet.

The tragedy of the Comet, which showed itself crash-prone at an early stage and claimed 110 lives between 1953 and 1954, has only recently been fully unravelled in a Channel 4 documentary screened in 2002, drawing on hitherto unseen De Havilland, BOAC and Royal Air Force Establishment documents, and on interviews with past De Havilland employees. As with the R101 airship disaster in 1930, the Comet's failure seems to have been at least partly the result of a desire to get this revolutionary plane into fare-paying service before full prototyping and testing had taken place – particularly in relation to the strength of the thinned-down aluminium outer skin.

Weight was an obsession because De Havilland initially insisted on its own Ghost turbo-jet engines, which were under-powered in relation to the Rolls-Royce Avons that BOAC wanted. On the Channel 4 programme it was alleged that De Havilland's production director, Frank Povey, had particular problems

Everyone's favourite car, The Austin Mini, 1959: above, designer Alec Issigonis

in getting the window frames bonded to the metal and proposed riveting them to meet the delivery time. These unplanned rivet holes later appeared to be the trigger for the fuselage exploding under stress. R .E. Bishop, the plane's designer, was

Fast mover: the Jaguar XK

said in the programme to have bitterly regretted agreeing to the short-cut. The Comet had been as exciting a project as the Concorde would be in the 1970s, and was even more beautiful a design. But in the four years it took to rebuild it for complete safety, the passenger jet market had been lost to Boeing and other US manufacturers.

The British car industry, meanwhile, was also looking deceptively good as the 1950s began. The greatest head-turner on the world's highways was the Jaguar XK sports car, the fastest production car in the world, which had been the sensation of the 1948 Motor Show. It remains a design classic to this day, coveted by collectors. At the end of the decade would come a true mass-market world-beater, the Austin Mini. Created by Alec Issigonis, designer of the popular Morris Minor, it redefined the small car, providing through an ingenious arrangement of engine and gearbox the same amount of room for four people as the Minor in a body two feet shorter.

The Mini was to become an icon of the Swinging Sixties, along with its namesake the mini-skirt. Rock stars and aristocrats drove Minis; they were fun and fashionable as well as practical in city traffic. But the car ran into labour troubles soon after its launch; assembly-line workers went on strike for more pay, and in a weird production fault, door hinges were put on the wrong way round, which caused water to leak into the car.

The sporty, souped-up Mini Cooper had a starring role in Michael Caine's famous 1969 caper film The Italian Job, in which three of the cars, painted respectively red, white and blue, daringly escape with $4m of stolen gold over rooftops and down church steps, making fools of the Turin police in their Alfas. Sixteen Mini Coopers were used in the film: all were wrecked. Caine has said that BMC refused to help with the production, but he was even more indignant to learn that a remake was planned in 2003 using VW Golfs.

In between the Jaguar and the Mini, the car industry grew apace, with domestic car ownership trebling between 1950 and 1955 and multiplying sixfold to six million between 1950 and 1960. The blueprint for Harlow new town, just after the war, had allowed for one car to every 10 houses, but by the time the town was finished, the ratio was one to every two. Sadly, success would not prove sustainable.

The designers of Harlow New Town underestimated car ownership by a factor of five

The forced merger (in effect, a takeover) of Morris and Austin in 1952 under Austin's Leonard Lord to form BMC never really jelled in its management culture. Lord was a sworn enemy of Lord Nuffield (see chapter 3) and it was the end of Morris as Britain's most profitable car maker.

THE CHANGING CENTURY

A snapshot of science and technology:

1950: Surgeons at the Little Company of Mary Hospital in Chicago performed the world's first kidney transplant operation

1950: The floppy disc was developed at the Imperial University in Tokyo and licensed to IBM. (The inventor, Dr Yoshiro Nakamats, already had 2,360 patents to his credit)

1951: The electronic computer went into regular production, with simultaneous launches of the Ferranti Mark I and the Univac I

1951: Operation Albert took place in North Mexico. Four monkeys, code-named Albert 1, 2, 3 and 4, were sent into orbit in a V2 rocket. They are thought to have been the first living creatures in space. Their "mission" was kept secret for fear of protest by animal lovers, but all four returned safely to earth

1952: The first tranquillizer, Resperine, was developed by the British biochemist Robert Robinson and the Swiss pharmacologist Emil Schittler. It would be produced for clinical use by Ciba Laboratories, Switzerland

1952: The first purpose-built drive-on, drive-off Channel car ferry went into service

1952: For the first time, Britain detonated an atomic bomb. The test site was the Monte Bello Islands off Western Australia

1952: The hydrogen bomb was tested by the US at Eniwetok atoll, part of the Marshall Islands in the Pacific. The megaton bomb was assigned the name "Mike"

1952: The world's first heart pacemaker (an external device) was developed at the Harvard Medical School by Dr Paul Zoll and used to restore the heartbeats of patient David Schwartz. Six years later, heart surgeons in Stockholm implanted the first internal pacemaker

1953: Dr Jonas Salk developed a vaccine against paralytic poliomyelitis. The Salk vaccine was to lead to the virtual eradication of polio in industrialised countries

1953: In Nature magazine, the geneticists James D. Watson and Francis Crick of Cambridge University announced the discovery of deoxyribonucleic acid (DNA)

1953: The first open-heart surgery was performed. Doctors at the University of Pennsylvania Medical School carried out a heart-lung bypass operation

1953: For the first time, the BBC gave a public demonstration of colour television, relaying by closed circuit a special outside broadcast of the Coronation procession to the wards of Great Ormond Street Hospital for Sick Children, central London

BMC became British Leyland in 1968, models proliferated and overlapped, there was lack of strategic focus, and endless union disruption; the steep decline of British volume car manufacturing was under way.

Elsewhere, science was creating new industries such as plastics (the first plastics exhibition was held in London in 1950), and new applications were developed for vinyl, which had enabled the wartime replacement of such scarce imported commodities as rubber, cellulose and linseed oil. The British Xylonite Company had been world pioneers in commercial plastics, and the Distillers' Company, improbably enough, was a research leader in the field, in collaboration with the Anglo-Iranian Oil Company, forerunner of BP.[6] Largely unnoticed outside the scientific community, but of historic significance for the future, was the publication in 1953 of the discovery by two Cambridge scientists, James Watson (top right) and Francis Crick (bottom right), of the "double helix"

structure of deoxyriboneucleic acid, the building blocks of life now known as DNA. In atomic energy, Sellafield on the Cumberland coast claimed to be the world's first industrial-scale atomic power station and was producing electricity for the National Grid by 1957.

Innovations were changing home entertainment well before the mass advent of TV. The summer of 1950 saw the first British long-playing record, issued by Decca, though the old 78rpm singles persisted for much of the decade. People wondered why these new unbreakable records were housed in stout cardboard sleeves while the breakable shellac 78s were only protected by paper. Purchase tax, the complicated forerunner of VAT, was to blame: the rate on gramophone records

1953: Twentieth-Century Fox studios made the first pictures in CinemaScope, a system with stereophonic sound

1954: At Obninsk, 55 miles from Moscow, the world's first atomic power station began producing electrical current for industrial and agricultural purposes. It was followed two years later by Calder Hall in Cumberland, which was designed to generate 90,000kw of electrical power and to manufacture plutonium, an artificial nuclear fuel, for military purposes

1954: The Rolls-Royce TMR, the first VTOL (vertical take-off and landing) aircraft took its maiden flight

1954: In America, the first clinical tests of an oral contraceptive were made. Dr Gregory Pincus of the Worcester Foundation for Experimental Biology at Shrewsbury, Massachusetts, and his co-worker, Dr John Rock, had spent five years trying to develop a form of birth control that was "harmless, entirely reliable, simple, practical, universally applicable and aesthetically satisfactory to both husband and wife". In 1956, 1,308 women involved in a slum clearance scheme in Puerto Rico took part in a three-year trial of what came to be known as "the pill"

1955: Christopher Cockerell, an electronics engineer and spare-time boatbuilder from Suffolk, patented the idea of the Hovercraft. His early

experiments famously used household objects – two tin cans and a vacuum cleaner – to demonstrate scientific principles

1956: The first transatlantic telephone cable was laid, stretching from Oban to Newfoundland

1957: Britain exploded its first hydrogen bomb. The bomb was dropped over the Christmas Islands as part of a series of tests in the Pacific

1957: The Russians launched the first space satellite, Sputnik 1. (The feat both amazed and horrified the West. Would the same rocket that launched the artificial satellite be used to launch a nuclear bomb?)

1958: President Eisenhower, not to be outdone by the USSR, set up an agency that would try to consolidate the efforts of American scientists to explore space. The National Aeronautical and Space Administration (NASA) was born

1959: The Russian spacecraft Lunik 2 landed on the moon

1959: At Dounreay, Caithness, Scotland, a fast-breeder nuclear reactor became operational

See also: business facts box

Main sources: Patrick Robertson: The New Shell Book of Firsts, 1994, Headline Book Publishing; Christopher Lee: This Sceptred Isle, Twentieth Century, BBC and Penguin Books, 1999; BBCi

was a swingeing 66⅔ and this also applied to their sleeves, so cardboard covers could have priced the old 78s out of the market.

Purchase tax was 10 years old in 1950, though it had been intended as a temporary wartime measure. It represented about a fifth of all tax revenue, most of it raised on clothing. On medicines, the rate was an unbelievable 33⅓; like records, silk and rayon carried a two-thirds rate, while leather goods attracted a full 100 per cent.[7] After 1951, when the Conservatives returned to power, they reduced income

Designers at work in Nissen huts, creating the new town of Crawley in West Sussex

and purchase taxes, which helped to launch the consumer boom. It was further pushed along by a 10 per cent fall in wholesale prices between 1951 and 1954, which damped down inflation.[8]

The main impetus to the recovery in the second half of the 1950s was the post-war reconstruction boom and the acceleration in new housing achieved under Harold Macmillan as Tory housing minister. Churchill's party had been returned in 1951 partly on the promise of building 300,000 homes a year, and Macmillan met the target in 1953 – another feel-good factor for Coronation year. In 1954, the figure reached 340,000. Under Labour, there had been a brave

A tower block under construction at Leamington Spa, Warwickshire

attempt to provide good-quality local authority housing for rent, built on a human scale with blocks of flats no higher than six storeys. The Tories realised that, with the new towns only able to accommodate a relatively small number of people – mostly skilled workers and their families – the solution to the housing crisis was to build more (and higher) new flats in the inner cities. This unfortunately led to the "new brutalist" architecture and shoddy concrete pre-fabricated slabs of tower blocks, one of which – Ronan Point in east London – tragically collapsed in 1968 following a gas explosion. But the real growth was in owner-occupied houses: between 1951 and 1963, the Conservatives progressively lifted controls and encouraged what they called "a property-owning democracy". Half the homes built during these years were owner-occupied.

The new homes came with integral bathrooms and lavatories and often, with fitted kitchens as well. In 1950, a survey had found that nearly half of all British homes had no bathroom.[9] The housing boom not only brought prosperity to the construction industry – despite lingering post-war controls and shortages – but it fuelled a comparable boom in household goods. The ending in 1952 of the wartime "utility" scheme for furniture encouraged the manufacturing of new-style furniture. Among the best known brands were Ercol of High Wycombe, owned by Lucian Ercolani, and G-Plan, made by the Gomme brothers. Their products represented a complete break from pre-war styles, featuring the "contemporary" look pioneered in the Festival of Britain, with clean lines, light colours and natural materials.

Electrical appliances still lagged behind other household goods, however. As late as 1956 only eight per cent of British homes had a refrigerator, and even fewer had a washing machine. By 1969, two-thirds of homes were equipped with both. The Kenwood Chef food blender was unveiled at the 1950 Ideal Home Exhibition, but sales did not take off until the 1960s, by which time it had been famously redesigned

Fanny Cradock, first and most flamboyant of the TV cooks

by Kenneth Grange. As for television, in 1950 there were only 350,000 sets in the whole country. A single event, the Coronation of Queen Elizabeth II on June 2, 1953, would change that dramatically; 20 million people gathered round TV sets in pubs or in their own or others' homes to watch the ceremony and pageantry (in black and white, of course) and in that year alone 100,000 sets were sold.

Television, along with Elizabeth David's pioneering books on Continental food, prompted a national interest in cookery. Fanny Cradock, resplendent in full evening dress, was the first TV celebrity chef, and whole advertising campaigns were built around Cradock and the wartime cookery adviser Marguerite Patten as the gas and electricity industries battled it out to sell their respective cookers. When meat, the last rationed food, at last went on free sale in June 1954, housewives tore up their ration books in London's Trafalgar Square. That was also the year in which Britain's first hamburger chain was launched by J. Lyons. The Wimpy Bar was at first installed as an added attraction in Lyons teashops but quickly became so popular that a separate company was formed to develop the concept, and Wimpy Bars spread all over the UK and into Europe. The freeing of meat from rationing prompted another restaurant innovation when two Italian immigrant brothers, Frank and Aldo Berni, set up a chain of US-style steak-houses. The first Berni Inn opened in 1955 and was to produce many clones on the high street.

Frozen food would soon be a familiar sight in the weekly shopping basket, Bird's Eye frozen peas (below) and fish fingers being early favourites. Legend has it that fish fingers, which went on sale in 1955, were originally going to be called frozen cod pieces until someone pointed out the unfortunate connotation.[10] That very basic convenience, the teabag, was introduced in 1952, the year that tea came off the ration. In 1957, tea consumption – around six cups a day per head of population – was twice that of today. And these new convenience foods would increasingly be bought at self-service grocery stores such as the one that the J. Sainsbury chain had recently introduced to the British public in suburban Surrey.

Tesco had experimented with one self-service store before the war, in St. Albans, and the Co-op had also tried the idea, but in 1949 Alan Sainsbury, the third-generation chairman of the family firm, was asked by John Strachey, Attlee's minister of food, to find out what could be learned from the US to help improve the British food industry. Strachey was thinking mostly of technical advances in frozen food, but Sainsbury did more. In two frenetic weeks of touring US supermarkets in New York, Buffalo, Chicago, Philadelphia and Boston he and a fellow-director became convinced that self-service was the wave of the future. The board selected one of the company's bigger stores for the experiment, on London Road, Croydon, and its counters were equipped with protective covers made of Perspex, the unbreakable transparent plastic developed by ICI for the cockpits of Spitfire fighter planes.

BIRDS EYE
FROSTED FOODS

The home freezer changed life for the 1950s housewife

Sainsbury's goes self-service: the first store in Croydon, 1950

Not every customer took kindly to the new dispensation. A judge's wife, accustomed to deferential counter service and home deliveries, threw her wire shopping basket at the Sainsbury chairman and swore at him for expecting

her to do a shop assistant's job. But the Croydon store quickly generated a bigger weekly volume of sales than any other food store in Britain, though the revolution was a slow one: it took 20 years for half of Sainsbury's stores to become self-service, and many of the chain's competitors such as Lipton's and Home and Colonial stuck to their belief that the British housewife still wanted personal service.[11]

Coronation year provided a feast of feel-good factors for the public. The great day itself coincided with the headline news that Mount Everest had been conquered at last; if not by a British climber, at least by two Commonwealth ones, the craggy New Zealander Edmund Hillary and his Nepalese Sherpa guide, Tenzing Norgay. Britain's Neville

THE CHANGING CENTURY

A snapshot of Britain:

1950: In February, the Labour government had a tough time at the polls. It seemed that Britons were tiring of the policies of chancellor Sir Stafford Cripps (a man as synonymous with austerity as Gordon Brown was with prudence in the late 1990s). Clement Attlee clung on to power by his fingertips. Returned with a majority of just four seats, his days were numbered

1950: In May, the French foreign minister Robert Schuman proposed the formation of a federation of coal and steel producing states. The Schuman Plan, as it came to be known, was the embryo from which the European Common Market would be born. Britain, perhaps putting too much faith in her "special relationship" with America and her ties to the Commonwealth, perhaps feeling reluctant to ally with Germany,

perhaps just being too busy (see panel, chapter 4), failed to get involved. When in August, France, Germany, Italy and the Benelux states met in Paris to launch the European Coal and Steel Community, she was conspicuous by her absence

1951: Two British diplomats Donald Maclean and Guy Burgess defected to the Soviet Union. They had been working for a spy ring that included Kim Philby and Anthony Blunt

1951: In an attempt to curb health service costs, charges were introduced for spectacles and dentures. The U-turn led to the resignations of Aneurin Bevan and of Harold Wilson, then president of the board of trade

1951: In May, the King and Queen opened the Festival of Britain on the South Bank of the River Thames (above right). Timed to commemorate the centenary of the Great Exhibition, the Festival was, as the official guide

explained, meant to be a showcase for British "Arts, Architecture, Science, Technology and Industrial Design". It was also meant to be a tonic for the war-weary people (see main text)

1951: Attlee, knowing he could hang on no longer, called an election for October. Winston Churchill, now aged 77, returned to Downing Street, winning 321 seats to Attlee's 295

1952: Far from setting the people free, the new chancellor, R. A. Butler,

introduced more restrictions. Seven years after the end of the war, the cheese ration was just one ounce (25 grammes) a week per person. Despite the Festival spirit of the previous year, austerity went on. Britain was broke; rationing would continue until 1954

1953/1954: The first signs of post-war social change started to emerge. The Teddy Boy arrived, to the tune of a new kind of music, rock 'n' roll (see main text). Young people, who previously had dressed and behaved in much the same way as their parents, were starting to rebel

1954: Britain got 340,000 new homes. The Conservatives were succeeding in fulfilling their election pledge to solve the post-war housing crisis. In doing so, they were helping to create the conditions for a consumer boom (see main text)

1955: From January to June, Britain was

Duke recaptured the air-speed record from the US, flying at 717mph in a Hawker Hunter jet fighter (a feat spectacularly exceeded by fellow-Briton Peter Twiss three tears later). There was much talk of a "new Elizabethan age" and modern versions of the bold ventures and creativity that had marked the reign of Elizabeth Tudor. The stock market reflected a new confidence, rising by two-thirds between 1951 and 1955. By the end of the 1950s, share prices had trebled.[12]

Apart from the government-propelled house-building programme, the foundations of great fortunes were being laid in these years for a new breed of entrepreneur, the property developer. Some of these had started as estate agents or in retailing and while German bombs were still

falling on London they had scrambled round still-smoking sites, buying prime London locations for a few hundred pounds. After the invasion of Normandy in June 1944, an Allied victory looked more certain and they could confidently bet on soaring real-estate values. Some later leading developers such as Jack Cotton and Harry Hyams would not become household names until they started changing the London skyline in the 1960s. (See Chapter 6.) Charles Clore, another property tycoon, soon diversified into industry, boldly taking over Sears Holdings with its Freeman Hardy and Willis shoe shops in 1953. (Sears would eventually own Selfridges department store, too.)

Three low-profile families – the Freshwaters, Sterns

hit by strike action. The electricians shut down national newspapers and the dockers and railwaymen walked out over pay differentials. One of Anthony Eden's first acts as prime minister (Churchill having resigned in April) was to declare a state of national emergency

1955: Labour shortages led London Transport and the Health Service to start a recruitment drive in the West Indies. Sadly, many of the immigrants who arrived hit a colour bar. (Unable to find decent accommodation, some were eventually to buy cheap housing in areas such as Brixton. This set a pattern of chain migration, grouping ethnic minorities in ghetto communities and sowing the seeds for the race riots of the 1980s)

1956: Two junior ministers, Edward Boyle and Anthony Nutting, resigned from the government over Suez. Meanwhile, Cabinet dissent grew: the Leader of the House, R. A. Butler,

was questioning the whole Suez enterprise, and the chancellor, Harold Macmillan, who at first supported the war, was changing his mind

1957: In January, Eden, having lost credibility because of Suez, resigned. He was succeeded by Macmillan

1957: In March, France, Belgium, Holland, Luxembourg, Italy and West Germany signed the Treaty of Rome, and what was then called the European Common Market was born; Britain stayed out

1957: The problem of Northern Ireland again exploded into violence. The Dublin government was forced to declare a state of emergency after a series of shootings and arson attacks on the North-South border. The Irish security forces arrested more than 60 IRA men

1958: Macmillan's team at the Treasury, the Chancellor Peter Thorneycroft and his two ministers

Enoch Powell and Nigel Birch, walked out in protest at increased public expenditure. Macmillan famously trivialised the resignations as "little local difficulties". Thorneycroft was succeeded by the tax-cutting chancellor Derick Heathcoat Amory, whose policies were to help sustain the "never had it so good" consumer boom (see main text)

1958: In September, white youths provoked blacks in Notting Hill and a violent confrontation ensued

1958: The Campaign for Nuclear Disarmament was founded. "Heavyweight" members included the philosopher Bertrand Russell, the politician Michael Foot, the dramatist John Osborne, the historian A. J. P. Taylor and the writer J. B. Priestley. The first marches were from London to the weapons research centre at Aldermaston, Berkshire

1959: The Conservatives were returned with a majority of 107. Licking his wounds, the Labour leader Hugh Gaitskell considered his party's future. Just as Tony Blair was to do some 30 years later, he proposed the abandonment of a central plank of the 1918 Labour party constitution, Clause Four

1959: Britain met with Austria, Denmark, Norway, Portugal and Sweden to form the European Free Trade Association. EFTA was Britain's way into Europe without damaging Commonwealth agreements. It was, however, to prove a double-edged sword, souring relations with France, which saw it as an attempt to spoil the EEC

Sources: Christopher Lee: This Sceptred Isle, Twentieth Century, BBC and Penguin Books, 1999; Juliet Gardiner: From the Bomb to the Beatles: the changing face of post-war Britain, 1945-1965, Collins and Brown, 1999; Miriam Akhtar and Steve Humphries: The Fifties and Sixties: a lifestyle revolution, Boxtree, 2001

and Bergers – all with a strict Orthodox Jewish background and much inter-connection by marriage, bought up vast swathes of London apartment blocks in the 1940s and 1950s and were often accused by tenants of providing minimum maintenance to their properties. In their own communities, they ranked as generous philanthropists, and in 2001 the Freshwaters' 35 acres of London alone was reckoned to be worth £350m, making Benzion Freshwater London's 16th richest landlord. At the lowest level of the property market, racketeers such as Peter Rachman were beginning their grim operations in the 1950s, overcrowding slum dwellings with immigrants and sending in gangsters with dogs as rent enforcers.

Post-war planning bungles enabled sharp operators to run rings around the municipal authorities, but equally, legislation was so complex that many opportunities were missed. The Church of England, one of the country's biggest landlords, lost out spectacularly on one prime London site. In 1958, it sold the freehold of Paddington railway station for a mere £43,000, after it had been leased to the Great Western Railway (abolished in the 1947 nationalisation of British Rail) for 2,000 years at £2,500 a year on condition that the company's locomotives "consumed their own smoke". Ironically, 1958 was the year in which the last British steam locomotive was built; steam was abandoned by British Rail in 1965.

As the decade began, despite nationalisations and other consolidations in industry, there were still only 833 companies in Britain employing more than 1,000 people. More than 17,000 companies employed between 11 and 24 workers.[13] Owner-managers were concerned about the crippling effect of estate duties on the inheritance of private businesses. Fewer new companies were being created than in the immediate post-war years – 13,726 in 1950 compared with 14,288 the previous year and 23,815 in 1946. Over a third of these new businesses were in engineering, food,

A London dock workers' delegate addresses a crowd of Liverpool dockers, who decide to strike in support of their London colleagues

building and clothing. In 1951, two national finance corporations – the Industrial and Commercial Finance Corporation (ICFC) and the Finance Corporation of Industry – were set up specifically to invest in industrial firms that were unlikely to get backing through conventional City channels.[14]

Until the return of the Conservative government in 1951 there was even a lingering threat of more state takeovers. In 1950, a famous stand-off took place between government and private industry when the Attlee administration proposed adding sugar to the nationalisation list. Tate and Lyle launched a ferocious public campaign against it, creating the battling character of "Mr. Cube", and the proposal came to nothing.[15]

Throughout the 1950s, managers in all industries were worried about Communist infiltration of the trade unions. There were over 40,000 paid-up members of the British Communist Party and many politically motivated strikes, notably in the docks, aimed at halting the flow of Marshall Aid. Most of the agitators were found in the engineering

Mods 'n' God: Reverend William Shergold discussing an outing with members of a Hackney youth club

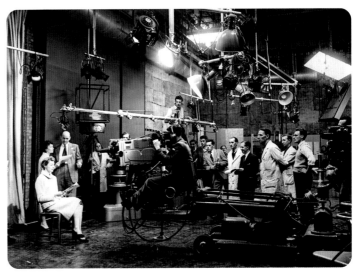

ITV launch: Shirley Butler, a station anchorwoman, rehearses her announcement in preparation for the opening night programme

industry and on "Red Clydeside", where shipbuilding with its complex layers of union "Spanish practices" such as demarcation presented a ripe target. After 1955, its peak post-war year, shipbuilding went into steady decline as world conditions and competition changed.

Productivity, then as now, was a major issue throughout industry. Surveys showed a noticeable decline from pre-war levels, and there was more absenteeism. An Oxford research group chaired by the economist Roy Harrod found that more than 60 per cent of business respondents thought their productivity was being impaired by restrictive labour practices.[16] Britain's productivity was low compared with that of the countries it had defeated in the recent war. It did grow by 40 per cent over the years 1950-59, but in the same period that of Germany and Italy rose by 150 per cent and that of Japan by 400 per cent.[17]

In late 1952, an American business view quoted in The Director was that Britain had become "a high-cost producer, unable to compete in mass markets". Unions in the building industry banned overtime at the height of post-war reconstruction, resulting in the backlog of demand growing faster than completed projects. The fault was not all on the side of organised labour, however. For many managers and City professionals it was still a culture of long lunches and weekends that began at noon on Fridays. "The antipathy of the British for work must be seen to be believed," scoffed The Director's US correspondent.

The mid-point of the decade, 1955, marked a definite change of gear into the Britain that most of us have grown up with; a country of service industries, consumer brands, advertising and the youth culture. The latter was now well under way, having been launched aggressively with rock 'n' roll in 1954. Bill Haley and his Comets pounded out exciting new sounds while the Teddy Boys, who aped Edwardian fashions and wore the first distinctive teenage hairstyle, greased into a quiff, tore up cinema seats and fought each other's gangs. Later, two distinctive groups emerged who regularly created street-corner mayhem, the nattily dressed "mods" and the black-leathered "rockers".

The year 1955 was memorable for the arrival of commercial television, against considerable opposition from the BBC and its allies among the great and the good. BBC radio, in its already addictive serial The Archers, famously launched a "spoiler" on ITV's opening night, September 22, by killing off the young bride Grace Archer in a burning barn. (See panel.) The lucrative new markets

opened up by independent TV would lead to one of the most memorable business comments of the century when the Canadian newspaper baron Roy Thomson floated Scottish Television in 1965 and observed that a TV franchise was "a licence to print money". (With the £13m he made from the flotation, Thomson bought The Times and Sunday Times from Lord Kemsley.)

Another landmark of 1955, though it would not be recognised as such until the following decade, was the opening of Mary Quant's shop Bazaar, which was to break

THE CHANGING CENTURY

Cold war, crisis and conflict: a snapshot of foreign policy

1950: Britain became more deeply involved in the anti-communist war in Malaya, which had begun in 1948. By the end of year, some 50,000 troops were fighting Malayan Communist Party (MCP) guerillas. (The British campaign lasted until 1958, by which time Malaya had become independent, and the MCP had demobilised. According to official estimates, dealing with the Malayan Emergency, as it was called, cost the government £520m)

1950: In August, the first British troops arrived in Korea. (War had broken out two months previously when forces from the communist north, controlled by Russia and China, invaded the south. The US and Britain had been given a UN mandate to go to the aid of the South Koreans. The conflict was to raise fears of nuclear holocaust: by now, the Soviets were known to have atomic weapons, and the

Americans were developing the hydrogen bomb. An armistice was not signed until 1953, by which time two million lives had been lost)

1950: In November, Britain's foothold in the strategically important Suez Canal Zone came under threat. King Farouk of Egypt demanded that British soldiers (there to keep the waterway neutral) leave the region so that Egypt could once more rule Sudan. Britain, which had owned part of the Canal since 1875, refused; instead, it sent in more troops

1951: Britain was in dispute with Iran. The cause was oil. The nationalist government of Dr Mohammed Mossadegh had seized control of the Anglo-Iranian Oil Company. In response, Britain announced that it would not allow Mossadegh's government to export any oil produced in factories previously controlled by Britain and sent a blockade of ships to the Persian Gulf. It took the removal of Mossadegh, cunningly engineered by British and US intelligence services in 1953, to end the dispute

1951: Cold war rhetoric became a feature of the October election campaign. For the Conservative leader, Winston Churchill, Britain had no choice but to build a deterrent force against the Soviet Union: "Unless you are armed and strong you cannot expect any mercy from the Communists; if you are armed and strong you may make a bargain with them which might rid the world of the terror in which it now lies and relieve us all from... the privations into which we shall otherwise sink"

1952: In October, British troops began to arrive at Nairobi airport. The enemy this time was the secret society known as the Mau Mau, which was committed to ridding its own tribal land of white settlers and which conducted a bloody campaign against members of the Kikuyu tribe loyal to the British. The war would last the decade

1953: Churchill, now ailing, tried to persuade the newly elected president of the US, Dwight D. Eisenhower, to hold talks with Stalin's successor, Malenkov. His hope, he told the Commons, was to try to stop the major powers tearing the "human race, including themselves, to bits". When the meeting eventually took place in July 1955 (by which time Churchill had stepped down as prime minister) it ended in deadlock. The

Mau Mau attack thwarted: how a contemporary artist portrayed the uprising in Kenya

the mould of the fashion store. The boutique had been born, aimed at the radical young, and Quant herself would soon stamp her look on the Swinging Sixties with her geometric Vidal Sassoon haircuts and sooty eye make-up. By the mid-1960s, there would be more than 1,500 boutiques in Greater London, most of them clustered in Kensington, Carnaby Street and along the King's Road in Chelsea.[18]

The curtain went up on the "never had it so good" era in July 1957, when Harold Macmillan, who had succeeded Anthony Eden as prime minister following the Suez debacle of 1956, told a meeting in Bedford: "Let us be frank about it: most of our people have never had it so good". Two years later, this would be adapted into the Conservatives' election slogans: "You've had it good. Have it better. Vote Conservative", and "Life's better under the Conservatives. Don't let Labour ruin it". The Tories in 1958 relaxed hire-purchase restrictions, allowing a boom in big discretionary purchases. "The whole nation has taken to buying everything on the instalment plan," the chairman of Great Universal Stores, Isaac Wolfson, cheerfully told his

Soviets said they would dissolve the Warsaw Pact (the Eastern bloc defence agreement, signed the previous May) only if the West disbanded NATO. More significantly, they declared total opposition to the reunification of Germany. The summit set the tone of East-West relations for the next 35 years

1954: In December, Britain embarked on a thermo-nuclear weapons programme to develop the megaton hydrogen bomb

1955: The "Cyprus situation" started to develop. Greek Cypriots rebelled against British rule, demanding "enosis", union with Greece. The militant group EOKA (the National Organisation of Cypriot Struggle), which was backed by Archbishop Makarios, began a campaign of terror. A state of emergency was declared. By 1956 (when Makarios was exiled to the Seychelles), there were 20,000 British soldiers on the island

1956: This was the year of the nadir of British post-war diplomacy – Suez. In accordance with an agreement signed in 1954 with Colonel Gamal Abdel Nasser, the new Egyptian leader, British troops began leaving the Suez Canal Zone in June. Less than a fortnight later, Nasser nationalised the Suez Canal Company. This gave Egypt command of oil supplies from the Gulf en route to Europe. Britain and France, which had run the Suez Canal Company, were outraged. They began covert talks with Israel, which, denied passage through the Canal, was bitterly antagonistic towards Egypt. Taking Nasser's refusal to accept the idea of an internationally controlled canal as their cue, they invaded the Canal Zone in October. The Anglo-French-Israeli action was condemned by President Eisenhower, who feared it would destabilise the region and play into the hands of the Soviets, who were already supplying Nasser with arms. Eisenhower forced through a UN resolution for a ceasefire, saying he would no longer support sterling if Britain went on fighting. By November, the war was over. It was a diplomatic and economic disaster – oil supplies were severely disrupted – and it cost prime minister Eden his job

1957: Macmillan and Eisenhower met in Bermuda. The talks marked the beginning of Britain's nuclear defence policy. A White Paper the same year declared that Britain's policy would be nuclear retaliation in the event of a Russian incursion into Western Europe

1958: Shootings and bombings continued in Cyprus. Macmillan had proposed a seven-year period of British rule to allow Greeks and Turks time to work out a way to govern the island. The British plan was rejected by both Greek and Turkish Cypriots

1958: To halt the spread of Nasserism Britain and America sent troops to Jordan and Beirut. (The Egyptian leader wanted to create a United Arab Republic. He had helped engineer a military coup in Iraq and was now backing nationalist movements in Jordan and Lebanon)

1958: The so-called "cod wars" began. Iceland imposed a 12-mile fishing limit, which Britain refused to accept. In Reykjavik, the British ambassador's house was stoned. Trawlermen and navies settled in for a long confrontation. (The dispute ended in 1961 when Britain accepted the limits but was renewed in 1972 when more restrictions were imposed)

1959: In Cyprus, the terrorist group EOKA declared a ceasefire. An agreement meant that the Republic of Cyprus would be established and that there would be a Greek president (Archbishop Makarios, now back from exile) and a Turkish vice president. Britain would keep two bases – as a much-needed foothold in the eastern Mediterranean. Independence for Cyprus conformed to a pattern of decolonisation that had started under Attlee, when Burma, India, Pakistan and Ceylon (Sri Lanka) had all been granted self-government

Sources: Christopher Lee: This Sceptred Isle, Twentieth Century, BBC and Penguin Books, 1999; Philip Deery: Malaya 1948: Britain's Asian Cold War?, International Center for Advanced Studies, New York University, 2002; Wikipedia; Guardian Unlimited; BBCi

Mr. Feelgood: Harold Macmillan enjoyed huge popularity in the boom years

out of pockets and wallets and handbags and changing into air tickets and oysters, television sets and caviar, art treasures and vacuum cleaners, cigars and refrigerators. Britain has launched into an age of unparalleled lavish living… It is the age of BOOM." (Queen itself was a symptom of the new media industry, an old-established society magazine that was bought by the talented, aggressive publisher Jocelyn Steven in 1957 and turned into the fashionable glossy that would set the tone of the Sixties)

The number of cars on Britain's roads doubled between 1952 and 1959, from two-and-a-half million to five million, and in 1959 the ribbon was snipped across the M1, often mistakenly described as the UK's first motorway, though in fact it was preceded by a short stretch of the M6 (see fact box) Average weekly earnings rose by 50 per cent between 1950 (£7.10s) and 1955 (£11) while the cost of living rose only 30 per cent. (By 1964, wages averaged £18 and were rising at twice the rate of prices each year.) In real terms, consumer spending rose by 45 per cent over the Conservative period of government between 1952 and 1964.[20]

Some historians now think the Macmillan feel-good era was a bit of a conjuring trick by an acknowledged master of political style. In his book Britain since 1918, Bentley B. Gilbert says: "Manifesting a political expertise seldom equalled, Macmillan… restored the illusion, if not the substance, of British prosperity". Gilbert's main criticism of Macmillan is that he failed to take the UK into Europe in 1957 when the European Common Market, as it was then known, was set up with France, West Germany, Belgium, Italy, the Netherlands and Luxembourg signing the Treaty of Rome. Joining Europe in the 1950s, says Gilbert, would have been "the best opportunity Britain had had since the war to re-establish genuine economic viability and to bring to an end the agonising triennial exchange crises that symptomised the unhealthy state of the British productive plant".

shareholders in 1958. GUS was already booming on a massive rise in mail-order buying – from £1m in 1950 to £130m in 1957.[19] Income tax was cut in spring 1959 from 8s. 6d. (42.5p) to 7s. 9d. (39p) in the pound, a rate not matched until Margaret Thatcher's tax cuts in the 1980s.

The patrician Macmillan, with his Edwardian drawl and drooping moustache, presided benevolently over what had suddenly become a national perception of good living. Queen magazine raved in 1959: "At the moment, there is more money in Britain than ever before. Nearly £2,000m is pouring

Macmillan, however, was treading in the path of previous PMs, both Labour and Conservative, who had been wary of anything smacking of a European federation dominated by France and Germany, and were also fixated on damage to Commonwealth trade and on maintaining the "sterling area" – itself deemed by one eminent economist of the time, Andrew Shonfield, to be an unacceptable burden on UK industry.[21] The biggest mistake, it was agreed by many politicians in 1957, was in failing to join the coal and steel community in 1950 (dismissed, in Herbert Morrison's famous put-down, because "the Durham miners won't wear it" – see chapter 4). Participation then, the argument ran, would have allowed Britain a truly formative influence over the nascent EEC.

Between 1950 and 1957, Britain had received another invitation to participate in EEC negotiations at Messina in 1955, but the Eden government hesitated and finally withdrew. At that time, the four old Dominions – Canada, Australia, South Africa and New Zealand – accounted for 25 per cent of Britain's trading, though the US was emphatically in favour of the UK joining. By the time France and West Germany had bonded in the late 1950s, it was already too late, and in 1963, when Macmillan's government finally girded itself to apply, President Charles de Gaulle brushed the application aside with an imperious "Non". Macmillan's compromise solution was to enter the European Free Trade Association (EFTA) with Austria, Denmark, Norway, Portugal, Sweden, and Switzerland, with special arrangements to continue allowing the import of key Commonwealth products such as Australian butter and New Zealand lamb.

Not everyone, of course, "had it good" in the election year of 1959. The previous year had seen unprecedented race riots in west London's Notting Hill, in those days a district of peeling stucco terraces shading into the slums of north Kensington where many West Indian immigrant

The start of something big: The Empire Windrush (top) brings the first black immigrants in 1948

Quiet riot: a peaceful moment during the Notting Hill Riots in London

families had settled. The first post-war Caribbean immigrants had arrived in 1948, on a ship called the Empire Windrush, taking advantage of recent legislation that made them automatic British citizens. These, many of them skilled war veterans, had been followed by growing numbers with fewer qualifications, attracted by the recruiting campaigns of labour-starved London Transport and the National Health Service. Ironically, even Enoch Powell, health minister under Macmillan, had encouraged West Indian immigration to fill menial NHS jobs that no Britons seemed willing to do: years later he would be sacked by Edward Heath for making the inflammatory "rivers of blood" speech about racial dangers in Britain.

Notting Hill apart, however, the worst explosions of inter-racial tension still lay 20 years ahead. As the 1950s ended with Macmillan's government returned in a landslide, it seemed as if the country and its industrial base were truly on an upward curve.

the ads we talked about

The very first TV commercial, which came on air shortly after 8pm on September 22, 1955, was for Gibbs' "tingling fresh" SR toothpaste. During the 1950s, with the advent of washing machines, some £7m was being spent annually on promoting the claims of rival washing powders.[24] By 1964, a quarter of all advertising would be TV-related (today, it is about a third).[25]

Advertising as a whole had scarcely been a recognised occupation before the 1950s – it was not even listed as one in the 1961 census. But the launch of many new products in the decade, along with commercial TV, meant the business grew rapidly. There was a year-on-year rise in real terms of eight per cent in advertising spending from 1952 to 1964.[26]

Slogans and catch-phrases in TV commercials and on roadside posters became part of the language: "Go to work on an egg" was coined by the young Fay Weldon, then working as a copywriter on the Egg Marketing Board account (1958). Other unforgettable phrases were "Snap Crackle and Pop" (Rice Krispies, 1955); "Don't forget the fruit gums, Mum" (Rowntrees, 1956); "Drinka pinta milka day" (National Milk Publicity Council, 1958) and "Unzip a banana" (Elders and Fyffes, 1959).

Equally memorable were the characters in TV commercials – the Oxo family (1958), the PG Tips talking chimps (1956) and the seductive Cadbury's Flake girls (1959). Many of these lasted for decades, and the first two have recently been re-conceptualised for a new generation.

Two of the Brooke Bond TV chimps, borrowed from Billy Smart's Circus, at Shepperton Studios in London

england swings sterling sinks

66 We are redefining and we are restating our socialism in terms of the scientific revolution. The Britain that is going to be forged in the white heat of this revolution will be no place for restrictive practices or outdated methods on .either side of industry. 99

Harold Wilson, opposition leader, addressing the Labour Party conference, October 1, 1963

6

Swinging London: Carnaby Street was a fashion mecca for the world

n 1960, a chirpy, self-made industrialist from Manchester named Ernest Marples was the new minister of transport in Harold Macmillan's "never had it so good" government. He had an 80-per-cent shareholding in the family construction business, Marples Ridgway, which specialised in building roads and had recently tendered for the new Hammersmith Flyover in west London. Marples had been appointed to his post in October 1959 but it was not until the following year that he sold his stake in the business for £2.5m – politics in the 1960s was less sensitive to questions of conflict of interest.

On November 2, 1959, Marples had opened the first 72-mile stretch of the M1, linking London (or, more precisely, St. Albans) with Birmingham and symbolically raising the curtain on the age of mass motoring. There were still only 2.8 million cars on Britain's roads (compared with 27.5 million today), but over the next four years, as a 2003 TV documentary on the motor industry expressed it, Marples "kick-started the car culture". In 1963, Sir Donald Stokes, the chairman of Leyland Motor Corporation, declared that he saw "no foreseeable limit" to the number of cars in Britain.

The prospect of family transport for all, and the mobility it unlocked, contributed greatly to the glow of prosperity that followed Macmillan's landslide election victory in the autumn of 1959. More people had more money in their pockets and they were buying more things. Materially, life was becoming more comfortable for the

In motorway heaven: transport Minister Ernest Marples

many, not just the few. The number of homes without a bathroom, for example, was to halve in the 1960s, from 3.2 million to 1.5 million.[1] Popular capitalism had arrived, a good 20 years before Margaret Thatcher. Even the Daily Mirror, that hallowed icon of working-class culture, had started to publish a City page so that its 13 million readers could feel part of the financial boom.[2]

As the motorway age began, however, the railway age that had been so proud a part of Britain's industrial heritage was under attack. In 1963, Dr. Richard Beeching, an industrial chemist on the board of ICI – and, one might think, a curious choice to determine the fate of the railways – produced his now-infamous "Beeching Report" on the future of Britain's nationalised rail network. The railways were eating money at the rate of £159m a year.

Beeching found that half of all the country's passenger train stations were producing only two per cent of revenue, so he closed them, axing in the process a third of the entire network. Branch lines were chopped out, leaving many rural towns stranded, and the crude surgery was unevenly distributed, with parts of East Anglia, south Wales and the West Country being hard hit while the densely populated south-east retained more routes.

Beeching's brutal prescriptions did produce results over the next four years: in 1965 alone costs were reduced by £90m, and productivity remained impressive considering the labour force had been cut from 500,000 to 340,000. But in 1967 the railways were still

Dr. Richard Beeching, railway axeman, with postmaster-general Tony Benn

spending £117 for every £100 they earned.[3]

Railway management was as professional and internally well-provided with information as it had been in its 1930s glory days, but it laboured under an incredibly complex and top-heavy bureaucracy – some 7,000 managers layered in hierarchies beneath eight board directors, 90 top executives and 600 "senior" managers. On top of that, in the mid-1960s the basic technology was in flux from steam to diesel and electric, so three different traction systems were in operation. Attempts to combine railway expertise on the board with commercial savvy from other industries such as vice-chairman Philip Shirley, formerly the chairman of Unilever's Batchelor's Foods, brought a new questioning approach to old assumptions but ultimately ran up against the buffers of an unmanageable conflict between financial realities and public expectations.

As the private car took over more and more from public transport in the 1960s, the motor industry in Britain might have been expected to flourish as never before. Yet it, too, was about to drive itself down a one-way highway to near-bankruptcy. The former editor

The two-millionth Mini rolls off the production line at Longbridge, Birmingham, 1969

of the Financial Times, Sir Geoffrey Owen, writing about the motor industry in his book From Empire to Europe, says "the BMC/British Leyland/Rover saga is part of Britain's most serious post-war industrial failure… At the end of the century, Britain was the only one of the larger European countries not to have a major nationally owned car company. Germany had three (Volkswagen, Daimler-Benz and BMW), France two (Renault and Peugeot) and Italy one (Fiat). Even Rolls-Royce Motors, the epitome of Britishness, was sold to Volkswagen in 1998."

In 1960, British Motor Corporation (BMC), which had merged the Austin and Morris businesses in 1952, ranked as one of the world's leading car manufacturers. It commanded 40 per cent of the UK market and in the Mini, the characterful little town car everyone wanted, it had a product that even tempted Continental motorists away from their national marques. Alec Issigonis, the gifted designer behind the Mini, came out with another winner in 1963, the Austin 1100/1300, which Ford saw as a real threat, and between them the two models had almost 25 per cent of the British market. Both, however, were inadequately priced for the cost of their manufacture.

From 1966, BMC could also boast the celebrated Jaguar cars in its stable, including the stunning V12 E-Type that had taken the 1961 Geneva Motor Show by storm. Jaguar, co-founded by William Lyons in 1921 as the Swallow Sidecar Company in Blackpool, had become SS Cars in 1931 and Jaguar in 1936, with the rakish SS Jaguar as its top model. (The prefix was dropped because of Nazi connotations when manufacturing resumed after World War II.) Post-war models such as the XK sports and the string of stylish saloons starting with the Mark V, maintained the company's reputation for exceptional design, build quality and high performance. Then in 1966 it merged with BMC to form British Motor Holdings: two years later, this in turn merged with Leyland Motor Corporation, which had swallowed up MG, Triumph and Rover. The unwieldy new beast was called British Leyland – soon to become a byword for labour unrest, unpopular cars and lack of management strategy.

BL's first new model, the Morris Marina, has been described as handling "like a skip on wheels". The Austin Allegro was another unattractive design with a bizarre square steering wheel. Changing gear in it has been likened to "trying to stir a bag of marbles with a knitting needle". The Allegro had several technical handicaps, one of the most irritating being that it would often refuse to start, then flood its engine.[4] At its upmarket end, BL introduced the Vanden Plas 3-litre Princess, an Austin in coach-built livery, and the 4-litre Princess R, with a Rolls-Royce engine developed for an army personnel carrier. Handsome though they were, these poor men's Bentleys were basically hybrid creations and never quite found their niche, although they had a highly visible role as transport for government ministers.

The few international successes that BL produced between 1968 and 1975, when it was rescued from financial meltdown by a partial nationalisation, came from its specialist division, notably the Jaguar XJ6 saloon and the Range Rover. In general, the patched-together company was a microcosm of British management failure, from its organisational tensions to its quality shortfalls to its incessant unofficial strikes. In mitigation, however, the Middle Eastern oil shocks of 1973 obviously affected the motor industry more than most. From profits of £38m in 1968, it went into the red by exactly twice that figure – £76m – in 1975. It would take the break-up of an over-centralised industry and the arrival of Japanese companies with their automated systems and interactive quality culture for the damage of two decades to be

repaired in the 1980s.

In the early 1960s, however, all still looked optimistic, and when Macmillan's government fell in 1964, battered by the Profumo scandal of 1963 and the rot that it had exposed beneath the ruling class of the day, Harold Wilson re-stoked that spirit of optimism by promising a modern Britain "forged in the white heat" of a technological revolution. (Like many political soundbites, his words have since been slightly amended in popular memory to "the white heat of technology".) Unlike Macmillan's short-lived successor as prime minister, Sir Alec Douglas-Home, who disarmingly (but fatally, as it turned out) confessed to using matchsticks to understand the economy, the Yorkshire-born Wilson was an Oxford-trained economist who spoke enthusiastically of change, science, youth and of "storming the frontiers of knowledge".

New broom: Harold Wilson narrowly wins No. 10

Initially, he seemed to deliver his promises. Labour invested heavily in education, and seven new universities – Sussex, Warwick, East Anglia, Essex, York, Kent and Lancaster – had opened by Wilson's second term in 1966. The prime minister's personal monument – perhaps the single biggest individual achievement of any British political leader – was the Open University, launched in mid-decade. The OU was the first-ever venture in distance learning, with courses broadcast through the BBC when normal programming had ceased, and it opened the prospect of degree qualifications to people who had never dreamed they would be possible.

By the mid-1960s, technology had its own cabinet minister – firstly, and singularly inappropriately, the veteran trade unionist Frank Cousins and secondly, from 1966 to 1970, the eager young Anthony Wedgwood Benn, scion of a publishing family who had shed his hereditary peerage (Viscount Stansgate) out of socialist convictions and progressively democratised the rest of his name to plain Tony Benn. In his diaries, Benn recounts a lunch with businessmen in the machine tool industry shortly after his

THE CHANGING CENTURY

Facts from the business archives:

1960: The Guardian newspaper coined the term "convenience food" to describe frozen fish fingers

1960: Roche Laboratories developed the tranquilliser Librium

1960: The Northamptonshire firm R. Griggs & Co. began to manufacture Doc Martens footwear – under licence from Dr Klaus Maertens of Munich, who had patented the air-cushioned soles in 1946

1960: Britax of Byfleet made the first British car seat-belts

1960: Charles Forte opened the UK's first motorway restaurant – on the M1 at Newport Pagnell, Buckinghamshire. (He had opened the first roadside Little Chef restaurant in 1958)

1960: The Swedish company Akerlund and Rausing produced the first plastic carrier bags

1960: ICI developed plastic refuse sacks. The first customer was Hitchin Council in Hertfordshire. By the mid 1990s, 1,500 million would be in use in Britain annually

1960: Pentel, the first fibre-tip pen, was manufactured by Japan Stationery Company in Tokyo

1960: Penguin Books, having been cleared of obscenity charges (see "social revolution" box), sold 200,000 copies (the entire initial print run) of the unexpurgated version of Lady Chatterley's Lover. (By the following year, two million Britons would have bought the book – at the then rather stiff price of 3s 6d)

1961: The first minicab service in Britain was introduced by Carline of Wimbledon

1961: Oral contraceptives became available in Britain. The first was Conovid, marketed by Searle Pharmaceuticals (now part of Monsanto)

1961: The American airline TWA introduced its first-class passengers to in-flight movies

1961: In France, the first hatchback, the Renault 4, was unveiled

1961: In New York, a cookie-addicted housewife formed the first Weight Watchers slimming club

1961: The British toy company Pedigree launched the Sindy doll

1961: At Southwark Bridge in London Britain's first self-service filling station opened for business

1961: The first fruit-flavoured yoghurt, Ski, came on to the British market, imported from Switzerland

1961: In New York, Kodak started to manufacture the world's first carousel slide projector

1962: In January, Decca refused to sign four boys from Liverpool in the belief they would never cut a hit record. Just 12 months later, Please, Please Me, on the EMI label, made it to Number One

1962: The Sunday Times launched Britain's first newspaper colour supplement. The cover showed 11 David Bailey photographs of Jean Shrimpton (in a Mary Quant dress) and one of footballer Jimmy McIlroy. Inside was a feature on Peter Blake (who was to produce the famous Sergeant Pepper album cover later in the decade) and a recipe by a then little-known chef, Robert Carrier

1962: Rowntree launched After Eight

1962: In Michigan, the Dow Corning Corporation developed the silicon breast implant

1962: Golden Wonder brought out cheese and onion crisps – the first flavoured potato crisps in Britain

1962: Aluminium kitchen foil was introduced in the UK with the launch of Bacofoil

1962: Manchester United broke the record for transfer fees, paying £100,000 for Denis Law of Turin

1962: The first official (legal) gambling casino opened in Britain: the Metropole in Brighton

1962: British United Airways launched the first hovercraft passenger service, operating a 60-knot, 24-seater Vickers-Armstrong VA-3 between Wallasey and Rhyl

1963: Valium was developed by Roche Laboratories. (The use, or abuse, of prescription tranquillisers such as Valium and Librium would be the subject of a sardonic Rolling Stones song 'Mother's Little Helper' in 1967)

1963: Dr Richard Beeching, the former technical director of ICI, published his now infamous report on the future of Britain's railways. As his axe fell, Ernest Marples, transport secretary, began to build more roads (see main text)

1963: The world's first disco, Whisky-A-Go-Go, opened in Los Angeles

1963: Inspired by the British invention of the hovercraft, Flymo (now part of Electrolux) brought out the Hover lawn mower

appointment. He told them of the history lessons he had learned as a boy, in which the achievements of Britain's great 18th and 19th-century engineers were overshadowed by "viceroys and generals, civil servants and diplomats… this country had simply opted out of industrialism". In the 1960s, he said, Britain should "give up being an imperial country and become an industrial one again, and only in this way can we reshape our society and encourage people to regard work in industry as the most worthwhile job that they can possibly do."

Benn had given a taste of this theme in the previous year when, as postmaster-general, he opened the visible

1963: The American Heart Association dealt a blow to the tobacco industry, becoming the first national organisation to launch an anti-smoking campaign*

1964: The American edition of Vogue carried reports in March of a new fashion – the above-the-knee hemline, as created by Paris couturier Andre Courreges. The following December, sightings were made in Chelsea of a skirt worn six inches above the knee; the car-stopping British "mini skirt" was in business

1964: In New York, Xerox unveiled the world's first office fax machine. (A vast piece of equipment, it required separate units for scanning, transmission and receiving, and could only be used over dedicated telephone lines or wideband microwaves. Xerox brought out a desktop version in 1966 but, again, there were drawbacks: it could only communicate with compatible models. The technology was not mature enough for general office use until the mid 1970s)

1964: Britain's new Labour government introduced corporation tax to replace companies and profits taxes

1964: Manchester Business School, the UK's first postgraduate business school, opened its doors

1964: IBM introduced the first word processor – a typewriter capable of making automatic adjustments to text

1964: In California, the toy company Mattel started to market a 12-inch figure dressed in World War II uniform and sporting a scar on his cheek. This was G. I. Joe, better known to Britons as Action Man

1964: Jiffy Packaging Company of Winsford, Cheshire, began production of Jiffy Bags*

1964: Terence Conran opened the first Habitat (see main text)

1964: The American Tobacco Company hit back against the anti-smoking lobby by launching the first brand of low-tar cigarettes, Carlton

1965: Express Diaries introduced Britons to longlife milk

1965: In America, Sony launched the first home video recorder; a colour version followed the next year

1966: Decca released the first record with Dolby sound (see science and technology fact box), a recording of Mahler's 2nd Symphony

1966: Midland Bank introduced Britain's first cheque cards

1966: BP piped the first North Sea gas ashore

1967: The first wine boxes were marketed by Tolley's of Hope Valley, South Australia. They quickly became known as "bladders" in Oz slang

1967: In Enfield, Middlesex, Barclays Bank unveiled Britain's first "hole-in-the-wall" automatic cash dispenser

1967: The first countertop microwave ovens were brought out in America. (Hitherto, microwaves had been the size of refrigerators and required installation by both electricians and plumbers)

1967: In Switzerland, watchmakers announced the development of a new product: the battery-operated quartz wristwatch

1967: The first lightweight, aluminium, baby buggy, the Maclaren Minor, went into production. It was designed and made by Owen Finlay Maclaren, a retired aeronautical engineer who had also designed the retractable undercarriage on the Spitfire

1968: In California, the agricultural pump manufacturer Roy Jacuzzi turned his attention to the production of something more

exotic: the whirlpool bath

1968: In Britain, the first 5p and 10p decimal coins were minted

1968: The advertising agency Boase Massimi Pollitt was set up in London. Founding partner Stanley Pollitt, who believed "proper understanding of the consumer" to be "at the heart of major advertising decision making," is widely recognised as the father of British advertising account planning. (BMP was to produce the celebrated 1974 Cadbury's Smash TV ad, which featured Martians mocking earthlings for their primitive skills in the kitchen)

1969: The first colour TV ad hit British screens. It was for the "convenience food" Bird's Eye frozen peas. (The debut spot, aired in the Midlands at 10.05am, cost just £23)

*By now, the health risks of tobacco were well-known. The British scientist Sir Richard Doll had published research on the relationship between cigarette smoking and lung cancer in the early 1950s. It was not until 1971, however, that health warnings on cigarette packets became a statutory requirement in the UK

**The first Jiffy bags had been invented in America in 1930

Main source: Patrick Robertson: The New Shell Book of Firsts, 1994, Headline Book Publishing; Guardian Unlimited

the £25 business that built dream machines

Victory on the motor-racing track had been a feature of success in the British car industry since the Bentley Boys drove their thundering machines to glory at Le Mans in 1928. In the 1960s there was no more glamorous figure in the car business than Colin Chapman, who had set up his Lotus Engineering Company in 1952 with £25 lent to him by his girlfriend Hazel Williams, later his wife.

Chapman, born in 1928, studied mechanical engineering at University College, London, learned to fly and, after national service in the RAF, bought and sold second-hand cars while tinkering with his own first model, a special modification of a 1930 Austin Seven that he entered successfully in a series of trials. The car was called a Lotus because he and his friends wore themselves out building it and decided it had the same soporific effect as the legendary lotus flower.

Lotus Engineering had enough early trials successes for Chapman to quit his job at British Aluminium and concentrate on the business, producing innovative aerodynamic designs and turning out racing and sports cars from workshops set up in stables behind the Railway Hotel in Hornsey, where his father was the manager. He also acted as consultant for the Vanwall and BRM racing teams and in 1956 built his first single-seater racing car, the Lotus 12.

Chapman now had his eyes on Grand Prix prestige and in 1958 entered a pair of Lotus 12s at Monaco for Graham Hill and Cliff Allison. The company's first big victory came in 1960 at Monaco, when Stirling Moss beat the powerful Ferrari team in his Rob Walker Lotus. Team

Lotus then notched up a famous win in 1961 when Innes Ireland won the US Grand Prix.

The road-car business was prospering too in the early 1960s, with the Lotus Seven, Lotus Elite, Lotus Elan and Lotus Cortina. In a 1970 interview with The Director, Chapman said Lotus sold less on high performance than on "sheer driving pleasure, on performance and agility rather than maximum speed". His customers, he said, were mostly 35 to 40-year-olds, in creative or professional jobs. The Elan was bought "chiefly by architects, doctors, engineers and advertising men".

The Lotus Seven was Chapman's seventh design for Lotus Cars and became an object of desire when it was featured as Patrick McGoohan's car in the late 1960s cult TV series, The Prisoner. As the Caterham Seven (Chapman sold the production rights to Caterham Cars in 1973), it is still reputed to be the world's fastest-accelerating production sports car.

In 1963, Jim Clark piloted the Lotus 25, which had the first monocoque chassis in Formula One racing, to seven victories in the same season, winning the world championship. Chapman and Clark, engineer and driver, had a symbiotic relationship, and Clark's death in 1968 in a Lotus 48 F2 car devastated his friend.

Team Lotus enjoyed a string of Formula One successes in the later 1960s, culminating in Graham Hill becoming world champion in the Lotus 49, the first car design to use the engine as a stressed chassis member. Chapman's innovative streak extended to commercial as well as engineering acumen: it was Team Lotus

Dynamic duo: Colin Chapman (right) with champion driver Jim Clark

that introduced sponsorship (by Imperial Tobacco) to F1 racing at Monaco in 1968. In the late 1970s it seemed that Chapman might gain control of the Formula One money circus over Bernie Ecclestone – a chance that fate would not allow Chapman to pursue.

The 1970s saw more international acclaim and championship wins for Lotus designs, and Chapman was beginning work on a new active-suspension development when he died in 1982 of a sudden heart attack, aged only 54. Later it would be revealed that Lotus was involved in some way in John de Lorean's car-building scam in Northern Ireland, for which the American had managed to extract £54m in UK government grants. A judge remarked that if Chapman had still been alive he would have been sent to jail for 10 years, but his exact role has never been fully explained.

The firm continued to have successes after Chapman's death, with Ayrton Senna scoring several victories in Lotus cars, but the innovative magic had gone, and the Lotus Group is now owned by Proton of Malaysia.[11]

symbol of the technological revolution, the Post Office Tower. In his speech, Benn compared the fussy Gothic grandeur of Big Ben, symbolising Victorian imperialism

that had been "built on the foundation of the first industrial revolution", with the "lean, practical and futuristic" telecoms tower that would represent "the technical and architectural skill of this new age". The 620-foot cylindrical tower, bristling with electronic equipment, had been built to serve the burgeoning telecommunications industry: by 1965, 22 per cent of British households owned a telephone, in contrast to a mere 3.3 million subscribers in 1940. The tower was the first purpose-built structure to transmit high-frequency radio waves, designed to allow the rapid expansion of telephone communications and to overcome the difficulty of laying cables in London. The sensitive narrow-beam transmitters needed to be sited on a stable base, and the tower's shape cut wind resistance to a minimum.

The Post Office Tower was an immediate tourist attraction with its viewing gallery and revolving restaurant high over London. In its first 16 months, it received 500,000 visitors, but the arrival of IRA terrorism in 1971 caused the gallery to be closed and the restaurant finally shut in 1980. In 2003, the BT Tower, as it is now known, became a listed building.

Tony Benn was – and remains, in old age – a charismatic speaker who, despite his left-wing convictions, could hold rooms full of leading businessmen spellbound as he enthused about the promise of new technology. He was quick to understand the potential of computers for saving time and money in business, although they were still at the cumbersome transistor stage. (Morgan Crucible in 1956 had become one of the first British companies to invest seriously in computerisation, along with Tube Investments. Both companies recorded in The Director their experiences of heavy costs and coming to terms with a longer-than-expected payback time, measured then in many years.)

At this time, Britain's sole remaining computer companies were International Computers and Tabulators (ICT), English Electric (which had bought the

Tony Benn backs the technological revolution

Symbol of a new age: the Post Office Tower

J. Lyons computer subsidiary LEO) and Elliott-Automation, which specialised in process control systems rather than office computers. The Wilson government believed it important to have a national competitor to IBM, despite the obvious disparity in scale, and to this end took a 10 per cent stake in the creation of International Computers Ltd. (ICL), whose other shareholders were those of ICT, English Electric and Plessey. It would take 20 years before realisation dawned that British resources were simply not equal to the challenge. British genius in the field would eventually emerge in the 1980s and 1990s in such vital creative niches as chip design and software writing.

Much more interesting to the general public, and the world at large, was Britain's sudden efflorescence of creativity in music, fashion and design, driven by the youth culture. The Beatles (left) burst upon the scene in October 1962 with their first EMI single, Love Me Do, laying the cornerstone of a mighty fortune for John, Paul, George and Ringo and a whole new industry based on the Mersey Beat. EMI had signed the Liverpool four after Decca had rejected them; one of the great oversights of business history. By 1963, they were topping the charts with Please, Please Me and She Loves You, and Beatlemania gripped the nation. It did not take long to spread across the Atlantic, with the foursome's first US tour in early 1964 sparking an unprecedented British invasion of the US pop scene. The Beatles' fifth single, I Want To Hold Your Hand, became America's No. 1 hit in February 1964 and by the time the year was out they would have a record 11 singles in the US top 10. Before 1964, British recording artists had accounted for only 1.25 per cent of major US hits: in 1964 alone, that figure soared to 26 per cent.[5]

On the back of the Beatles' phenomenal impact, US companies began competing for British rights. Suddenly,

THE CHANGING CENTURY

A snapshot of science and technology:

1960: Searle Laboratories carried out the first British field test for the oral contraceptive. Fifty women in Birmingham took part in the trial

1960: The physicist Theodore Maiman of Hughes Research Laboratories in Malibu, California, invented the ruby laser. (Work on the laser, which stands for "light amplification by the stimulated emission of radiation", had begun at Bell Laboratories in 1958. Maiman's achievement was to develop the technology for use in industry and medicine)

1960: The first ballistic-missile submarine, the USS George Washington, was launched. It was armed with 16 Polaris missiles

1960: In Wigan in Lancashire, the engineer and surgeon John Charnley developed the first artificial hip joints

1961: The Russian cosmonaut Yuri Alexeyvich Gagarin became the first man to return safely from space

1961: The first industrial robot, Unimation 1900, was developed for use in General Motors' die-casting plant in New Jersey

1962: America's Bell Telephone launched the world's first television communications satellite, Telstar I. More than 200 million viewers in Europe could now receive live American TV programmes

1962: The Americans' space programme caught up with the Russians': the astronaut John Glenn, like Major Gagarin had done the year before, orbited the earth

1963: International direct dialling was introduced between London and Paris

1963: In Auckland, New Zealand, the world's first pre-natal blood transfusion was carried out. The following year, a similar procedure took place at Lewisham Hospital in Britain

1963: Britain commissioned its first nuclear submarine, HMS Dreadnought

1964: On April 30, BBC2 began transmission. (The launch was somewhat inauspicious: a power failure meant it was impossible to broadcast from Television Centre as planned; Alexandra Palace had to be used instead)

1964: Britain got its first hydrofoil service, between the Channel Islands and France

1964: London got its first automatic (driverless) tube trains, running between Woodford and Hainault on the Central Line. In the same year, the first automatic Underground ticket barrier was introduced (at Stamford Brook station)

1965: The world's first commercial telecommunications satellite was launched at Cape Kennedy

1965: The New York Stock Exchange introduced a talking computer to provide stock quotations in response to telephone enquiries. The machine, which had a 126-word vocabulary, was the first of its kind in public use

1965: In an old dressmaking factory

England was where all the innovation in pop music was happening, with the Dave Clark Five, the Animals, Manfred Mann, Herman's Hermits, the Kinks, and eventually the Rolling Stones. The last were relatively slow to build in the US, their rebellious, destructive image being a touch extreme for American taste, but there was no doubting the massive British takeover. The US trade paper Billboard declared: "Great Britain has not been as influential in American affairs since 1775". The Beatles became the first group to gross more than $1m from a tour, and their merchandising quickly earned them 50 times that amount.[6] It is difficult to quantify the Beatles' contribution to the UK economy at that time, but Wilson's decision to award each of them the MBE in 1964 was a clear recognition of their services to exports.

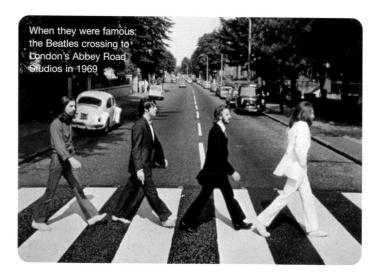
When they were famous: the Beatles crossing to London's Abbey Road Studios in 1969

in Fulham, London, Ray Dolby and four co-workers developed a new sound recording system. The noise-reduction Dolby system was to become a quality mark for record companies

1965: The Post Office Tower was opened in the heart of London. Built to serve thousands of new telephone subscribers, the 620ft space-age tower, complete with revolving restaurant and public gallery, was a symbol of Harold Wilson's new, technologically-driven Britain. (It became a listed building in 2003)

1966: The first British-built Polaris submarine was launched at Barrow Dockyard

1966: At the Standard Telecommunications Laboratory in Harlow, Essex, Dr Charles Kao and

Dr George Hockham developed fibre optic telephone cables

1966: The Russians' Lunik IX made a soft landing on the moon. The experiment proved that the moon's surface, hard enough to withstand the weight of a space craft, could be walked on by man

1966: The first transatlantic television programme was transmitted by satellite

1967: The first public colour TV service was launched in Britain. The first transmissions were mainly of lawn tennis from Wimbledon

1967: The Hawker Harrier took its maiden flight. The first vertical take-off and landing (VTOL) aircraft to enter military service, it was a triumph for British design and engineering (see main text)

1967: In London, the GPO started to test market push-button telephones

1967: In Cape Town, Professor Christian Barnard performed the world's first heart transplant operation. The surgery lasted for six hours and involved a team of 30 doctors and nurses. The patient survived for 18 days. The first heart transplant surgery in Britain took place the following year, the patient living for 46 days. (By the 1980s, two centres of excellence for transplant surgery had been established in England; see chapter 8)

1968: The first Channel hoverferry, a 168-ton vessel, with a carrying capacity of 609 passengers, or 254 passengers and 30 cars, went into service

1968: Surgeons in Cambridge performed the first liver transplant

operation in Britain

1968: A 15-year-old boy became Britain's first lung transplant patient

1969: The supersonic craft Concorde took its maiden flights. (It was not, however, to enter commercial service until the mid 1970s)

1969: The American astronauts Neil Armstrong and Buzz Aldrin walked on the moon. (The flight was somewhat eventful. Just before descent, fuel levels were low. Flight director Gene Krantz told controllers: "You'd better remind them up there, there ain't no damn gas stations on the moon!")

See also: business facts box

Sources: Patrick Robertson: The New Shell Book of Firsts, 1994, Headline Book Publishing; Christopher Lee: This Sceptred Isle, Twentieth Century, BBC and Penguin Books, 1999; Buzz Aldrin: speech at the IoD annual convention, 2003

EMI as a company prospered mightily on Beatlemania, having bought the rights to the Fab Four from their original discoverer, the former record shop manager Brian Epstein, who later committed suicide. After the war, Electrical and Musical Industries had seemed stuck in a time warp, still living off its pioneering work in radar. It had managed to secure the UK rights to Elvis Presley's singles and nurtured homegrown talent such as Cliff Richard and Adam Faith, but it was the Beatles who, thanks to the producer George Martin, managed to crack the huge US market for EMI. Beatles' record sales worldwide reached 200 million. In November 1969, the journalist and MP Julian Critchley listed EMI's global achievements in The Times: by then, it owned and operated major record companies in 28 countries, including America's Capitol Records, and was responsible for one-fifth of the billion records sold every year throughout the world.

If the new bands provided the dance beat to Swinging London, immortalised as such by a Time magazine cover story in 1966, the visual impact on the streets of a revitalised city came from a bold, youth-oriented new fashion industry. Julian Critchley wrote in The Times: "The rise of 'pop' music has been mirrored by the change in clothes. With the cult of youth has gone the end of middle age. Mary Quant has said we can all stay young until 65."

Mary Quant undoubtedly did for British fashion what The Beatles did for pop music. She had been around well before the 1960s, having opened her first Bazaar shop on the King's Road, Chelsea, in 1955, but the decade of liberation and youth met her moment. Looking back at the 1960s nearly 40 years later, she said: "I wanted everyone to retain the grace of a child and not to have to become stilted, confined, ugly beings. So I created clothes that worked and moved and allowed people to run, to jump, to leap, to retain their precious freedoms."

With her provocative doe-eyed make-up and trademark fringe, Quant dealt openly in sex appeal. Her jumpers, miniskirts and dresses, coloured tights, hipster belts, PVC garments and sleeveless, crocheted tops were a complete break from the way young women had dressed in the 1950s – basically, like younger versions of their mothers. It is unclear whether she was the actual creator of the mini-skirt – John Bates and one or two French designers have claims to that achievement – but she was certainly the populariser, selling short skirts and dresses through her Bazaar outlets in London and elsewhere, and through her international wholesale company, the Ginger Group.

Mary Quant,
fashion queen, wanted
"everyone to retain
the grace of a child"

the hunt for hidden assets

The second half of the 1960s saw a rush of bare-knuckled merger and takeover activity that would not be matched again until the 1990s. So rough were some of the tactics employed that Harold Wilson was stung into challenging the City to set "formal and clear" ground rules on takeover battles and to be responsible for seeing them implemented. Otherwise, as Sir Leslie O'Brien, deputy governor of the Bank of England, warned the Square Mile, the government would introduce a securities and exchange commission on the US model.

One of the biggest mergers, in 1967, was GEC's takeover of Associated Electrical Industries, in an industry that had already been subject to much hectic consolidation. There was also much activity in the food sector, with the Rank Hovis McDougall and Cadbury-Schweppes mergers leading the field. The latter, in 1969, would prove one of the most enduring corporate marriages of the time: the fit was exceptionally good, with Schweppes lending a sharp financial edge to the business and Cadbury – still run by its Quaker family – offering experienced management. (The Cadbury board had all been hands-on managing directors.) Alliance with Schweppes also opened up new geographic markets for the Cadbury brands, especially in the US.

In the late 1960s there was a heady atmosphere – as there would be 30 years later – of mergers being good for unlocking shareholder value, although that phrase had not yet been born.

The Wilson government also favoured the "big is beautiful" approach – hence the ill-fated union of British Motor Corporation and Leyland in 1968.

According to David Kynaston's authoritative history of the City of London, Wilson was "swayed by emphatic assurances from Warburg that Donald Stokes (the Leyland chairman) was a brilliant executive capable of forging British Leyland into an unbeatable national champion in the worldwide motor industry". The Wilson government's perpetual search for the holy grail of "national champion" industries was as doomed to failure in cars as in computers (with ICL).

Another aspect of unlocking hidden value surfaced in the shape of the asset-stripper, than whom there was no sharper practitioner than Jim Slater (right). Born in 1929, Slater had been right-hand man to Donald Stokes at Leyland and in 1963 turned his hand to journalism, writing a monthly share-tipping column in The Sunday Telegraph under the nom-de-plume of Capitalist.

His methodology, he explained, would be to "spot anomalies on the basis of existing information before the market does". Within three months, his tips were showing a 30-per-cent profit, and in less than two years Slater had amassed a tidy profit for himself of £25,000, despite assuring Nigel Lawson, then the paper's City editor, that he would not personally exploit his position.

Slater teamed up with Peter Walker (left), a Conservative MP who had built a small fortune in property, insurance and unit trusts. In 1964, the pair launched Slater Walker Industrial Group, with the intention of taking large holdings in badly managed companies and injecting efficiency into them. In fact, as the property developer Nigel

Broackes observed in his memoirs, the policy became one of "taking over sleepy companies, ripping out (and selling off) the loss-making sectors to build up a profitable core…"

During 1967, in a bull market and with merger mania in full spate, Slater Walker was the darling of the City, and the group was valued at some £10m. Slater lectured British management to run its businesses "like an investment portfolio – cut your losses and let your profits run. In other words, concentrate your efforts on the profit-makers rather than the loss-makers. A lot of British boards seem to do the opposite…"

The Slater Walker rocket fell to earth in the mid-1970s, partly the result of a property and stockmarket collapse and partly over rumours of dubious Slater Walker operations in Singapore. Slater bowed out, handing over the chairmanship of his securities business to James Goldsmith, a flamboyant entrepreneur in foods and property. The Daily Telegraph called it "the end of one of the most remarkable stories in the City's long history – the rise of builder's son Mr. Jim Slater and his creation of possibly the most remarkable investment machine ever seen".

Years later, the asset-stripping king re-surfaced in a most unlikely new career, as a successful children's author, but he still writes the occasional book on investment strategy.[12]

Like the Beatles, the mini-skirt was one British export the US went wild about: when it was launched there in 1965, sales leapt to $2m in one year alone. So successful was it at home that British tax regulations were changed: before the mini-skirt, any garment under 24 inches in length had been categorised as children's clothing and exempt from purchase tax. The mini-skirt, exposing so much more of women's legs, also changed the hosiery industry from conventional nylon stockings to tights. By 1970, sales of stockings, which had accounted for 80 per cent of the hosiery market in 1962, had sunk to a mere five per cent. The Nottinghamshire manufacturer Pretty Polly launched its first range of nylon tights in 1968.[7]

Quant popularised a total look, from mini-skirt to mascara, and all her products were marketed under a distinctive daisy-petal logo. Part of "the look" was the angular Vidal Sassoon haircut that would forever be associated with Mary Quant. Sassoon, who had served a 1950s apprenticeship under the first celebrity hairdresser, "Teasy-Weasy" Raymond, began opening salons specialising in the precision-cut geometric bob and soon ranked as society's favourite crimper. The 1960s was the first period in history

THE CHANGING CENTURY

A snapshot of Britain:

1960: National Service was abolished; young men were now freer to make the transition from their teenage years to adulthood on their own terms. No more would they be forced to conform to the discipline of the armed forces. It was a fitting start to what would be remembered as a decade of liberation and libertarianism

1960: The rising standard of living meant that the young had the money to enjoy their new freedoms. In 1959, teenagers had been spending an average £8 a week (£830m in total) on clothes, cigarettes, records and cosmetics. The post-war baby boom meant that the young were now a major economic force: by the early 1960s, almost 40 per cent of the population was under 25

1960: At the Edinburgh Festival, the careers of Peter Cook, Dudley Moore, Alan Bennett and Jonathan Miller were launched with the review

Beyond the Fringe. The following year, they took their show to the Fortune Theatre and lampooned, among other people, Church of England vicars and the prime minister. All in their 20s, the Beyond the Fringers, together with other young satirists such as John Wells, John Fortune and Eleanor Bron, symbolised the spirit of the new age. Members of the younger generation were not going to bow and scrape to people just because they were older, wealthier and more influential and powerful than they were: deference was dying; iconoclasm was here

1960: At the Old Bailey, Penguin Books was tried under the Obscene Publications Act. Its "crime" was to publish the full text of D. H. Lawrence's across-the-class-divide love story, Lady Chatterley's Lover, 30 years after it had been banned. The trial became a flashpoint for changing attitudes and mores, for old and new Britain. Having pinpointed 13 passages describing sexual intercourse, Mervyn Griffiths-Jones, one of the prosecution

barristers, famously asked: "Is it a book you would... wish your wife or your servants to read?" The jury said it was; Penguin was cleared of the charge and given a lucrative licence to print. (The literary merit of the book, which formed the basis for Penguin's defence, would lead comedians Morecambe and Wise to christen the author Dirty Hardbacks Lawrence)

1961: The anti-establishment paper Private Eye was launched. (It was deemed too scurrilous by W. H. Smith, which banned it from its shelves)

1961: The first oral contraceptive was made available. (At first it was prescribed for married women only)

1962: The irreverent That Was The Week That Was, featuring David Frost, Christopher Booker and Willie Rushton, came on air. The first satirical TV show, it was to prove too much for the BBC board, which, despite viewing figures of 12 million, took it off at the end of 1963

1963: John, Paul, George and Ringo

made it big (see main text). All from working-class backgrounds, they seemed to stand for the new meritocracy, the new freedoms and the new opportunities. As The Times put it in 1980: "The Beatles enabled millions more to crack the barriers that existed between classes, between London culture and that of the provinces, between Scouse and Geordie and the accents of the BBC and Oxbridge. Their style of dress and their irreverent behaviour led the youth of Britain to a new and independent identity"

1964: Helen Brook, a banker's wife who had for years worked in family planning, opened her first clinic. Brook Clinics would give single girls easy access to contraception. Soon, the take-up rate of the pill grew to half a million

1964: The so-called battles of the beaches (a feature of bank holidays for the next couple of years) began as hundreds of members of rival gangs the Mods and the Rockers clashed on the south coast, many

Icons of the swinging sixties: l to r, Vidal Sassoon styling Mary Quant's haircut; colourful Carnaby Street

of them high on amphetamines

1965: There were almost 1,134,000 detected crimes; a decade earlier, there had been fewer than 440,000. (Some blamed the increase on less discipline in schools and the more relaxed style of parenting, promoted by childcare expert Dr Benjamin Spock)

1965: Roy Jenkins, home secretary, began a programme of social reform, abolishing capital punishment. In the next couple of years, he would relax the laws on homosexuality, divorce, censorship and abortion, and introduce the parole system for prisoners. His reforms would earn him the title "architect of the permissive society" by the right-wing press; to him, they were attempts to "civilise" Britain

1965: In a break with tradition, the Beatles were given the MBE. (The award of the honour to "mere" pop stars caused a storm of protest. Nine previous recipients returned their decorations)

1965: Appalled by the growing incidence of bad language and sexual explicitness in the broadcast media, Mary Whitehouse set up the National Viewers' and Listeners' Association to try to police the standards of the BBC

1967: The hippie movement took off in the so-called Summer of Love. The same year, nearly 2,500 people were prosecuted for the possession of marijuana. (Fifteen years earlier, prosecutions had been in single figures.) The flower power hippies with their dislike of materialism were, even more than the leather-clad motorbiking Rockers, the antithesis of the sharp-suited, flashy Italianate Mods. (Many came from middle-class backgrounds and many were students)

1967: In September, Radio 1, the youth music station, was launched. (On TV, meanwhile, there were the youth shows Ready, Steady Go and Top of the Pops)

1968: Mounted police had to be called in to tackle anti-Vietnam war demonstrators in Grosvenor Square,

home to the American embassy. (US soldiers had burned the My Lai village to the ground, killing hundreds of people in the belief they were harbouring Viet Cong guerrillas.) Many of the protesters were students and hippies

1970: John Lennon told Rolling Stone magazine that the 1960s had been a decade when "everyone dressed up but nothing changed". There were probably many people who believed he was right. The "winds of change" might have swept through Africa, reducing the British Empire to a handful of colonies, but in most developed countries things had gone on much as before: the Cuban missile of 1962 had brought the world to the brink of nuclear war; America had become deeply involved in a brutal anti-communist campaign in Southeast Asia; the British government had lurched from one economic crisis to another and had yet again been defeated by the Irish problem. (In 1969, rioting and violence in Northern Ireland had reached almost unprecedented

levels. What came euphemistically to be known as the "troubles" had begun; the British Army was sent in to take over responsibility for the security of the province)

NOTES:
The rise in youth culture and the growth of the anti-establishment movement pre-dates the 1960s. The first youth cult, the Teddy Boys, emerged in the mid-1950s, dancing to the tune of a new, youth-oriented music, rock and roll. Meanwhile, Angry Young Men such as John Osborne and Colin Wilson were railing against "the system". (Osborne, whose play, Look Back in Anger, opened at the Royal Court in 1956, was a fierce critic of the establishment, calling the Royal Family "the gold filling in a mouthful of decay")

Sources: Christopher Lee: This Sceptred Isle, Twentieth Century, BBC and Penguin Books, 1999; Juliet Gardiner: From the Bomb to the Beatles: the changing face of post-war Britain, 1945-1965, Collins and Brown, 1999; Miriam Akhtar and Steve Humphries: The Fifties and Sixties: a lifestyle revolution, Boxtree, 2001; Guardian Unlimited; BBCi

that opened up the possibility of celebrity and huge earning power to working-class people with a particular flair or technical skill – whether in hairdressing, photography (David Bailey cut a swathe through young society women) or entertainment, where suddenly all the chart-toppers had accents from Liverpool, Glasgow or east London.

What Mary Quant did for young women's fashions in the 1960s, John Stephen was doing for young men. Stephen had come to London from Glasgow in the 1950s, opening his first clothing shop in Beak Street, Soho, in 1957. His clothes were taken up by the "mods" – those who wore the nattily tailored, round-collared look so diametrically opposed to the leather-clad "rockers" – and by 1965 Stephen had four shops in Carnaby Street, a narrow back-street parallel to London's Regent Street. Carnaby Street became the mecca of Swinging London. That year, a US journalist, John Crosby, wrote in the Daily Telegraph: "England leads the world in young people's fashions, both female and male. Buyers from American department stores come here and

are absolutely astounded at what is happening… The impact of Carnaby Street is becoming worldwide. Tony Curtis wears Carnaby Street clothes. So do Peter Sellers and the Beatles."

The age of the boutique had been born, for shoppers of both sexes, and US retail buyers would go home and fit out shops like John Stephen's within the bigger department stores. Another iconic boutique of the time was Biba, founded as a mail-order business by Barbara Hulanicki and her husband Stephen Fitzsimon in 1964. Its guiding philosophy was to provide designer fashion at knock-down, throw-away prices and Hulanicki designed her own fabrics, a blend of Art Nouveau and Art Deco. Her big breakthrough came when the Daily Express offered her gingham dress and matching headscarf to readers "for 25 bob." (£1.25) Seventeen thousand readers responded with orders and the couple set up their first two small boutiques.

Biba became a way of life for many. The shops were designed like discos, with rock music playing, and dark mahogany screens everywhere. Customers were encouraged to come in and try on anything – and they did, in droves. In 1969, Biba opened its celebrated flagship shop in Kensington, following Quant's one-stop philosophy. It offered everything from lipstick to leggings under the Biba brand but by 1973 the glory days were over and Biba's over-ambitious translation to the Art Deco salons of a nearby department store, the former Derry and Toms, did not last for more than a couple of years.

The London fashion and design industry of the 1960s could offer classic quality as well as trend-setting flair. Caroline Charles, a former protegee of Quant's, launched her own label in 1963 when she was barely into her twenties, and soon became the stylish choice of pop stars on both sides of the Atlantic. Jean Muir, who started her own label in 1966, made classically cut, elegant clothes in rich but simple fabrics. More quirky was Zandra Rhodes, who launched her first collection in 1969, and John Bates, who designed the leather cat suit for Diana Rigg in the TV series The

The Biba boutique, founded by Barbara Hulanicki (left), became a way of life for many

Avengers, and made it a signature fashion statement. In 2003 he recalled in a BBC radio interview how he had designed mini-skirts before Quant, but did not have her advantage of being able to market through his own boutiques and was dependent on persuading the big department stores – which turned his mini-skirt down.

Laura Ashley, whose business would take off globally in the 1970s (see chapter 7), had begun in a tiny way with husband Bernard in 1953, hand-printing headscarves. In the 1960s they moved to cheap factory premises in Wales and their first London shop – in Pelham Street, South Kensington – opened in 1968. Sales rocketed after The Observer newspaper ran a feature on them in 1970. They established a fashion look that was in direct opposition to Quant, the Andre Courreges "moon boots" and all the white plastic and pelmet-like skirts of the period. It was a throwback to Victoriana and gained accidental fashion kudos from the kind of outfit worn by Katherine Ross in Butch Cassidy and the Sundance Kid; long, floaty, ruffled cotton dresses sprigged with country flowers and buttoned high to the neck.

"She was very much making a moral statement," Laura's daughter Jane Ashley said in a 2002 TV documentary – a statement against the sexual suggestiveness of mini-skirts and in favour of demure dressing, church on Sunday and the moral values of the past. The designer who "sexed up" the Ashley look was Ossie Clark, who

Ossie Clark (right), ill-fated fashion leader

had begun by working in far-out materials such as metallic leathers and snakeskins – he made a famous snakeskin suit for the singer Marianne Faithfull – but by the late 1960s he had become known for soft tailoring

Laura Ashley's romantic retro styles celebrated Victorian values

and romantic evening wear, often in floral crepes and chiffons designed by his wife Celia Birtwell. His career, begun in 1961 with a much-publicised fashion show staged at Chelsea Town Hall, ended in bankruptcy in 1981, after which the Inland Revenue claimed 14 years' back taxes. Tragedy followed in 1996 when he was stabbed to death by a homosexual lover.

All these names promoted a powerful image of Britain, and particularly London, as the centre of the youth universe. Design was innovative in other areas, too. In furniture, a designer called Robin Day devised an injection-moulded stacking chair made in polypropylene for Hille and Company around 1962-63. It became, according to a TV programme on 1960s design, "the biggest selling British design classic ever". It was bought in bulk for conferences, church halls, meeting rooms and business venues of all kinds. Over the 40 years from 1963 to 2003 more than 14 million chairs have been sold in 23 countries, sometimes proving to have unexpected uses. On a trip to Botswana, Day was surprised to find the bases of the chairs being separated from the legs to form seating for canoes.[8]

Taste-makers: the stylish Terence and Shirley Conran and their revolutionary shop, Habitat

For furnishing the home, however, there was only one place for the trend-conscious buyer to go in the 1960s and that was Terence Conran's bright new Habitat store on London's Fulham Road, opened in 1964. It represented a revolution in retail; not only were the usual serried ranks of upholstered sofas and armchairs replaced by clean-cut furniture in natural woods and fabrics, but Conran set out to offer a "complete home concept" of modern design that could literally be bought off the wall.

Shelves against painted brick walls carried masses of well-designed homewares that reflected the move towards Mediterranean-style cooking popularised by the books of

THE CHANGING CENTURY

The fall of Supermac, the rise of Wilson: a snapshot of politics, 1960-1964

1960: It was becoming clear that the consumer boom, which had helped the Conservatives win the 1959 election, belied serious weaknesses in the economy. The trade balance was awry; Britons were spending more than they were making. High demand levels and low unemployment levels were leading to higher pay claims. Industrial unrest was growing; by autumn, the dockers were out, and car workers had embarked on a series of damaging stoppages. (A strike by rail workers had been averted earlier in the year – but only by the intervention of Macmillan to increase pay)

1961: By now, the gap between imports and exports and between wage increases and output was perilously wide. Public spending was reined in – the health minister Enoch Powell raised NHS prescription charges – and a "pay pause" was introduced by the chancellor, Selwyn Lloyd. The National Economic Development Council was formed in an attempt to bring unions, industry and politicians together in a co-operative forum. No amount of good intentions from "Neddy", however, were going to be enough to set the economy to rights

1962: In March, a by-election was held in Orpington. The Liberal candidate Eric Lubbock turned a Tory majority of nearly 15,000 into a Liberal one of nearly 8,000. As often happens in by-elections, disaffected Tory and Labour supporters were making a statement by voting tactically. The result did not mean that the government would inevitably lose a general election; nonetheless, it rang a loud alarm bell in the prime minister's ears

1962: In July, Macmillan sacked Selwyn Lloyd and then seven other ministers from the Cabinet in what became known as the Night of the Long Knives. The move, designed in part to inject new life into a tired government, backfired: Supermac was now Mac the knife. The Liberals' Jeremy Thorpe* quipped: "Greater love hath no man than this, that he lay down his friends for his life"

1963: Hugh Gaitskell died. The Labour leadership was now up for grabs. George Brown, deputy leader and a future foreign secretary, was considered too much of a loose cannon for the top job and came second to the more left-wing Harold Wilson. (Legend had it that Brown had once, the worse for

Elizabeth David. One icon of the time will be remembered by many home cooks – the terracotta "chicken brick" in two pieces that was designed to cook a bird in its own juices.

Habitat sales staff wore Mary Quant uniforms and had their hair styled by Vidal Sassoon. Like Quant, Conran had a fairly simple commercial philosophy: "My belief is simply that if reasonable and intelligent people are offered something that is well made, well designed, of a decent quality and at a price they can afford, then they will like and buy it." Conran, as ever, had his finger on the pulse. Habitat became one of the most famous British brand names, opening a big second store on central London's Tottenham Court Road in 1966 and in Manchester the following year.

Behind all this buzzing, colourful and upbeat commercial activity that has helped, in many middle-aged memories, to make the 1960s seem a golden age when youth was at the helm and Britain a hive of creative new businesses, lay a darker, grittier reality about the economy. Like the tower blocks that had transformed its city skylines and won

architectural plaudits, only to degenerate into grubby slums of cracked concrete – and in the notorious case of Ronan Point in 1968, to collapse entirely, killing five people – Britain's economy had serious structural defects. There was more money in everyone's pockets – especially young people's pockets – but by 1960 the nation was spending more than it was producing. The structure of manufacturing industry encouraged imports rather than exports, despite the post-war drive for dollars. The trade balance was going out of kilter again, and rising consumer demand, coupled with virtually full employment, was about to stoke up wage demands.

The Conservative government of Harold Macmillan, in its declining years between 1960 and 1964, tried a variety of measures, from raising interest rates to imposing a credit squeeze to introducing a so-called "pay pause". Nothing worked. Eight Cabinet ministers including chancellor Selwyn Lloyd lost their jobs in the wake of a by-election defeat in July, 1962, in what became known as Macmillan's "night of the long knives". Once admiringly cartooned as Supermac,

---

drink, mistaken the papal nuncio at an embassy reception in South America for a woman in a red dress and asked him to dance)

1963: This was Macmillan's "annus horribilis". In January, he suffered humiliation at the hands of de Gaulle, who imperiously turned down Britain's application for full membership of the EEC, and later in the year he suffered humiliation at the hands of Wilson, who accused him of "indolent nonchalance" as he faced the House over the Profumo affair. (John Profumo, Secretary of State for War, had at first strenuously denied allegations of an "improper" relationship with the former cabaret

dancer Christine Keeler, who counted Captain Ivanov, an attaché at the Soviet embassy and a supposed KGB spy, among her lovers. When he at last came clean and resigned, questions were inevitably raised about Macmillan. Had the premier known that Profumo had lied? And if he had not known, why not? The government had slid further into the quagmire when Dr Stephen Ward, the society osteopath who had introduced Profumo to Keeler, committed suicide after being found guilty of living off the immoral earnings of Keeler and her friend, Mandy Rice-Davies. It seemed as if Ward had been made

to pay for hypocrisy and duplicity at the heart of government)

1963: In October, Macmillan, worn out and ill, resigned. He was succeeded by the aristocratic Alec Douglas Home, a man who seemed to symbolise the old Britain, with its class divisions and ruling elite, as much as Wilson, the Yorkshire-born grammar school boy, who talked of youth, progress and meritocracy, symbolised the new

1964: Labour won the October general election. With a majority of just five seats, Wilson became prime minister. His government, which introduced social reforms, took Britain

further into the communications age, extended educational opportunities by building new universities and launching the Open University, achieved many things. Sadly, economic stability was not one of them

*The urbane Thorpe became Liberal leader in 1967 and subsequently stood trial for the attempted murder of former male model, Norman Scott, with whom he was alleged to have had an homosexual affair. He was acquitted, but the scandal ruined his political career

Sources: Christopher Lee: This Sceptred Isle, Twentieth Century, BBC and Penguin Books, 1999; Juliet Gardiner: From the Bomb to the Beatles: the changing face of post-war Britain, 1945-1965, Collins and Brown, 1999; Guardian Unlimited; BBCi

Prime Minister Harold Macmillan, French President Charles de Gaulle, Yvonne de Gaulle and Lady Dorothy Macmillan at their home in Sussex

the ageing prime minister was now "Mac the Knife". Then on January 14, 1963, French president Charles de Gaulle imperiously told the world that Britain was not a continental nation and not qualified for full membership of the European Economic Community. He accused Macmillan of setting up the EFTA free trade group of seven non-EEC countries to prevent progress by the EEC. De Gaulle was obsessed by Britain's continuing close links with the US and by the fact that France had not played a key part in the formation of NATO in the late 1940s.

Labour's jubilation at winning a narrow victory over the burned-out Conservatives in 1964, and their taunts about "13 wasted years" were to prove hollow satisfactions. When Wilson's new administration examined the nation's accounts, concluding that the balance of payments deficit would be more than £800m, the cabinet's first reaction was to impose an import surcharge of 15 per cent and a price review body.

International currency speculators were causing havoc with the pound – the first of many such runs – and James Callaghan, the new chancellor, was forced to bring in an

emergency budget, raising income tax by six per cent and introducing a new capital gains tax together with a corporation tax to replace companies and profits taxes. The first emergency action against the speculators came on November 23 with a two per cent hike in interest rates – interpreted by the world at large as a panic measure. Two days later relief came when the central bankers of 11 nations offered $3bn to shore up sterling.

But in 1966 the ferris wheel of fiscal crisis came around again, and in July Callaghan imposed a year-long price freeze, increases in purchase tax, another squeeze on hire purchase and a six-month pay-and-dividends freeze. Could things get worse? Yes. On November 19, 1967, the pound was devalued from $2.80 to $2.40. Wilson went on television to make his infamous assurance to the nation that "the pound here in Britain, in your pocket or purse or in your bank" had not been affected. As recorded by Barbara Castle in her memoirs, The Castle Diaries, Callaghan had told his Cabinet colleagues of his decision to devalue with the words: "This is the unhappiest day of my life… the most agonising reappraisal I have ever had to do and I will not pretend that it is anything but a failure of our policies."[9] It did not save his job, and he was replaced by Roy Jenkins. Next year, however, sterling was at its lowest since devaluation and, as Christopher Lee writes in This Sceptred Isle, "the situation in the second week of March was so desperate that Britain was asked by the World Bank to close the London Gold Market – in other words, to shut down the banks… The London Gold Market was actually shut down for two weeks."

Wilson's government believed in state dirigisme, and was heavily interventionist – acting, as Management Today described it, like a management consultancy on a national scale. The National Plan, grandly unveiled in 1965 by George Brown, the minister for economic affairs, but abandoned within a year, was intended to achieve overall annual growth of 3.8 per cent until 1970 – total growth over the six years of 25 per cent.

Targets were set for each industrial sector, and the government brought in a "selective employment tax" intended to divert labour from the service industries to export-oriented manufacturing. Even as the Plan was being published, many economists predicted that a growth rate of 3.8 per cent was unattainable: their pessimism was "amply justified", said an editorial in Management Today, assessing the first year. One critical factor for the Plan's success was investment in new plant and equipment, which in the first year had already been scuppered by short-term economic pressures forcing cutbacks.[10]

Nor was the Labour government helped by its chums in the trade unions. By the end of the decade, industrial unrest had reached such a pitch that Barbara Castle, the employment secretary, published a most un-Labour-like White Paper called In Place of Strife, which would have allowed the government to take trade unions to court over unofficial strikes. Callaghan, an old union man, strongly opposed it as home secretary and the battle lines were enduringly drawn between him and Castle (when he succeeded Harold Wilson as prime minister in 1974, he dropped her unceremoniously from his cabinet). The unions, sensing that they had had a lucky escape, made a token agreement to put their house in order, but the strike-ridden 1970s would prove the bitter legacy of Castle's defeat.

Wilson's government was also plagued with problems in the defence industry, having to cancel costly projects just as they came to fruition, as the Conservatives had done

Steve Shirley: what's in a name?

When Stephanie Shirley (right) set up one of Britain's first computer services companies in 1962 with £6 capital and the dining-room table as her office, the business world was still so patronisingly male-dominated that she decided to sign her business correspondence Steve, "so as to get through the door before anyone realised my gender".

The ploy worked, and the FI Group, which started as a network of freelance computer programmers enabling women to work from home while bringing up children, is today an international software group in the FTSE-250 called Xansa, with a turnover of £454m.

Dame Stephanie, as she has become – though everyone still knows her as Steve – retired in 1993 with the title of honorary life president and is one of Britain's 100 wealthiest women and most generous philanthropists. Since 1996, her

Shirley Foundation has committed more than £50m to causes supporting autism – she had an autistic son, who died aged 35 in 1998 – and better use of IT in the voluntary sector.

Shirley, 70, arrived in Britain in 1939 as an unaccompanied six-year-old refugee from Nazi Germany. Her surname was then Buchthal, changed to Brook on naturalisation, and to Shirley when she married in 1959. By 1951, aged 18, she was working in the Post Office research department at Dollis Hill, north London, helping to develop the first electronic telephone exchanges. She also worked on the first prototype of ERNIE (Electronic Random Number Indicating Equipment), the mechanism used to pick winning Premium Bond numbers.

After three years at ICL, the computer company that was then hoped to become Britain's technology flagship, she set up her fledgling

business, motivated, as she says, "by a social crusade for women rather than money". She was also looking for a new way of working, and the FI Group

became a template for a participative, team-based organisation well ahead of its time.

Its success has enabled Shirley to realise her belief that wealth from business is for ploughing back into society. Her business hero is Andrew Carnegie, the Scottish-American steel tycoon who gave away much of his fortune to social causes, most famously to founding the public library system. "When you have made a lot of money, you need to give meaning to that," she says.

The amazing jump jet: the Hawker Harrier,
a British world-beater, c. 1970

earlier with the nuclear missiles Blue Streak and Blue Water (De Havilland and English Electric respectively). Wilson cancelled the supersonic attack aircraft TSR2, which was abandoned in 1967 in favour of the US-built F111 – only to see that, too, cancelled in later defence cuts. It has been said that if the TSR2 had gone ahead, it would still have been in service today, such was the quality of its concept and design. There still remained some stunning examples of leading-edge British design, none more so than the Hawker Harrier, the world's first VTOL (vertical take-off and landing) jet aircraft to enter military service.

First developed by Sir Sidney Camm in 1957, its prototype flew a few inches from the ground in 1960; by August 1966, six aircraft were being built and the first production aircraft made its maiden flight at the end of 1967, entering RAF service in July 1969. The Harrier proved its military worth in the Falklands War of 1982, when the aircraft carried laser-guided bombs, 50mm rocket pods and Sidewinder air-to-air missiles.

Then to crown the decade with a global aviation first, the Anglo-French Concorde, the world's first supersonic airliner, made its maiden flight; the French version from

Toulouse in March 1969 and the British prototype from Filton aerodrome, Bristol, a month later. It had been a long and troubled development saga that might have been stalled in 1964 except for a no-cancellation clause inserted by the French. In the end, only 13 of the beautiful white birds went into service with British Airways and Air France, the expected market having shrunk because of regulations in the US and elsewhere about flying supersonic overland. Concordes would never after all span the globe to Tokyo and Australia, and their amazing ability to race the time zones would only be exercised on scheduled routes across the Atlantic. But they remained in service for 27 years, an unparalleled tribute to Anglo-French engineering despite their ruinous cost. (The original development estimate of £70m swelled to £2bn, around £29bn in today's terms.)

They would certainly have gone well into their fourth decade but for the devastating crash outside Paris in July 2000 that grounded the Anglo-French fleet. By the time the Concordes took off again with kevlar-reinforced fuel tanks (the source of the explosion after a tyre ruptured on the runway), the shattering events of September 11, 2001 had blown a massive hole in the airline industry. The business chiefs who mostly used Concorde found other ways to bridge the Atlantic, including video-conferencing. Despite a bold bit of chutzpah by Sir Richard Branson, offering to buy BA's Concordes and keep them flying in Virgin livery, they were destined at the end of 2003 to sit in a museum, alongside the Bristol Britannia, the Comet and all the other past glories of British aviation.

ail-out
Britain

66 Britain faces the most precarious
crisis in its peacetime history with the
most precarious Government it has
had for nearly half a century. 99

The Economist, March 9, 1974

7

T he forward-looking optimism and faith in progress that ended the 1960s, with the Anglo-French commitment to Concorde and the US moon landings, was short-lived. By the spring of 1974, Britain was at the edge of an economic and industrial abyss unequalled even by the Great Depression, facing what the Economist called "the most precarious crisis in its peacetime history". Paralysed by the power struggle between striking coal miners and Edward Heath's Conservative government, the country had been on a three-day week since the New Year, and as for technological progress, many small businesses were struggling to carry on by candlelight. Inflation roared unchecked through the decade, touching an apocalyptic 26.8 per cent in August 1975. Earlier, the Economist had warned: "No country which has sustained a rate of inflation of over 20 per cent for long has been, or has remained, a democracy."[1]

What had brought the high hopes of 1969 crashing down? Heath's surprise victory over Wilson in 1970 resulted in an expansionist climate for business – too expansionist, as it happened. Anthony Barber's tax-cutting budget of 1972 helped to unleash an avalanche of imports and to stoke up inflation. After years of shilly-shallying about joining the European Economic Community, Britain had finally signed the Treaty of Rome in 1972, supposedly the key to the

Into Europe at last: Prime Minister Edward Heath signs the Accession Treaty, 1972

continent's future peace and prosperity. But the country was still, in the mordant phrase of the time, "the sick man of Europe", plagued by the twin British diseases of under-investment and industrial disputes. Invited to a private lunch at the Institute of Directors, then housed in adjoining townhouses in Belgrave Square, Prime Minister Heath berated a group of leading businessmen for failing to invest sufficiently – in spite, he said, of his government's incentives to do so.

Strikes flared one after another in key industries. "British cars are still the best in the world," declared Lord Stokes, chairman of British Leyland, the ill-fated successor to British Motor Corporation, adding bitterly: "People would buy them – if there were any in the showrooms." In 1973, production by the four major domestic car manufacturers was up by 10 per cent, but new registrations had increased by 27 per cent. The gap was filled chiefly by imports from Japan, which soared from 10 per cent in 1969 to 30 per cent in 1973. For every 1,000 car workers in Britain, 2,650 days were lost through strikes. Later in the decade, British Leyland's shop steward Derek (Red Robbo) Robinson would become the epitome of trade union militancy, his big face a familiar sight on TV screens, haranguing noisy mass meetings outside the Longbridge plant. Robinson continued to stir up action against the closure of loss-making plants until he was sacked in 1979

Public enemy No.1? Derek (Red Robbo) Robinson, militant strike leader at BL

Michael Edwardes, BL's South African chairman, challenged union power by sacking Robinson

by Michael Edwardes, the feisty South African businessman brought in as British Leyland's last hope of recovery. The volume car industry in Britain was in any case suffering through changes in global markets. International competition accelerated as tariffs came down and manufacturers rationalised their operations across regional and national boundaries, setting up plants for local assembly. Sixty per cent of so-called British cars were actually made by US companies with subsidiaries in the UK.

The state-owned transport sector was in even worse shape. Far from regaining health after Dr. Beeching's radical surgery in the mid-1960s, the railways seemed to be in terminal decline. After a long-unchallenged dominance in freight transport, rail in 1972 carried only one-tenth of the annual tonnage moved by road. Further cutbacks to the network led inexorably to further losses of traffic, so that any cost savings were immediately cancelled out. Capital write-offs by government only made things worse by rewarding failure. They temporarily turned bottom-line losses into profits, but the deficits soon came

back. In 1973, the BR chairman, Richard Marsh, was forced to admit publicly that BR could not pay its way, despite assuring a freight conference that public opinion would not allow the roads to become swamped with HGVs – "mechanical triffids", as he called them. Unfortunately, the customers weren't listening.[2]

Industrial money pits were opening up everywhere for the new Conservative government, which had stoutly declared its resistance to bailing out the losers. Shipbuilding, a dinosaur still clinging to life, delivered a humiliating kick to Whitehall in 1971 with the "work-in" at Upper Clyde Shipbuilders, a loss-making group that included the once-great John Brown yard, builder of the QE2. With public opinion largely behind the shipyard workers struggling to keep the yard open, the government was forced into the first of many U-turns on industrial subsidies (this was when the phrase U-turn was coined as a political term of abuse). A new company was formed to take over three of the yards, while John Brown was sold to a US oil rig business.

Two other particularly embarrassing lame ducks in 1971 were International Computers Ltd. (ICL), the national flagship formed only three years earlier, and the iconic Rolls-Royce, which collapsed from inability to finance aerospace contracts, including the government-backed RB211 engine. The Heath government was forced to nationalise the aero-engine part of the company as Rolls-Royce and to float the car division. In a desperate attempt to save ICL, it injected more than £14m, which soon escalated to £40m, to develop a new range of computers, but, like its continental counterparts, ICL could not hope to beat IBM in global markets. After many vicissitudes, it was sold to Fujitsu of Japan in 1990.

More bail-outs of bankrupt companies would come in the mid-1970s: British Leyland, which swallowed £900m over eight years and eventually became state-owned; BSA motorcycles (makers of the famous Norton and Triumph bikes), which struggled on for a while as a workers' co-operative; and Alfred Herbert, once the most respected machine-tool maker in Europe. Steel and textiles also consumed vast amounts of public money as the failures of earlier business strategies were painfully revealed.

Ironically, the nadir for the Heath government came in the one industry that had not had a major strike since 1926 – coal. After a previous run-in with the Communist-led National Union of Mineworkers in 1972, when the union had demonstrated a ruthless use of flying pickets and intimidation, Heath chose to take them on in late 1973. The NUM called an overtime ban to back up its demand for a £3 to £5 a week pay increase. The pay demand was extreme in relation to what it covered – the time that miners spent preparing for and leaving their work, including their pithead baths – and would bust the government's wage guidelines wide open. Heath and his ministers thought they had a strong case and were well prepared for a state of emergency.

What no-one foresaw was the thunderbolt that came that winter from the Middle East. Oil supplies had become

Computers in 1970 were the size of industrial fridge-freezers

more expensive and less stable as a result of the so-called Yom Kippur War the previous October. Then, at the end of 1973, the Gulf states in OPEC, the oil-producing cartel, suddenly doubled the price of a barrel of oil – making it four times more expensive than it had been in September. They also cut back production. Every developed economy dependent on imported oil now faced recession; the outlook had changed irrevocably. As Management Today put it in an editorial that January: "The Arab oil offensive... probably marks the end of an epoch. The Western world is unlikely ever to be the same again". That prediction proved true enough, though not the accompanying optimistic belief that the world would henceforth concentrate on substitutes for oil, rehabilitating coal mines and developing nuclear energy and electric cars.

For Britain, whose North Sea oil and gas discoveries were not yet on stream – BP's Forties field began exploration in 1970 but the oil did not flow until late in the decade – the coincidence of the two energy crises was lethal. Furthermore, it came on top of an enormous balance of payments deficit and inflation that was already around 12 per cent. Output for each British worker was less than half what it was in West Germany, the US or Sweden. Britain ranked 14th for productivity among industrialised nations. Its current account deficit amounted to four per cent of the whole GNP. Profligate borrowing abroad and manipulation of the currency – letting the pound sink just low enough but not too low – had created a disastrous scenario, "heavily mortgaging the future", as critics from the business world put it.

The champagne corks had barely ceased popping for the New Year of 1974 when Britain's economic position was being described as "the worst since the Great Depression".[3] The pumping of excess money into the economy, coupled with the government's attempt to restrain prices and

THE CHANGING CENTURY

A snapshot of Britain:

1970: The age of majority was now not 21 but 18. Legislation the previous year had lowered the voting age

1970: Crime was continuing to rise. Thirty-nine thousand people were in prison; 12,000 more than 12 years earlier

1971: Britain's currency went decimal on February 15 at 100 new pence to £1. Banks were closed for four days before D-Day to clear old £sd cheques. There were many complaints of retailers "rounding up" prices, but the changeover went more smoothly than expected – in two months rather than six

1972: Miss Rose Heilbron QC became the first female judge to sit at the Old Bailey

1973: Trevor MacDonald of ITN became Britain's first black newscaster

1973: The first graduates of the Open University received their degrees at a ceremony at Alexandra Palace

1973: The first 10 female members of the London Stock Exchange were elected. At the end of March, Mrs Susan Shaw became the first woman to set foot on the floor of the Stock Exchange

1976: Princess Margaret and Lord Snowdon announced that their marriage had broken down. Twenty-

one years earlier, the princess had made the decision not to marry divorced Group Captain Peter Townsend, saying she was "mindful of the church's teaching that Christian marriage is indissoluble"

1977: BBC Radio 1 banned the Sex Pistols' single, God Save the Queen. Released for the Queen's Silver Jubilee Year, the single was a two-fingered salute to the Establishment. It went to Number One, selling 150,000 copies in just one day

1979: Margaret Thatcher became the first woman in British history to enter Number 10. The archetypal "strong woman", she was resolute from the start. Before long, her Cabinet colleagues had nicknamed her Tina – "There is No Alternative"

Margaret Thatcher with husband Denis celebrating election victory in 1979

Sources: Sources: Christopher Lee: This Sceptred Isle, Twentieth Century, BBC and Penguin Books, 1999; Patrick Robertson: The New Shell Book of Firsts, 1994, Headline Book Publishing; The Office for National Statistics; Guardian Unlimited; BBCi

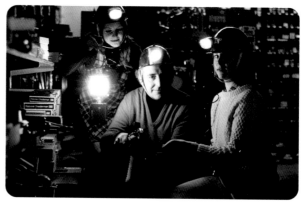

Half-time Britain: the three-day week hits industry. Clockwise: headlines tell the story; women at the Slumberdown factory wearing quilts to beat the cold; miners' lamps or gas lamps combat the power cuts. Bottom right: rubbish lies uncollected in a street

incomes, would have the effect of fuelling domestic demand and diverting supplies away from the export market. Dearer imports would then lead in a deadly spiral to workers seeking higher wages. "A more irresponsible and profligate mishandling of the nation's external finances than even Mr. Wilson achieved," was the verdict of Management Today; hardly the sort of endorsement a Tory government might have expected from the business press.

Nevertheless, the government was confident it could weather a coal strike through the winter. It dusted off emergency legislation drawn up a year earlier for the threatened coal strike and put industry on a three-day week to conserve power. At one grim point in early February, it even looked as though a two-day week might be necessary.[4] Sir Michael Clapham, president of the CBI, said things were "almost as serious as an outbreak of war". In the CBI's quarterly industrial review, a question about prospects in March if the dispute continued got the following response from several companies: "Not applicable; we shall no longer be in business".

Two-thirds of Britain's workforce was affected by the three-day week, but business coped with the brown-outs, power failures and shutdowns remarkably well. After the first month of short-time working, production had only dropped by 20-30 per cent. Shops somehow contrived to spread their allowance of electricity so as to be open every day,

even if for a short time, or in dim light. Then, six weeks into the struggle, Heath went for broke and called a general election on the issue, "Who governs Britain?" When the votes were counted at the end of February, the answer to the fateful question was: not Prime Minister Heath. And, as the Economist and other commentators had predicted, the miners were paid their Danegeld. The incoming government of Harold Wilson settled the strike at a cost of £103m, representing an increase in wages of 30 per cent.[5]

The 1970s were terrible years in which to manage a business. The whole decade was scarred by industrial disputes (culminating in the "dirty jobs" public sector strike of the 1978/79 "winter of discontent"), inflationary pay settlements, the constant fear of oil prices going out of control and desperate attempts by government to bandage the bleeding wounds of unemployment in one region of the UK after another. Manufacturing was falling behind lower-cost competition from the developing world, and the

THE CHANGING CENTURY

Facts from the business archives:

1970: The Ann Summers Sex Supermarket opened in London; the sex shop had arrived in Britain

1970: The world's first jumbo jet, the Boeing 747, went into service, flying Pan Am passengers between New York and London

1970: Canon Business Machines unveiled the world's first hand-held electronic calculator, the Pocketronic

1970: Philips developed the first car cassette player

1970: Record company Decca released the first Dolby cassette tapes; the Dolby system subsequently became a byword for high-quality sound

1971: The Dutch company DAF introduced the Variomatic, the first car with stepless automatic transmission

1971: Vickers built the world's first full-size tracked hovercraft, the RTV 31 High Speed Passenger train

1971: ICI developed Biopal, the first fully biodegradable and recyclable plastic

1972: Plessey Communication Systems of Surbiton brought out a

facsimile transmission machine, the Remotecopier KD111; it took another 10 years, though, for the technology and the word "fax" to come into general use in Britain

1973: The first commercial radio station in mainland Britain, news station London Broadcasting Company (LBC), came on air. The launch of the general entertainment station Capital Radio followed a week later

1973: Fisons introduced the Gro-Bag

1974: In France, Bic introduced the disposable lighter

1974: Philips launched the world's first domestic video cassette

recorder, billing it as "the start of a revolution in home entertainment". The VCR, the N1500, cost £388.62 and played half-inch tape with a maximum duration of one hour. The N1700, which had a playing time of up to two hours, came on the market three years later*

1975: Britain's first pop video had its debut on Top of the Pops. It was made on a budget of £4,500 to promote the Queen single Bohemian Rhapsody for EMI

1975: BP's Isle of Grain refinery in Kent took delivery of the first crude oil from the North Sea – 14,000 tons had been shipped from the Argyll Field

UK economy was becoming more dependent on services, but there was a reluctance – on both political and industrial fronts – to acknowledge this.

Central Scotland was dependent on coal, iron and steel and shipbuilding; South Wales on coal, iron and steel; south Lancashire on cotton, textiles, coal and shipbuilding. All were fast-declining, uneconomic industries and all were politically sensitive Labour heartlands. Short-term measures to buffer the impact of job losses and retrain workers continually hampered the public policy stance that such industries could not be supported indefinitely.

Regional planning, so much a feature of 1960s central government, had been exposed as an inexact science because private investment could not be forced into needy areas, only persuaded there by tactical financial carrots. By 1970, it was already obvious from the statistics – including the TUC's own research – that despite £1bn being pumped into regional development areas, unemployment in these

areas was up to five per cent higher than elsewhere. Nationally, Britain was spending so much more than it earned from exports that by 1976, chancellor Denis Healey had to go cap in hand to the International Monetary Fund (IMF) for a $3bn loan to be rescued from a desperate balance of payments crisis and two successive runs on the pound. The IMF only agreed in return for a package of strict budgetary curbs, which covered subsidies for loss-making industries.

One former icon of British manufacturing – the motorcycle firm of BSA – had already collapsed the preceding year. Badly managed until the late 1950s by the notorious Sir Bernard Docker and resting on an historic reputation for heavy, well-engineered machines like the Norton, it failed to exploit the new global demand for nippy, light bikes such as the Vespa that had emerged in the 1960s. It was clearly riding for a fall against the new power of the Japanese, who by 1975 had collared three-quarters of the world's motorcycle exports.

Concorde takes off on its first commercial flight, 1976

1976: Smith Kline and French started to manufacture Tagamet, the miracle cure for stomach ulcers. Launched worldwide the following year, it was to become the world's first billion-dollar-selling drug

1976: Loctite UK of Welwyn Garden City brought out Super Glue

1976: Concorde went into passenger service, flying between Heathrow and Bahrain and Paris and Rio de Janeiro

1976: Rowntree brought out the Yorkie bar

1977: Freddie Laker started the first low-cost airline, Skytrain. The bus-stop type service cost just £59 from Gatwick to New York; a regular flight on another airline would have set you back more than £180

1977: Britain got its first low-fat spread, St Ivel Gold. It contained half the fat of butter or margarine

– mainly because it was 51 per cent water

1978: The bar code made its British debut, appearing on the packaging for Melroses 100 Century Tea Bags

1978: Key Market in Spalding, Lincolnshire became the first UK retailer to use bar code scanning at point of sale. The system used IBM hardware

1979: In Japan, Sony launched the Walkman

1979: In Minnesota, 3M started to produce Post-It Notes

1979: The Rubik Cube, devised in 1974 by Professor Erno Rubik of

Budapest, was put into commercial production by Ideal Toy of New York

1979: British Rail inaugurated the Intercity 125 High-Speed Train. The first service was between London and Bristol

*The breakthrough for home video was the VHS format, launched in Britain in 1978. Nonetheless, the mass market was still some way off. A survey of December 1979 showed that although there were 230,000 VCRs in use in Britain, one in five Britons had not even heard of video. Of those who had, most did not know you could record off-air with the TV set switched off

Main sources: Patrick Robertson: The New Shell Book of Firsts, 1994, Headline Book Publishing; Christopher Lee: This Sceptred Isle, Twentieth Century, BBC and Penguin Books, 1999

141

Ian MacGregor, cost-cutting chairman of British Steel, was far less effective as coal board chairman in the 1980s

Another to fall to the aggressive challenge from the East was Alfred Herbert, the once innovative and globally respected machine tool maker, which went bankrupt in 1975, was taken into care by the National Enterprise Board – the Labour government's industrial casualty ward – but was finally liquidated and broken up in 1980.

The NEB was the successor to the Industrial Reorganisation Corporation, one of the monuments of the second Wilson government's dedication to planning in the 1960s. It was basically an instrument for quasi-nationalisation by another name, investing in companies that the banks could not or would not help in return for a controlling equity stake. British Leyland, Ferranti and ICL were others that came under its wing in the 1970s.

Public money poured out of an open tap into lame-duck industries. Steel was a prime example. It had been on a political see-saw since the late 1940s – nationalised in the dying days of the Attlee Labour government, denationalised under Churchill in the 1950s, re-nationalised by Wilson in the 1960s. In the wake of the IMF deal, British Steel plants were closed, reversing a

previous reprieve and sparking furious labour unrest. Chairman Sir Charles Villiers tried to soothe the unions by importing the German idea of a supervisory board with worker participation, but the well-meaning plan – never favoured by the Institute of Directors or most business leaders – did not work and was scrapped in the 1980s by the aggressive new Thatcherite chairman, Ian MacGregor.

The apocalyptic atmosphere of energy crises, soaring inflation and ungovernable labour relations made it seem as if the ground was giving way under old political and economic certainties, and to an extent this was true. The 1970s were the decade when the business world entered the era of discontinuous change. Managements everywhere had to learn to cope with this new and unsettling phenomenon, for which there were no guidelines or precedents. Since 1945, a comfortable consensus had ruled, held up by the pillars of full employment, incremental improvements in living standards, generally stable commodity prices (especially in oil) and a producer-driven business environment in which customers were content to buy what they were offered and competition was small-scale and easily handled. It was certainly not global, or driven by technology, but both these things were about to change.

Despite the fact that the world's first large operational computer had been built in Britain – the EDSAC at Cambridge University in 1949 – and despite Harold Wilson's famous 1963 pledge to harness "the white heat of the technological revolution" to British industry, computer use was still largely confined to big companies until the late 1970s. Only then did the widespread arrival of the microchip spawn a new awareness of the likely effects of technology on business efficiency, competitiveness and employment prospects. The last seemed bleak indeed – and this had an impact on the whole attitude of business and government. In 1979, the Social Policy Research Unit looked ahead 20 years and predicted a further four million job losses in the UK; a French government report put total unemployment at 13 per cent by the end of the century.

A doom-laden book called The Collapse of Work, by two trade union thinkers, Clive Jenkins of the Association of Scientific, Technical and Managerial Staffs and his director of research Barrie Sherman, confronted latter-day Luddites with this Faustian choice in 1979: "Remain as we are, reject the new technologies and we face unemployment of up to five and a half million by the end of the century. Embrace the new technologies, accept the challenge, and we end up with about five million." There were other predictions that if unemployment went above three million, there would be social revolution.

The jobless total was, in fact, to peak at around three and a half million in the mid-1980s, but where Sherman and other pessimistic pundits of the time went wrong was in their underlying assumptions that no new industries – and therefore no new jobs – would be created by technology. No-one, it seemed, foresaw the rise of the information economy and "knowledge workers" in business services – no-one, that is, except the American polymath and godfather of the guru industry, Peter Drucker, whose book The Age of Discontinuity, published in 1969, accurately predicted the post-industrial age and coined the very term knowledge workers.

MFI: furniture that walked out of the store

Innovation was the key to one of the biggest retailing success stories of the 1970s – the flat-packed furniture company, MFI. The DIY culture, which originated in the early 1950s, had really taken hold by this time, and two mail-order entrepreneurs, Noel Lister and Jack Seabright, saw the idea of selling furniture direct from stock, with customers collecting and assembling their purchases, as a way to rescue their collapsing company. In less than five years, MFI was one of the UK's fastest growing retailers. It helped make Britain a ready market for the Swedish furniture "warehouse" IKEA, which, ironically, was to prove one of its fiercest competitors.

The concept was simple: to apply mass-marketing techniques to what was then a bulky, staid and unprofitable business, with upholstered wooden frames occupying massive inventory space. MFI prices were kept low, often undercutting the traditional products by a third. The range was restricted, but volumes were high. The

furniture was mostly made in (still-Communist) Eastern Europe or Asia Pacific, with some from British suppliers who were kept on a tight rein, supermarket-style, to provide consistent quality and long production runs.

The result brought new furniture within reach of low and middle-income buyers. Turnover leapt from £15.2m in 1975 to £87.5m in 1979. By the end of the decade, pre-tax profits had rocketed from a mere £78,000 to £18m. Lister and his merchandising director Sid Cody travelled the world in search of new ideas – from Levitts in the US to Conforama in France and, of course, IKEA in Sweden. Lister acknowledged that his kind of business did best in hard times and once the more prosperous 1980s and 1990s arrived, along with IKEA and its more contemporary image, he was not surprised to see its fortunes diminish.

Flat-pack living: a kitchen fitted out with MFI products in 1979. The firm is now upgrading its image to chase market leader Magnet

Early in the new century, however, MFI appeared to be re-positioning itself for a move upmarket, particularly on its kitchens side, where its products had been thoroughly overshadowed by market leader Magnet. The company appointed an unlikely non-executive director in the shape of Peter Wallis, a management consultant who, in his public persona of Peter York, co-inventor of the Sloane Rangers, is known as a leading style guru and expert on rebranding.

Among the few British business readers who latched on to Drucker's revolutionary message was the then principal of Ashridge Management College, Philip Sadler, whose thinking was entirely changed by The Age of Discontinuity. For Sadler, the book pointed clearly to the coming decline of Britain's manufacturing industry, an idea then considered sacrilege.[6]

Even in the US, companies were slow to take up the new technology. It was still seen as an optional choice when Silicon Valley was getting under way in the late 1970s. A manufacturer of railway points in Cleveland, Ohio crystallised one pervading attitude: knowing that its control equipment was out of date, the management feared bringing in consultants from Silicon Valley because, as a micro-computer manager in Menlo Park put it, "they would feel threatened by young whiz-kids with long hair, wanting to play tennis in the afternoons and ride bicycles".[7]

Negretti and Zambra, the UK scientific instruments company, encountered resistance from its auditors when it switched to microelectronics in the late 1970s. The accountants were worried about the need to redefine overheads (sales support and service for a computer-based system, for example, could become a profit centre rather than a cost) and to change depreciation policy to take account of shorter life-cycles. It took six years of financial review, from 1974 to 1980, according to one Negretti and Zambra executive, for the main board to appreciate the need for ongoing investment in technology. Another problem was that traditional instruments requiring highly skilled makers were still in demand, while at the same time the company needed to recruit and train assembly workers and build a knowledgeable sales force for its new MPC80, a computerised control system for process plant. The result was a fragmented use of skills and resources. To be fair, however, managements were being faced with making a quantum leap greater even than the internet would mean in the 1990s.[8]

Change management was a concept not yet dominating the business book market – that market itself

---

THE CHANGING CENTURY

A snapshot of science and technology:

1970: The Russian space probe Venera 7 landed on Venus

1970: Telephone direct dialling was introduced between London and New York

1971: The first digital watch was introduced

1971: New medical technology, the CAT scanner, developed by Godfrey Hounsfield of EMI, was used to diagnose a brain tumour in a patient at the Atkinson Morley's Hospital, London

Personal computers arrive on office desktops, 1975

1974: The term personal computer was invented by Ed Roberts of Albuquerque, New Mexico, creator of the first microcomputer designed for home use, the MITS Altair 8800. The microcomputer, named after a planet in Star Trek, was not for the uninitiated: there was no keyboard and 25 toggle switches had to be pressed in the right sequence to start the machine

1975: The BBC made its first Ceefax teletext transmissions

1976: The US space probe Viking 1 landed on Mars

1978: The world's first test tube baby, Louise Brown, was born in Oldham, Lancashire. She owed her life to the work done by in-vitro fertilisation pioneers, the British medical scientists, Dr Robert Edwards and Dr Patrick Steptoe. By 2003, one million children worldwide had been born using their IVF technique

1979: The UK Post Office launched Prestel, a teletext system delivered via telephone lines and accessed via TV screens. The technology, developed by Post Office engineer Sam Fedida was, in effect, a forerunner of online information services. High costs meant take-up rates were low, and Prestel had to be withdrawn in 1994 by the inventor's son, BT executive Clive Fedida

See also: Business facts box

Main source: Patrick Robertson: The New Shell Book of Firsts, 1994, Headline Book Publishing

would not become a sales phenomenon until the publication of Peters' and Waterman's In Search of Excellence in 1982. But already in the mid-1970s, Michael Porter at Harvard Business School was working on his theory of competitive strategy and in the UK Charles Handy, having analysed business structures and cultures in Understanding Organisations, was carrying out research for his coming bestseller, The Future of Work, which forecast the rise of "portfolio" working as the old-style lifetime career ebbed away.

Something else in the early 1970s was undermining management confidence in itself – the revelation, or partial revelation, of wrongdoing and unethical behaviour in large corporations. Edward Heath, whose premiership foundered on the iceberg of organised labour, also ran up against what he famously called "the unacceptable face of capitalism" – a corporate boardroom crisis that foreshadowed those of Guinness and Enron and led to the first stirrings of a genuine corporate governance movement.

Lonrho was a pan-African trading company that had been built up by the buccaneering Roland "Tiny" Rowland from profits of £500,000 in 1962 to £29m in 1973. Its expansion had been fuelled by acquisitions and soaring commodity prices, but Lonrho's non-executive directors were unhappy at Rowland's methods, which were railroaded through the board; in several cases, it turned out, on the back of grossly misleading figures. Half the equity in one copper mine, in which £3m of group funds had been invested, was revealed as belonging to Rowland and two

Unacceptable faces of capitalism: Robert Maxwell, left, who plundered his company's pension fund, and Tiny Rowland, who ran Lonrho like a personal fiefdom

other directors via offshore companies. Other corporate scams included the purchase of lavish accommodation for the chairman. Eight of the directors, led by Sir Basil Smallpeice, launched a boardroom revolt to remove the chairman, but Rowland boldly made it a voting issue for shareholders (the main shareholder being himself) and won. Shareholders were too dazzled by his delivery of year-on-year dividend growth to worry about how the results were being achieved.

The Lonrho revelations followed hard on the heels of Robert Maxwell's first run-in with City regulators. The Czech-born Maxwell was a genuine war hero who had won the Military Cross fighting with the British army but who had developed into an habitual manipulator of balance sheets – not for nothing was he known as "the bouncing

Czech". Maxwell had built an impressive business in Pergamon Press, a technical and reference publisher, but when he tried to sell it for a vastly over-valued £25m to a US computer services company, Leasco Data Processing, Leasco insisted on a rigorous examination of the books. After three DTI inquiries, its profits were found to have been vastly overstated; Maxwell was publicly deemed unfit to be a director.

In time, however, he bounced back and in the 1980s succeeded in his ambition to be a newspaper owner, taking over the Mirror Group after losing first The Sun and then The Times and Sunday Times to the Australian Rupert Murdoch. Had the cards fallen otherwise, it might have been employees of Times Newspapers who had their pension fund plundered to meet business shortfalls. His mysterious death, falling from his yacht in 1991, unravelled a shocking saga of fraud that left many retired Mirror employees in penury.

Lonrho and Pergamon were early examples of the impotence of non-executives against a determined chairman or CEO, and vividly demonstrated how ineffective boards sometimes were in safeguarding shareholders' interests,

Real-life Monopoly: seven investment experts play the board game for BBC TV's Money Programme, 1970: l. to r. Jim Slater, Oliver Jessel,

THE CHANGING CENTURY

Politics in Britain:

1970: Strikes forced the new prime minister, Edward Heath, to declare a state of emergency

1971: Reds-under-the-bed fears were stoked and, it seemed, confirmed by intelligence reports that 300 out of the 550 Soviet officials in London were spies. The Foreign Office, led by Sir Alec Douglas-Home, expelled 105 of them

1971: Unemployment was more than 800,000, the highest figure for more than 30 years

1972: The lights went out: 12 power stations were shut down in another state of emergency; official black-outs were imposed; school children were sent home; hospital services were disrupted. Less than two years later, the three-day working week was announced to conserve energy supplies (see main text)

January 30, 1972: British paratroopers opened fire on demonstrators in the Bogside district of Londonderry, killing 13 people in what became known as Bloody Sunday. The British army tried to plead self-defence but convinced few people. The Provisional IRA (the violent wing of the IRA, formed in 1971) immediately announced that its policy was "to kill as many British soldiers as possible". The following March, Heath removed security powers from the Ulster government

and made William Whitelaw Secretary of State for Northern Ireland

1972: Twenty-seven thousand British passport holders in the former colony of Uganda were given refuge in Britain. They were the Asians savagely expelled by dictator Idi Amin. Their arrival brought protests from Enoch Powell, the Monday Club and the National Front. Cabinet papers released in 2003 show that the government, fearing a further influx of British Asians, was

Victor Watson, Tesco chief Sir Jack Cohen, David Malbert, actor
Robert Morley and property entrepreneur Nigel Broackes

as well as how passive shareholders themselves tended to
be when the money was rolling in. The Lonrho affair in
particular threw a lurid light on how companies handled
other people's money, and there were strong calls in the
business press for company law to lay down the duties of
independent directors and what proportion of a board they
should comprise. But it would take another 20 years
before the Cadbury Committee, led by Sir Adrian Cadbury
of the confectionery and soft-drinks company Cadbury
Schweppes, became the first of several "great-and-good"
bodies to set out guidelines for a voluntary code of
practice. Directors, and the City in general, had preferred
to think cases such as Lonrho, Guinness, Blue Arrow and
the rest were just a few bad apples and that self-regulation
in corporate governance should be enough.

The 1970s, both at the time and in retrospect, were
years of almost unmitigated gloom and struggle for British
business, though a few industries seemed to glow star-like
out of the darkness. Since the early 1960s, when the Beatles
had burst on to the world scene from the unprepossessing
surroundings of the Cavern Club in Liverpool, British talent
in popular music had created an enormous money-spinner

scouring the Commonwealth for a
suitable resettlement island*

1974: In Northern Ireland, the
"troubles" claimed their 1,000th
victim, a Catholic man. By now, the
IRA bombing campaign had moved
to England. This was the year of
the Guildford and Birmingham pub
bombings and of attempts to kill
Edward Heath and the Labour
sports minister, Denis Howell

1974: The Ulster parliament,
Stormont, was finally shut down;

Northern Ireland was now to be
ruled from London

1975: Inflation hit a post-war high,
reaching 26.8 per cent in August

1975: Britain held its first referendum.
The people were asked whether
they wanted to stay in Europe or
get out. (See Britain in Europe box)

1976: The jobless total topped
1.5 million

1978: All Metropolitan Police leave

was cancelled over Christmas as the
government mounted Operation
Santa to try to anticipate IRA attacks
on London shoppers

1979: In the spring, Airey Neave MP,
who believed Sinn Fein should be
banned, was killed by a terrorist
bomb planted in his car; in the
summer, Earl Mountbatten of Burma
and his 14-year-old grandson were
killed when an IRA bomb blew up
in their boat. The new prime
minister, Margaret Thatcher,

formulated plans for a ban on TV
and radio broadcasts of the views
of terrorists and their sympathisers

*Several Ugandan Asians now hold
senior positions in public life. They
include Shailesh Vara, vice-chairman of
the Conservative Party, and Tarique
Ghaffur, deputy assistant commissioner
of the Metropolitan Police. In business,
industrialist Manubhai Madhvani
appears regularly in the rich lists. His
global empire, with interests in sugar,
brewing and tourism, is worth £160m

Rolling Stones gather moss: the British rock industry led by the Beatles and Mick Jagger of the Stones (r), was generating a substantial slice of the economy by the mid-1970s

for the country and for individual musicians such as Paul McCartney of the Beatles and Mick Jagger of the Rolling Stones. Britain was suddenly seen as the world's major source of new pop talent, both in composers and performers, and a massive new industry grew up to promote it. In the late 1960s, foreign record companies moved into Britain, and, by the early 1970s, small, independent home-grown labels started to appear such as Island Records, which established the Western market for Jamaican reggae. For much of the 1970s, the pop music industry seemed immune to the pressures elsewhere in the economy. Retail sales of records and tapes doubled in two years, from £103m in 1972 to £207m in 1974 and moved up to £277m in 1977. In 1978, a particularly high-spending year, the figure jumped by a third to £354m.

But the growth in turnover was more in inflationary cash terms than in units sold, as the chairman of CBS in Britain observed in 1980. Sales of LP records were actually declining, while the fees paid to artists rocketed. In 1979, the records and tapes side of Lord Grade's Associated Communications Corporation, which owned the Pye label,

showed a pre-tax loss of £43,000 compared with a profit of £1m the previous year. At Decca, sales of records and tapes slumped that year by £9m, pushing the company into an overall net loss of £5.2m. At EMI, profits in the music division dived from £16.8m to £1.8m. The industry would recover with the coming of CDs in the 1980s, but for the time being the shine was definitely off one of Britain's greatest post-war business successes.

Pop records laid the foundation of the youthful Richard Branson's business empire in the 1970s, when he began selling LPs by mail order from a phone box in Brighton. In the same decade and in the adjoining town of Hove, Anita Roddick and her husband Gordon set up behind an uninviting shopfront in George Street selling beauty creams and potions made from natural products. The Laura Ashley fashion business, started as a cottage industry in Wales in the 1960s, took off in the 1970s and its nostalgic country prints, using natural materials, were an international trademark by 1975, when the company had 40 shops worldwide. Virgin Records and The Body Shop would become two of the most charismatic British

Lord Forte, the catering king, ran grand hotels and motorway services on the same cash metrics as his first milk bar

Arnold Weinstock: cash-builder extraordinary

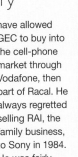

"The object is to be efficient, not big. Growth comes through efficiency." It was through following such simple maxims that Arnold Weinstock (right) became the most successful post-war manager in Britain. Had his arrogant successors heeded this precept, the tragic destruction of Marconi, Weinstock's carefully stewarded legacy at GEC, would never have happened.

The orphaned son of Polish Jewish immigrants who endured a lonely childhood as an evacuee in World War II, Weinstock learned the hard way how to rely on his own resources. This may have shaped the way he ran GEC; hands-on and tight-fistedly, with a strict emphasis on accountability and rigorous monthly reporting to the managing director. "Every manager now knew that if he failed to meet his budget, he would be in trouble, and possibly out on his ear," wrote Weinstock's biographers, Alex Brummer and Roger Cowe, of the period when he took over the flagging electrical giant in 1961.

But success in business also requires luck at the right moments. Weinstock's was marrying the boss's daughter when he was 24, although at that time he was not yet working for Michael Sobell, who became Britain's radio and TV king after his company won a contract to assemble sets for EMI. When Sobell floated his business in 1954 as Radio and Allied Industries (RAI), both

he and his son-in-law became instant paper millionaires. Seven years later, Weinstock's managerial skills were so legendary that GEC took over RAI primarily to acquire him.

Weinstock believed in simplicity above all. He sent one of his managers to benchmark practices at Texas Instruments and General Electric in the US, and adopted seven key performance metrics from them – return on capital, return on sales, sales as a multiple of capital employed, fixed assets and stocks, sales and profits per employees. It was straightforward enough to be understood by the engineers who largely ran GEC's business units. By the time Weinstock retired in 1996, GEC had absorbed such famous names as AEI, English Electric and Plessey, and was a £10bn multi-business company spanning the globe. It was also sitting on a "cash mountain" of £1.4bn which Weinstock had resolutely refused to spend despite the pressures from City analysts to put it to work.

"He believes profoundly in the stewardship of time and money," the Observer had noted admiringly at the time of the AEI takeover, describing Weinstock as "one of the first British exemplars of the managerial revolution".

He was not infallible, though. He failed to launch a takeover bid for Racal that would

have allowed GEC to buy into the cell-phone market through Vodafone, then part of Racal. He always regretted selling RAI, the family business, to Sony in 1984. He was fairly criticised for failing to invest adequately in R&D. And he also failed to plan adequately for the succession at GEC, which fell apart after his son Simon died of cancer in his 40s. Ironically, the one successor he did approve personally was George Simpson, who was to wreck everything Weinstock had built up by selling off GEC's core defence businesses, buying overpriced telecoms businesses and declaring his intention to spend the cash mountain "as fast as I can".

Weinstock used to say that if he had stayed in the property business of his youth, before he met Netta Sobell, he would have ended up "very, very rich" instead of just "very rich." His last days in 2002 were darkened by seeing hundreds of millions of his personal fortune evaporate as the Marconi share price plummeted from £12.50 to just over four pence.

---

businesses of the next decade, and their founders would join the otherwise thin ranks of British business heroes.

In the 1970s, these heroes included Sir Charles (later Lord) Forte, who had built an international catering empire on the basis of a single London milk bar, and Sir Arnold (later Lord) Weinstock, the architect of GEC. (See panel.) Forte and Weinstock shared a hard-working immigrant background – Forte from Italy and Weinstock from Poland

– as well as a taste for simple, powerful management tenets such as tight financial controls and rigorous budget targets for managers.

"Percentages and ratios are the basics of the business," Forte would say. Each unit of his empire, which had doubled in size in 1970 with the Trust Houses merger and came to include some of the grandest hotels in Europe, continued to be run on the principle, established in his

1935 milk bar, of being measured against one another in percentage and ratio terms of likely income, gross profits, overheads and minimum sales needed. Forte remains one of a small, elite band of entrepreneurs in Britain who successfully made the transition in one generation from founding a family business to managing a huge international group. The loss of control and subsequent breakup of the business after a hostile takeover by the Granada leisure group in the 1990s was a bitter defeat for Lord Forte and his son Rocco. The latter, now Sir Rocco Forte, has since created his own small, upmarket hotel group under the RF logo, but the loss of the family empire still rankles.

On the whole, the 1970s were a sterile time for entrepreneurship and innovation. There was little incentive in the provision of venture capital, or in the general business climate, for risk-taking or even new ideas. One unlikely entrepreneur who became a household name, identifying his broad Norfolk accent with his product – "bootiful" turkey – was Bernard Matthews. In 1950, his company had consisted of himself, his wife, 20 turkey eggs and an incubator. By persuading people that turkey was not just for Christmas he led the business to a turnover of £5.3m by 1974. Matthews hired a marketing genius named Bill Marlow from Unilever,

who took the company into a diversity of turkey-based products such as roasts, fillets and escalopes. "It's the same product," said Marlow at the time of his appointment. "But it's marvellous the different things you can do with it."[9]

Eventually, the organically-minded 1990s would downgrade the appeal of processed turkey. But almost single-handedly, Matthews created a new market for what had been a once-a-year industry and pioneered a "big but small" culture in his Norfolk farm-factory that would later form much of the appeal of the Branson and Roddick empires. He also realised, years before the 1980s enterprise culture, how to unlock wealth in any industry. His marketing man Marlow summed it up: "The company's success has been entirely based on innovating and then going on to something else before the innovation is dead."

Innovation was becoming more identified with services than with manufacturing as the decade ended, and so was growth. In Management Today's Profitability Growth League of 1979, six out of 10 top companies were engaged in some form of distribution, from food to antiques. This league table, based on share price and dividend growth rather than sales, could still spring a few surprises: the old-style manufacturing conglomerate BTR, for instance, was only five

THE CHANGING CENTURY

Britain in Europe: key developments

June 1971: After tough negotiations, which began the previous year, Britain won an agreement that would allow it to join the Common Market on equal terms with France, Germany and Italy

October 28, 1971: The House of Commons voted by 356 to 244 to approve the government's decision

to negotiate entry. Then, as now, the issue divided political parties: thirty-nine Conservative MPs voted against Heath; 69 Labour MPs voted with him

January 22, 1972: Heath signed the Accession Treaty

January 1, 1973: Britain, together with Ireland and Denmark, joined the EEC

February 1974: In his general election campaign, Harold Wilson

(below) promised to get better terms for Britain and to give the people the right to decide whether to stay in Europe or get out.

March 1975: At a meeting with the other nine members of the community in Dublin, new terms were at last agreed. They included the principle that Britain should pay a "fairer", i.e. lower, contribution to the Common Market budget and new arrangements for the import of Commonwealth sugar and New

Christmas all year round: Bernard Matthews and a model of one of the "bootiful" turkeys from his Norfolk farm factory

places behind Racal, the electronics wonder, and although so-called "casino growth" companies such as Ladbroke (No. 2 in the table after Dixons Photographic) rode high, the aerospace and engineering company Hawker Siddeley also turned in a textbook example of good management – seeking profitable growth rather than expansion for its own sake, building up cash flow and returning exceptional yields.

Property began its meteoric asset rise under the Heath government, as the "Barber boom", which made credit more easily available, doubled real-estate values in a year. As early as 1973, Trafalgar House, a property development and investment company led by Nigel Broackes, showed a 2,125 per cent return on its shareholders' capital over a 10-year period, beating any of the industrial giants.[10] Other stars of shareholder value included the investment company Slater Walker, which subsequently became derided as a mere asset stripper. In that year, the business journalist Robert Heller wrote: "Great money power has come into the hands of men who sought the money rather than the power. But it is how they use the latter, and in whose interests, which will determine how they are judged." Many 1970s money makers would have their reputations drastically reassessed on those criteria.

Zealand dairy products. The so-called "new deal" also sought to remove what the government, in its referendum pamphlet, described as a "threat to employment in Britain from the movement in the Common Market towards an Economic and Monetary Union".

April 1975: The Dublin agreement went before the Commons to be ratified. Again, there were no signs of consensus: Wilson had to rely on Conservative support as 145

Labour MPs voted against him. Seven members of the Cabinet, including Peter Shore, Tony Benn, Michael Foot and Barbara Castle, were opposed to continued membership.

June 6, 1975: Wilson won. Sixty-seven per cent of voters said they wanted Britain to remain a member. The "yes" camp had been backed not only by the media (no national newspaper had campaigned against Europe) but also by big

business; the Confederation of British Industry (CBI) had said that around 98 per cent of its members were in favour of the Common Market.

June 1979: The new prime minister, Margaret Thatcher, went to a summit in Strasbourg to argue for a major cut in Britain's contribution. The Common Agriculture Policy (CAP) was then eating up 70 per cent of the EEC budget, providing subsidies for which Britain's relatively efficient

farmers had little need. Thatcher scored a victory the following May when it was agreed that Britain's £1bn-a-year payment should gradually be reduced to £250m but the battle was not yet over. Thatcher would be back for more; it was the start of a period of increasing tension between Britain and her European partners.

Main source: Christopher Lee: This Sceptred Isle, Twentieth Century, BBC and Penguin Books, 1999

In the meantime, bail-out Britain was due for a dose of radical rehabilitation to dry out its dependence on the limitless stimulants offered by central government. In the process, it would suffer a dreadful manufacturing recession, losing much capacity permanently. Services would take over most of the economy. Institutions from Clydeside shipyards to City banks would be turned upside down. But the virtues of hard-grafting enterprise would be fashionable again after decades of corporatism, and union muscle power would be reined in.

After a winter of discontent when reeking black rubbish bags were piled high in the heart of London's entertainment district and Merseyside gravediggers refused to bury the dead, whatever the untried Conservative leader Margaret Thatcher had to offer looked better than the status quo – and not only to the business community.

Anthony Barber, the Tory chancellor who unleashed the property boom in 1974 through easier credit. Values doubled in a year

Garbage fills Leicester Square, London's entertainment hub, during the winter of public-sector strikes that helped propel Margaret Thatcher into power

the enterprise years

66 Our objective is clear: it is to return to steady economic growth, earned by people's own efforts in a free and responsible society. 99

**Prime Minister Margaret Thatcher,
House of Commons speech, February 28, 1980**

8

"Loadsamoney!" Harry Enfield's gross character sets the tone of some boorish young City dealers who got rich fast

argaret Thatcher's government came to power in May 1979, after a winter of unprecedented industrial conflict. Driven by the twin ambitions of disciplining the nation's housekeeping and creating a land fit for entrepreneurs, it was, in one decade, to change British business more profoundly than any single event apart from a world war had done before.

At the start of the 1980s, Britain was mired in industrial disputes and in hock to the IMF; a flock of lame ducks – in both the state and private sectors – was being sustained by treasury corn. By the end of the decade, major state industries such as British Airways, British Telecom and British Steel had been privatised; an injection of Japanese working practices and inward investment had introduced total quality management and no-strike deals; the proportion of women in the workforce had risen from a third to a half; inflation had been tamed along with the unions; the City had been shaken to the core by Big Bang; high technology was revolutionising the way we worked; and business heroes were the fashion, from the exuberant Sir John Harvey-Jones of ICI to the impish, bearded Richard Branson of the ever-expanding Virgin Group. At the same time, corporate scandal – though, as we have seen, hardly unknown in previous decades – was setting in train a governance revolution that would change Stock Exchange rules and British boardrooms in the 1990s.

The dark side of the decade was the emergence of a near-grotesque sub-culture among the newly affluent, personified by yobbish young City traders who swigged champagne out of bottles as they boarded their commuter trains – those who weren't driving Porsches or Ferraris. The phenomenon was mocked by the comedian Harry Enfield in a loutish TV character who boasted "loadsamoney!" as he waved his wad of banknotes. Some, including the then Archbishop of Canterbury, Robert Runcie, seemed implicitly to blame Thatcherism for creating an uncaring "Pharisee"

society at odds with the old British virtues of public service and community spirit. But if some of that ethos had vanished since the 1950s, it may have been, as the economist Ralf Dahrendorf acknowledged in a Director interview in 1989, a necessary price to pay for shaking the daylights out of sluggish and complacent British business practices.

The sea-change in industry was hastened by the first great impact of the new government's determination to throttle back the money supply. This was the deep recession of 1980/81 that cut into the bone of manufacturing and made lasting changes to patterns of employment. Thatcher's government was the first in living memory not prepared to trade off inflation for a policy of full employment, and the brunt was taken by manufacturing, which had already suffered the worst of the industrial

The nation's housekeeper arrives at No.10: Margaret and Denis Thatcher signal a new era of self-reliance

relations and investment problems of the 1970s. Nearly all the 1.5 million jobs lost between 1979 and 1981 were in manufacturing, most of them in the core engineering-related industries. Days lost through strikes were still running at horrendous levels; 11 million in 1980 and twice that in 1984, thanks to the bitter miners' dispute. Both of these figures, however, paled in comparison with the shocking total of 30 million in 1979, the year that had begun with the infamous "winter of discontent" in the public sector.

Chancellor Geoffrey Howe: his 1981 budget aimed to cut consumption and encourage enterprise by redirecting taxation

Though only a few were prescient enough to see it at the time, Britain and the US were entering the post-industrial age, a traumatic and painful rebirthing. By the end of the decade, services accounted for about two-thirds of the nation's GDP, manufacturing for less than a quarter. The latter's slide continued and today its share is under one-fifth. (Such figures, moreover, do not tell the whole story: many manufacturing companies now outsource non-core activities to companies that are classified as service suppliers.)

The first Thatcher administration set about its task of tightening the screw on inflation by closing the public purse. Chancellor Geoffrey Howe's radical budget in 1981 simultaneously signalled a green light for entrepreneurs and a red light for state subsidies by lowering personal taxes (the top rate of income tax came down from 83 per cent to 60 per cent) and taking a massive £3.5bn out of the public sector borrowing requirement. Bank rate rose to a swingeing 17 per cent. The thrust of taxation moved instead towards consumption, and VAT was virtually doubled to 15 per cent from eight per cent. Exchange controls were lifted, allowing investment to flow abroad as in the palmy days of Edward VII, though possibly to the detriment, as then, of home industry.

There was a "mad rush to buy a lot of things", as one investment banker commented, especially companies in the US. The 1980s began with about 200 UK companies a year making transatlantic acquisitions. The charge was led by Barclays, which purchased banking interests on both the east and west coasts, by the pharmaceutical group Beechams and by tobacco-based Imperial Group, which bought the Howard Johnson chain of motels. Before the decade was out, the City's Big Bang revolution had modernised stock market trading practices and opened the door to foreign investment houses, virtually returning the market, as City historian David Kynaston put it, "to the seamless capital flows that had characterised the pre-1914 world".

Many more big-name companies got into the US market in the late 1980s, including GrandMet, which bought the Pillsbury baking business and Burger King, and Marks and Spencer, whose 1988 purchase (for nearly twice its true value) of the venerable east coast men's outfitters, Brooks Brothers, proved a liability. It was not always the case, as British boards discovered, that a common language meant interchangeable business skills, though some companies managed it better than others. Hanson, the industrial conglomerate run by the formidable pairing of Lords Hanson and White, was one notable success, and it advertised its transatlantic achievements on

Ian Martin, chief executive officer of Grand Metropolitan food sector, meets the Pillsbury Doughboy after GrandMet buys the US bakery business; one of several ambitious purchases by UK firms as exchange controls were lifted

Over here, over there: Lords Hanson and White, partners in the industrial conglomerate that advertised its transatlantic success

television with a motif of the Union flag and Stars and Stripes tied in a bow.

The manufacturing heartlands of the midlands and the north of England took a hit in the recession of the early 1980s from which they never really recovered, despite valiant efforts over the ensuing years to increase productivity. Much of these efforts centred on the adoption of Japanese techniques, such as total quality management, lean production and no-strike deals, brought in by the Japanese companies setting up in Britain.

Japanese inward investment had started in 1970 with YKK Fasteners, the world's largest zip-fastener manufacturer, setting up a factory in Runcorn, Cheshire, and before long Wales was the favoured location, attracting a third of the incomers, with major electronics firms such as Sony (Bridgend, 1974), Matsushita (Cardiff, 1976) and Hitachi (Hirwaun,

Working the Japanese way at Nissan

1979) in the vanguard. Later, the area known as Silicon Glen in Scotland drew NEC semiconductors; Maxell set up in Telford; Worcester pulled in Yamazaki, the machine-tool giant, and Washington in County Durham bagged the biggest prize, car manufacturer Nissan.

The first no-strike agreement, between the electricians' union and Toshiba Consumer Products (UK), based in Plymouth, Devon, was signed in April 1981. Similar deals followed with Sanyo at Lowestoft, the Norwegian company NEK Cables in Tyne and Wear, and Hitachi in South Wales. Part of the reason for union co-operation was that both sides were starting from a blank sheet; production facilities would be modernised as a quid pro quo, and many of the plants affected were in depressed, job-hungry areas. The no-strike record was not quite so promising in UK-owned companies, though quality circles began to be widely adopted: Rank Xerox claimed that it took out about 80 per cent of defects from the products of its Micheldever plant in Hampshire between 1979 and 1984, while reducing its costs of quality control from six to one per cent and increasing the number of units produced by 400 per cent.[1]

Later in the decade, TQM would also revolutionise the UK car industry, notably at Rover in its joint venture with Honda, where a new working structure won union agreement to removing all restrictions on overtime and accepting frontline employee responsibility. The structure was based on cells, each with two teams of 40-50 workers reporting to a team leader, and single status collective bargaining was adopted. A similar team-based system was introduced at Rolls-

Royce Motors in Crewe, along with new manufacturing technology that cut assembly time by three-quarters and enabled the company for the first time to build the bodywork of its cars, instead of having it done by a subsidiary of Rover's. A continuous improvement programme called "Strive for Perfection" ran alongside lunchtime forums where staff were able freely to question and exchange ideas with senior managers. Strategic leadership at plant level was also thrown open to team leaders, which proved a significant incentive.[2]

All these innovations administered much-needed therapy to the ailing UK manufacturing sector but, as events turned out, by the time many companies were ready to move into the recovery ward, globalisation was in full

THE CHANGING CENTURY

A snapshot of Britain:

1980: James Callaghan resigned as Labour leader. He was succeeded by the left-wing veteran Michael Foot. Foot's election, at a time when a Trotskyite movement, the Militant Tendency, was allegedly plotting to win control of Labour, exasperated those who believed the party's future was the centre ground (see 1981, below)

1980: Steel workers went on strike over plant closures and job losses. Unemployment, 1.59 million at the start of the year, hit two million by the autumn. Nonetheless, at the Conservative party conference in October, the prime minister defiantly declared "she was not for turning"

1980: The SAS stormed the Iranian embassy in Kensington, killing four of the five terrorists who had held 19 people hostage for six days. Coming in the wake of a bungled attempt by President Carter to rescue 53 hostages from the American embassy in Tehran, the operation (rightly or wrongly) gave the impression that Britain, just like the Conservatives were saying, really could be great again

1981: The so-called Gang of Four, Shirley Williams, David Owen, Roy Jenkins and William Rodgers, broke away from Labour and formed the Social Democratic Party. There were several reasons for the schism. One of them was the Common Market – unlike the majority of Labour party members, the Gang of Four wanted to stay in

1981: In March, convicted IRA terrorists went on hunger strike in the Maze prison, demanding to be treated as prisoners of war, not criminals. By August, 10 were dead. By October, the IRA bombing campaign had been resumed in England

1981: Women began arriving at Greenham Common, the US airbase in Berkshire, to protest against the decision to store 96 cruise missiles at the site. They set up an all-female peace camp and went on to make the news for the rest of the decade

1981: Racial tension, which had been manifest in race riots in Notting Hill in 1976 and in fighting in the St. Paul's area of Bristol in 1980, spilled over into large-scale violence. In April, the streets of Brixton exploded in petrol bomb flames. The following July, rioting also broke out in

Liverpool (Toxteth), Birmingham, Hull, Wolverhampton and Preston. The police and minority groups seemed polarised; in Brixton, black community leaders blamed the violence on years of police harassment

1982: In April, Argentina invaded the Falkland Islands. Britain had dismally failed to anticipate the event, withdrawing the last Royal Navy vessel in the area in 1981. When war broke out, Lord Carrington, the foreign secretary, immediately resigned. Britain's chances of recovering the territory were increased by support from President Ronald Reagan; America supplied air-to-air missiles and satellite intelligence. The British flag was back by June – but 900 people had died in the conflict

1982: An IRA car bomb exploded in Hyde Park, killing two mounted soldiers on route to the Changing of the Guards ceremony. Seventeen onlookers were injured and seven horses had to be put down. A few months later, an IRA bomb killed 16 people in a pub in Londonderry

1982: Concerned by the crime statistics, residents of the Cheshire villages of Lea and Mollington set

up Britain's first Neighbourhood Watch scheme. Working with the local constabulary, they saw crime fall by a third in a year

1983: In the June election, Margaret Thatcher won an overall majority of 144. No prime minister since Clement Attlee in 1945 had had such a mandate

1983: Neil Kinnock, the bridge between old and new Labour, became leader of the opposition

1983: Cecil Parkinson, the trade and industry secretary and the linchpin of the Tories' election campaign, resigned over revelations that Sara Keays, his former secretary and mistress, was expecting his child. For a party that had been championing old-fashioned values it was embarrassing and potentially damaging publicity

1984: The jobless total went above three million

1984: In March, the National Union of Mineworkers, led by the militant Arthur Scargill, went on strike over the National Coal Board's proposal to close 21 pits. The dispute, which lasted a year, was one of the most bitter and violent in trade union history. On May 29, more than 60

swing and the labour-intensive business of making things was being relocated to lower-cost areas of the world such as South-east Asia and Latin America. (In the first few years of the 21st century, this process was repeating itself even within these regions: much South Korean manufacturing, for example, is being shifted to lower-cost China. In 2003, BMW, the epitome of German precision engineering, announced it was setting up in China, using 40 per cent locally produced components.)

Worst affected by the manufacturing recession of the early 1980s were the car factories (by 1982, Britain had lost half its two million production of 1972 and was making fewer cars than Spain) and the shipyards, which were largely reduced to making oil rigs. Cutbacks in both of these

people were seriously injured in a clash between pitmen and police at Orgreave Coke Works in South Yorkshire

1984: In October, the IRA blew up the Grand Hotel in Brighton, the conference headquarters of the Conservative party. Four died, including the MP Sir Anthony Berry and the wife of John Wakeham, the chief whip. The trade and industry secretary Norman Tebbit and his wife Margaret were severely injured

1984: Thatcher declared that there was now a man in the Kremlin she could do business with: the reforming Mikhail Gorbachev

1984: Bob Geldof and friends cut "Do they know it's Christmas?" All proceeds from the record went to relieve the suffering caused by famine in Ethiopia. The following year, the Live Aid concert took place, raising an estimated £40m

1985: The British prime minister and the Taoiseach, Dr Garrett Fitzgerald, signed the Anglo-Irish Agreement, which gave the Irish Republic a consultative role in the running of Ulster. Hard-line Unionists felt betrayed. One of Thatcher's ministers, Ian Gow,

resigned in protest. Five years later, he was murdered by the IRA

1985: The government earmarked about £1m for research into AIDS. A major public awareness campaign followed, using the slogan "don't die of ignorance"

1985: Police shot dead a black woman during a search of her house in Brixton; rioting followed. Subsequent riots on the Broadwater Farm housing estate in Tottenham North London reached a violent conclusion when PC Keith Blakelock was hacked to death

1986: A Somerset-based business, Westland Helicopters, became a flashpoint for Cabinet infighting. The ailing helicopter manufacturer was being stalked by the American company, Sikorsky. The defence secretary, Michael Heseltine, tried to put together an alternative rescue plan from a European consortium, but he was opposed by both the prime minister and her ally, the department of trade and industry secretary, Leon Brittan. Both ministers subsequently made exits from the Cabinet, Brittan after the apparently "tactical" leaking of a letter from the attorney general accusing Heseltine of "inaccuracies"

1986: The journalist John McCarthy was captured in Beirut; the following year, he was joined in captivity by hostage negotiator Terry Waite

1987: Labour's Paul Boateng, Diane Abbott and Bernie Grant became the first black people to be elected to parliament. All won their seats in the June General Election. Two years later, Boateng was appointed shadow treasury minister, becoming the first black MP to sit on the front bench

1987: An IRA bomb exploded during the annual Remembrance Day parade in the town of Enniskillen in Northern Ireland. Eleven were killed; 63 were seriously injured

1988: The sitting of the Commons had to be suspended for 10 minutes as Labour MPs barracked the Chancellor's budget speech. Nigel Lawson introduced one high-rate income tax, 40 per cent, and a basic rate of 25 per cent. Critics denounced it as a budget for the rich. Meanwhile, Lawson had other battles to fight: he and Thatcher had fallen out over the Exchange Rate Mechanism

1988: The Liberals, now called the Social and Liberal Democrats after merging with the SDP, elected a

new leader, Paddy Ashdown

1988: Britain had its first Red Nose Day: 3.8 million plastic clown noses were distributed in aid of the telethon charity Comic Relief

1988: For the first time in Britain, a witness in a child sex abuse case was allowed to give evidence on video. (The issue of child abuse had been highlighted by the foundation of the Childline charity by TV presenter Esther Rantzen in 1986.)

1989: Frustrated by his prime minister's habit of listening to her financial guru, the anti-ERM economist Alan Walters, rather than him, Nigel Lawson resigned

1989: Britain joined in the condemnation of the massacre of hundreds of pro-democracy student demonstrators in Tiananmen Square in Beijing in June. There were fears for the future of Hong Kong, due to be transferred to China in 1997. Few could have foreseen that by the time of the hand-over China would have begun its long march to capitalism

Sources: Christopher Lee: This Sceptred Isle, Twentieth Century, BBC and Penguin Books, 1999; Patrick Robertson: The New Shell Book of Firsts, 1994, Headline Book Publishing; Guardian Unlimited; BBCi

industries naturally had an enormous impact on the steel industry, their core supplier. But in the southern half of England, and among the pundits of the City, the sickness in manufacturing was little appreciated. Even those who did perceive it were inclined to suggest that it had a positive side, arguing that Britain could earn a good living internationally by exporting invisible services, instead of what Tom Peters, the US business guru, has called "hard lumpy objects".

Perhaps no business more symbolised this shift in the 1980s than the advertising agency colossus built by two Iraqi-born brothers, Maurice and Charles Saatchi. It had begun in a modest way in 1970 but by 1978 had captured a major prize in the Conservative Party's election advertising. The main poster, purporting to show a queue of unemployed under the slogan "Labour Isn't Working", put Saatchi and Saatchi on the map and was widely credited with putting Margaret Thatcher into Downing Street. The agency roared ahead, growing globally by acquisition and aiming to become the world's first "one-stop shop" for advertising and marketing. One of the talents it nurtured, finance director Martin Sorrell, quit in 1986 to create WPP, now one of the world's top three marketing companies.

The Saatchi brothers were ousted from control of their now-public company in 1995 by directors unhappy with their over-weening ambition and spending to match. They

One who got away: Martin Sorrell quit the Saatchis' employment to build one of the world's top marketing businesses, WPP

proceeded to set up another small agency but gradually diverged into other activities: Maurice into politics as a working Tory peer speaking on Treasury matters and Charles as an avant-garde art patron responsible for backing such

Saatchi and Saatchi on the rise: the reclusive advertising genius Charles (L) and his brother Maurice. For years they refused to issue any new photographs

controversial artists as Damien Hirst and Tracey Emin. Saatchi and Saatchi, now controlled from New York, remains a powerful name and in 2002 harvested more new business than any other agency – $1.2bn in net terms.

Invisible wealth on a vastly greater scale was also pumping from beneath the North Sea. As early as 1980 Britain was self-sufficient in her own oil, producing 100 million tonnes a year, on a par with Kuwait and Iraq. Since the 1970s, the UK has harvested some £190bn in taxes from North Sea oil and gas, and attracted £205bn of investment.[3] It is still questionable whether enough of those glittering revenues were re-invested in industry.

The 1981-82 recession cut deeply into employment patterns, quite apart from the tens of thousands of jobs lost. Unemployment doubled between the summer of 1979 and that of 1981, and by 1986 peaked at 3.3 million. It would remain around the three million mark for three more years, despite a spell of boom-level prosperity in the late 1980s. Though few saw it at the time, this was essentially the end of the jobs-for-life culture that had informed employer-employee relations since the Great Depression. In its place came the nebulous concept of "employability", in which employers undertook to keep their workers' skills up-to-date to enable them to switch jobs either within or outside the company as required. The new buyers' market for employers soon encouraged companies to "downsize" for efficiency even if they were not faced with outright crisis; a trend that was already sweeping giant US corporations such as General Electric, which removed a quarter of its workforce between 1980 and 1990 under its then-controversial CEO, "Neutron Jack" Welch.

The other big switch in employment was towards part-time working and outsourcing. All the jobs that replaced the million lost to full-time working between 1981 and 1985, and some 300,000 additional ones, were temporary, part-time or self-employed posts.[4] This, however, created growth opportunities in at least one industry: by the end of 1986, the number of companies registered under the Employment Agencies Act was above 9,250, an all-time high. In the same year, the Institute of Manpower Studies calculated that at any given moment, 75 per cent of employers were using temporary staff somewhere in their organisations and that 7.5 per cent of the total UK workforce was temporary. Nearly all the new jobs were in seven key service industries – retailing, wholesaling, hotels and catering, financial services and general business-to-business services such as accountancy, management consultancy and software systems. In one year in the early 1980s, Manpower, an agency specialising in outsourcing, registered an 800 per cent increase in demand for word-processing and other computer skills.[5]

"The economic cutbacks in 1980/81 changed the fabric of the market," said Mike Crosswell, group managing director of the Blue Arrow Group, which in 1984 comprised just two small chains of employment agencies specialising in office and industrial staff. Unfortunately, the boom prompted Blue Arrow to embark on an over-ambitious series of acquisitions. It took over the Reliance chain and the Brook Street Bureau in 1985 and the specialist executive search agency Hoggett Bowers in 1986. A year later, it engineered its own downfall by trying to acquire Manpower, the world's largest work-contract agency through a rights issue based on questionable accounting of its assets. The resulting scandal damaged the group, which only recovered on a smaller scale, and discredited its chief executive, Tony Berry.

The part-time working boom had extensive social implications too, bringing far more women into commerce and industry. By 1987, women formed more than half the workforce, a cultural change comparable with that brought about by the First World War. The British Institute of Management suggested in 1988 that in industries as varied as textiles, construction, financial services and IT, women had more than doubled their share of management posts over the previous decade. But the glass ceiling was already becoming obvious: despite the emergence in the 1980s of female boardroom dynamos such as Jennifer d'Abo of stationery chain Rymans, Anne Burdus of advertising agency McCann-Erickson (a council member of the IoD) and a number of high-flying finance directors at major companies such as Sainsbury's, the IoD recorded in 1988 that women still held less than five per cent of UK directorships.

Jennifer d'Abo, who multiplied Rymans' profits tenfold by bringing colour into office products

D'Abo, who died in 2003, was an unusual mix of entrepreneur and corporate strategist. An instantly recognisable figure with her heart-shaped spectacles, she bought Ryman's from the Burton Group in 1981 and multiplied its value almost tenfold in six years before selling out to Terry Maher's Pentos bookshop group and buying Moyses Stevens, the fashionable florists. By introducing colour and style into Ryman's products, d'Abo showed that office equipment need not be dull or mundane. Box files and folders in hues of scarlet and purple, commonplace now, were something new in 1981.

Entrepreneurs were the heroes of the hour, a good number of them women. The 25-year-old Sophie Mirman flashed like a comet across the business pages with her Sock Shop chain, started with £45,000 from the government's Loan Guarantee Scheme in 1983. Four years later, she and her husband had 120 shops, and the business was floated on the Unlisted Securities Market. Such was the public enthusiasm that the issue was oversubscribed 52 times and the shares doubled in value on the first day. A year later, in 1988, the over-borrowed business went into administration, destroyed by such unforeseen events as a national rail strike, which closed half the chain's outlets, based in underground and train stations. Mirman bounced back in 1990, opening a much more modest children's store with just two outlets, but at the peak of Sock Shop's success she was worth £50m. Another, but more substantial business founded by a woman whose initial share offering was massively over-subscribed – 34 times – was that of Laura Ashley, by now a diverse and international company stretching as far as Japan. Its flotation in 1985 came just two months after its founder died in a freak accident, falling down stairs at her home.

THE CHANGING CENTURY

Facts from the business archives:

1980: The Sony Walkman personal stereo hit Britain. At first, it went under the name Stowaway, Sony's marketing department having been misinformed that "Walkman" would not work in English

1980: In Detroit, General Motors put a "seeing" robot to work on its production line. Electronic eyes meant the robot could select and separate components on a conveyor belt

1980: At the Salzburg Festival, the conductor Herbert von Karajan demonstrated the future of recorded music: the compact disc. The CD had been developed in the Netherlands by Philips over a 15-year period

1980: IBM and Bill Gates of Microsoft met in secret to discuss Project Chess, the development of a new personal computer. Gates was to supply the operating system. He bought the Disk Operating System from Seattle Computer for $50,000 and supplied IBM with MS-DOS. The rest is history: by 1991, Microsoft was making $200m a year from sales of MS-DOS alone*

1981: The IBM PC came out. It was the first machine to have the abbreviation "PC" as part of its name and is therefore credited with popularising the term "personal computer"

1982: In Japan, Sony launched the first compact disc players. The following year, the players were marketed in Britain, France, West Germany and Holland

1982: Britain's first satellite TV channel was launched by Satellite Television of London; three years later, Rupert Murdoch bought an 80 per cent stake in the company and renamed it Sky

1982: Diet Coke made its debut in the US

1983: In the US, Tandy Corporation launched the first laptop computer. Battery operated and weighing less than 4lbs, it included built-in software, a full-size keyboard and a built-in 300 band modem

1983: British Telecom launched the UK's first cordless telephone, the Fidelity Wanderer. It could take calls or dial out up to 600ft from its base. It cost a princely £170 – or an even more princely £223 if you got it from Harrods

1983: Apple Computer launched the Lisa, the forerunner of the Macintosh. Although rather slow and prohibitively expensive, the Lisa was a breakthrough in user-friendly computing. It was the first

Other profound, though less visible, changes were taking place in the world of work. The idea of "portfolio" working gained ground in the 1980s as talented people displaced from lifetime careers sought to fill the gaps in their time and income by taking on more than one part-time occupation. The Irish-born business consultant and social philosopher Charles Handy promoted the positive virtues of this in his 1984 book The Future of Work, and those of the "shamrock" organisation, using a mix of full-time, part-time and contracted-out employment, in The Age of Unreason (1989).

The loss of full-time (predominantly male) jobs in manufacturing and the rise in part-time female working in services gradually led to a perception of a "North-South divide" across the UK. Certainly, the services-heavy south

The Laura Ashley phenomenon: Laura and husband Bernard in the early days and (inset), the retro style that spawned a fashion empire

Laura Ashley New Shop opens May 4th at 157 Fulham Road, S.W.3, with the summer collection (and Laura Ashley) Smalls Custom collection) also in Laura Ashley fabrics printed and dyed in Wales. Children's clothes a new red and dyed in South will be at 23 Pelham Street, S.W.3 shop South Kensington Station for both shops

---

commercial PC with point-and-click technology – i. e. a graphic user interface and a mouse (see science and technology box)

1985: Racal-Vodafone and British Telecom introduced Britain's first mobile phone services. The BT venture went under the name Cellnet. The phones cost between £1,200 and £1,500 each and there was a monthly service charge of between £50 and £60. Nonetheless, within four months, Vodafone and Cellnet were attracting over 300 new users a week

1985: Coca-Cola made what has often been described as one of the biggest blunders in marketing history, changing its famous 99-year-old recipe in an attempt to outdo its arch

rival, Pepsi. The decision was made on the back of expensive research suggesting that 55 per cent of buyers would prefer the new, sweeter formula. Unfortunately, that still left 45 per cent craving the "real thing". After a storm of protest, the company was forced to bring back the original

1985: Panasonic introduced Britons to the camcorder

1986: Eddy Shah launched Today, the first British national daily newspaper to be printed in colour

1986: The broadsheet newspaper The Independent was founded

1986: Nissan unveiled the first car with four-wheel steering, the Skyline

1986: Fuji brought out the first

disposable camera

1987: The building society Nationwide Anglia introduced Britain's first interest-bearing cheque account

1987: Barclays Bank launched its Connect Card, the UK's first debit card

1988: In Aberdeen, solicitor Frank Lefevre set up Britain's first "no win, no fee practice", Quantum Claims Compensation Specialists

1988: The first Mercury call boxes appeared: 26 were installed at Waterloo Station

1988: Keith Mills of British Airways developed the free-flight promotional scheme Air Miles

1989: Associated Newspapers printed

the first British papers in non-rub ink. From now on, what you read in the Daily Mail, the Mail on Sunday and the Evening Standard would stay "in your head, not on your hands"

1989: Sky Television went national. Four of Rupert Murdoch's channels could now be beamed direct to viewers' homes via dish-decoders. Viewers had to pay a subscription fee of £250 – plus, of course, the cost of a dish. The sceptics dubbed the service "money for old soap" – a swipe at the American repeats that dominated Sky One's early schedules

Main source: Patrick Robertson: The New Shell Book of Firsts, 1994, Headline Book Publishing

*Figures cited in Hard Drive, Bill Gates and the Making of the Microsoft Empire by James Wallace and Jim Erickson, John Wiley & Sons, 1992

was less affected than the old manufacturing heartlands (which also included Wales) by the recession of the early 1980s. This imbalance would not be redressed until a decade later when white-collar staff were severely shaken out of their well-paid employment in the City of London and elsewhere.

However, the radical programme of the new Conservative government was, by and large, accepted as necessary therapy for the arthritic 1970s economy, and a great part of the new spirit of dynamism was engendered by the first big privatisations. These began in 1981 with British Aerospace, the National Freight Corporation and Cable and Wireless, but it was the British Telecoms privatisation in 1984 that captured the public's imagination on a grand scale, showing gains of more than a third on the opening

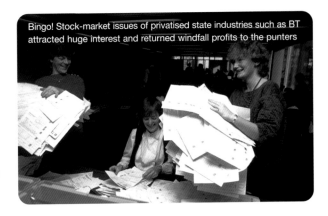

Bingo! Stock-market issues of privatised state industries such as BT attracted huge interest and returned windfall profits to the punters

price within a week of the issue. Two years later, people who had never before gone anywhere near a stockbroker responded eagerly to the "Tell Sid" advertising for the

THE CHANGING CENTURY

A snapshot of science and technology:

1980: At Harefield Hospital in Middlesex, the Egyptian-born surgeon Professor Sir Magdi Yacoub performed his first heart transplant operation. By 2000, he and his team had given new cardiothoracic organs to 2,330 patients – 1,121 of whom were still living. Together with Papworth Hospital in Cambridge, Harefield became synonymous with transplant surgery

1983: The US president Ronald Reagan announced the controversial Strategic Defence Initiative (SDI). Popularly known as "star wars", SDI aimed to explore the use of science and high technology – including space-based systems – to

knock out incoming Soviet missiles

1983: The computer mouse made its commercial debut. Apple introduced the first computer with a graphic user interface, revolutionary technology developed at Xerox's Palo Alto Research Center (PARC). Instead of just typing commands on a keyboard, users pointed at and clicked on tiny images on the screen

1985: Nature magazine published a paper on "genetic fingerprinting", discovered at the University of Leicester by Dr Alec J. Jeffreys. Two years later, the technique, which finds a DNA match for samples of blood, saliva or semen, was being used by Leicestershire police in a rape and murder investigation

1986: The Soviet Union launched the Mir ("Peace") space station

1988: Computer and linguistic experts of London University developed a desktop machine able to respond to voice commands

1988: The first transatlantic optical fibre cable was laid by BT, AT&T and France Telecom. The cable, consisting of six hair-thin strands of glass fibre able to carry 40,000 simultaneous telephone calls between America and the UK or France, cost £220m

1989: The B2 stealth bomber, the most costly aircraft in the world ($516m), was developed by Northrop and the US Air Force. The bomber combines low observability with the capability to deliver massive firepower

1989: At Guy's Hospital London, surgeons performed the first heart operation on an unborn child. The

baby was given a balloon valvuloplasty (a procedure to stretch open a narrowed heart valve) when her mother was 33 weeks pregnant

1989: The World Wide Web was developed by the English computer scientist Timothy Berners-Lee while working for the European Particle Physics Laboratory (CERN). The internet protocol had been developed 16 years earlier by the American computer scientist Vinton Cerf and the American engineer Robert Kahn as part of a project sponsored by the United States Department of Defense Advanced Research Projects Agency (ARPA)

See also: business facts box

Main source: Patrick Robertson: The New Shell Book of Firsts, 1994, Headline Book Publishing

British Gas flotation. From then on, especially when water and electricity were privatised, there was such a rush to cash in on quick "stagging" gains that some observers drew comparisons with a casino – this, they said, was a cheap punt, not popular capitalism, not genuine investment.

Serious questions were also raised about the way many senior executives in those industries were simply transferred to more lucrative private-sector status for no tangible improvement in performance. The combative Sir Denis Rooke, chairman of British Gas, was reported by a rival in the electricity business to have commented within a year of privatisation (when, of course, deregulation of the energy market was still a long way off) that his company had not changed a jot from its public-sector self.[6] When asked if people would buy shares in his company, one water authority chairman remarked: "Of course, because a monopoly always makes money".

But the first wave of privatisations did turn in some impressive performances. The profits of BAe and Amersham International, an early biotechnology and speciality chemicals company, doubled in five years, while those of Cable and Wireless trebled. National Freight Corporation had made a profit of £4.3m in its last year of state ownership (1981); by 1986 this had soared to £37m. Jaguar Cars, released from the straitjacket of state ownership under British Leyland, went from profits of £50m to £121m in two years. Other leading names in engineering and technology such as Rolls-Royce, Ferranti and ICL were let out into the big world from the well-meaning but stifling embrace of the old National Enterprise Board.

Jaguar – one of the most spectacularly improved companies – had actually been turned round while still state-owned. It was rescued by Sir John Egan, a serially successful chief executive who had already made his mark managing Unipart, BL's components division, subsequently spun off as a separate business. In the 1970s, Jaguar had

become notoriously erratic in quality, badly damaging its reputation in the key US market, and Egan worked magic on it by applying rigorous quality management.

National Freight offered an inspiring example of what wider share ownership could achieve when a company became owned by its employees rather than by members of the public out for a gambling win. NFC chief executive John Mather observed that "the real spur to improved profitability has come from the deep involvement of our employee-shareholders. It is this that has had a continuing impact, has encouraged us to communicate [better] and has encouraged a participative management style".[7]

More common was the cultural revolution that privatisation effected in forcing previous state-run businesses to take notice of the paying customer. Nowhere was this better illustrated than at British Airways, which went public in 1987 with £900m worth of shares. The national airline, formed out of British Overseas Airways Corporation and British European Airways in 1972, had been making big profits in the late 1970s, heydays for first and business class air travel, but the new Tory government wanted it out of

British Airways takes off into the private sector under aggressive new management, 1987

Hard man at the helm: BA chairman Lord King

state hands to avoid the Treasury having to shell out £1bn for its investment programme.

Under the forceful chairmanship of Lord King, a seasoned entrepreneur with an aggressive manner brought in by Thatcher to mastermind the transition to the private sector, and his customer-minded chief executive, Sir Colin (now Lord) Marshall, who had once worked for Avis, the "we try harder" US car rental firm, the airline's corporate culture was rapidly and radically transformed. From a transportation-oriented company run largely by ex-RAF officers, it was moulded through dedicated training programmes called "Putting People First" into a thoroughly commercial, customer-conscious business – and it prospered accordingly for the next 10 years.

Privatisation – a term invented by the management polymath Peter Drucker, though he called it "re-privatisation" – created one of the most sweeping redistributions of wealth in British history. In seven years, the sum of assets removed from state ownership totalled more than £12bn, and 500,000 employees were switched from state to private bosses.[8] The programme would be one of Thatcherism's most durable legacies. Its philosophy outlasted the Conservative years in government and was embraced for pragmatic reasons by Tony Blair's New Labour administration. Blair's government went even further than that of Thatcher in trying to offer air traffic control for privatisation, despite fervent pledges by Labour in opposition not to "sell our air".

The last and most ambitious privatisation, that of British Rail, however, has done nothing for the denationalisation cause. The project was rushed through under John Major's government in 1995 and the chance of reform was fudged by the incoming Blair administration; the whole thing was fatally flawed by the separation of train and track ownership. The railways are still swallowing public money while offering few of the benefits of competitive service because of an infrastructure that had been under-funded for decades.

Not all Conservatives favoured the massive state sell-off. Lord Stockton, the former prime minister Harold

THE CHANGING CENTURY

Two years that shook Britain: 1987-1989

March 7, 1987: The roll-on roll-off ferry The Herald of Free Enterprise sank as it left Zeebrugge harbour in Belgium. The bow doors had been left open after departure, and water flooded the car decks. Nearly 200 people lost their lives.*

October 15, 1987: The south east

was hit by a hurricane-strength storm: the London fire brigade had more than 6,000 emergency calls in one day – the highest number in its history. In Kew Gardens, more than 30 per cent of specimens were uprooted. For a week afterwards, about 300,000 homes in the south of England were without electricity

October 19, 1987: Black Monday: falls and heavy selling on Wall Street

triggered a wave of stock market crashes. In London, 10 per cent of the total share value disappeared, and the value of publicly quoted companies fell by £50bn

November 1987: Thirty people died when fire spread through King's Cross underground station in London. The tragedy led to the introduction of a no-smoking policy on the tube

December 12, 1988: Thirty-five people

died when two trains collided outside Clapham Junction in south London**

December 21, 1988: As the result of terrorist action, a Pan-Am jumbo jet crashed at Lockerbie, killing all 259 passengers plus 11 people in the town

April 15, 1989: Ninety-six football fans were crushed to death in the crowds that converged on the Hillsborough stadium in Sheffield

Macmillan, caused a sensation when he attacked the programme in the House of Lords as "selling the family silver". How he would have felt seeing essential industries such as water, energy and rail subsequently sold off to foreign buyers can only be guessed at: in later decades, many British institutions would be owned on the Continent, from Christie's the auctioneers (the French group Pinault) to Rolls-Royce (BMW) and Bentley (Volkswagen).

Privatisation did, however, inject more freedom for managers – the desire to "get government off our backs" had run high. Turnround masters such as Egan and Marshall were a breath of fresh air in erstwhile nationalised industries as the climate became more enterprise-friendly.

In the private sector, meanwhile, the most high-profile exponent of corporate change – and one who shattered the accepted image of British corporate chairmen – was Sir John Harvey-Jones of ICI. Shaggy-haired, gravelly voiced and flamboyantly dressed, sporting psychedelic ties more in keeping with Carnaby Street than the City or the imposing Millbank headquarters of ICI, Harvey-Jones had been a submariner in World War II and had joined the company from the Royal Navy in 1956 as a work study officer. He was the surprise choice as chairman in 1981 after the company, a major stock market barometer, had just reported the first

Kipper ties and charisma: Sir John Harvey-Jones of ICI became an unlikely business hero and, later, TV personality as the 'troubleshooter'

deficit in its history, a net loss of £20m on sales of nearly £6bn. This bluest of blue chips was forced to cut its dividend for the first time since its founding in 1926, leaving shareholders and employees shell-shocked.

Harvey-Jones brought a tough nautical discipline and plain-speaking frankness to the awesome task of bringing the mighty ICI vessel round. The process imposed severe strains on the structure, leading to the loss of 30,000 jobs in the UK – a third of the domestic workforce – the closure of plants and the withdrawal from whole areas of manufacturing.

for the FA Cup semi-final between Liverpool and Nottingham Forest. (It was the third disaster to strike the sport in four years. In 1985, a fire at the Bradford City ground had killed 40; in the same year, a similar number of people had died at the Heysel stadium in Brussels after Liverpool and Juventus fans fought on the terraces, causing a wall and fence to collapse. The Heysel tragedy led to a five-year

ban on British clubs in European competition.)

August 20, 1989: Fifty-one people died as the Marchioness pleasure cruiser collided with the dredger, Bowbelle, on the River Thames

FOOTNOTE:

*After a public inquiry into the disaster, Lord Justice Sheen published a report that identified a "disease of

sloppiness" at every management level of P&O, owner of the ferry operator Townsend-Thoresen. P&O European Ferries and directors at the company were subsequently charged with corporate manslaughter. The case against them collapsed but it set a precedent for the charge of corporate manslaughter being admissible in court

**A public inquiry into the crash recommended the installation of

automatic train protection (ATP) for the whole rail network. ATP equipment controls the speed of trains and automatically stops them at red lights. But both the government and British Rail ruled it out: the £750m price tag was thought too high for an industry limbering up for privatisation.

Sources: Christopher Lee: This Sceptred Isle, Twentieth Century, BBC and Penguin Books, 1999; Guardian Unlimited; BBCi

Even the production of polythene, which ICI scientists had accidentally invented in a laboratory experiment in 1933 and which was, therefore, a deep part of the company's history, was abandoned.

The old, bureaucratic management system was flattened out; the old baronial divisions were turned into internally competitive businesses; reporting lines were shortened. Harvey-Jones even revolutionised the way board meetings were held, preferring shirt-sleeved informality in his office to leading proceedings in the imposing Art Deco boardroom at Millbank with its octagonal table.

After three years, ICI emerged triumphant from its ordeal to become the first British company to announce pre-tax profits (for 1984-85) of over £1bn. The achievements of the Harvey-Jones turnround strategy – which also set a new direction in moving away from bulk chemicals and into speciality products – provided a template for others in the 1980s. If imitators failed it was usually because their approach was top-down rather than collectively pursued. ICI had always had a collegiate management culture and its so-called "parliament", dating back to the 1920s, was one of the earliest examples in the UK of workers being empowered to question senior management decisions. An executive director said at the time of the Harvey-Jones reforms: "On major issues, if more than two people are against a proposal the majority are unlikely to take it forward, although they might try again after." The chairman himself

Branson the brand: the informality and daredevil stunts of Richard Branson identified his Virgin Group products and services with youth and vigour

remarked that although there had been a few occasions where he overruled the wishes of the majority, "a company of this size can only be run in a collegiate fashion".

A self-confessed "passionate advocate of change", Harvey-Jones once said: "any company that thinks it is a British institution is on the way out". In practical business terms, this was not a decade of conservatism. The visionary and energetic corporate executive capable of injecting new life into the company or spinning off entirely new businesses became a more common phenomenon in the 1980s.

Above all, however, this was the age of a new kind of entrepreneurial business hero, in new kinds of youth-oriented businesses. Richard Branson was – and remains well into the 2000s – the epitome of this breed. Branson had begun flexing his business skills when still a teenager at Stowe public school, selling record albums by mail order and launching a student magazine. His first start-up was a discount record shop over a shoe shop in London's Oxford Street in 1971. Ten years later, his Virgin Group had a small, not very profitable book publishing operation as well as the music side, and interests in film and video.

The breakthrough came in 1981 when Branson recruited Robert Devereux, a 25-year-old who had been working for the publishers Macmillan, to expand the film and video side. By 1987, these activities accounted for 75 per cent of the communications division and had a turnover of £43m.

In 1981, Branson also: made a protracted takeover of W. H. Allen to get the marketing and distribution network needed to build a sizeable publishing business; bought a minority stake in a computer games firm to gain an early entry into electronic publishing; and became a founder shareholder in British Satellite Broadcasting (BSB). Meanwhile, he was exploring possible deals to broaden the record side away from the pop market.

Twenty years later, Branson was to be criticised for boldly stretching the Virgin brand into markets as diverse as vodka, cola and privatised train services, but for now his scatter-gun approach proved hugely successful. He was one of the first to recognise the potential of corporate brand management over a varied field. "I like getting my teeth into new challenges," he said in one interview. "I like making things work when others are sceptical and surprising the pundits."[9] In 1986, the Virgin music publishing and retailing business went public, supported enthusiastically by small investors but not by the City, which cast a cool eye on the bearded, publicity-minded Branson with his penchant for inter-continental ballooning. Branson reciprocated the analysts' mistrust and in 1988 took the business private again through a buy-back of shares. He subsequently built up a complex web of holding companies linked by the Virgin brand and involving many joint ventures to provide capital.

Two things stand out from Virgin's rapid growth in the 1980s. The first was Branson's ability to delegate the running of his businesses to competent professionals. He enjoyed – and excelled at – breaking into and shaking up complacent existing industries, but he never made the mistake of assuming he had the skills to manage the follow-through himself. "My skills are finding the right people to run companies and coming up with new ventures," he said.

On the music side, Virgin's original core, free rein was given to chairman Simon Draper to build and develop Virgin's record labels for nearly 20 years. (Branson, as it happens, is tone deaf.) The group had an informal top structure with just one or two financial "suits" balancing the sweater-clad Branson with his nose for new businesses, and the whole organisation enjoyed a culture of decentralisation. In 1987, it had 2,500 employees, who worked in units of up to 80 people, each unit having its own director.

The second innovative feature of Branson's strategy was the linking of cross-interests in seemingly diverse businesses. Foreshadowing the way Time Warner would operate a decade later, Virgin would, for example, set up a children's series for TV and link it to complementary book-publishing rights, music rights and merchandising rights, all carried out by Virgin facilities.

At this time, Branson's businesses were mostly in what would become known as the "old" or "legacy" economy. But by the mid-1980s, all the fashionable macroeconomic talk was about investing in "sunrise" industries, which meant high tech. Technology was still, in the UK, largely the preserve of giant companies such as Plessey, British Aerospace, Cable and Wireless and Racal Electronics. Britain did have its equivalents to the garage start-ups of Silicon Valley but they often foundered; Applied Holographics, a sadly short-lived company that specialised in reproducing the hologram symbols on credit cards, was one example.

Despite brilliant technology, the young firms could not compete with the big boys. There was also a notable absence of fast-growing middle-weight companies in the technology sector. One of the few exceptions was Oxford Instruments, a company that proved a rare combination of advanced technology and strong commercial management. It had been founded as early as 1959 by Martin Woods, a researcher in physics at Oxford University who had invented the nuclear magnetic resonance (NMR) spectrometer used for analysing bio-chemical particles. Woods set up Oxford Instruments to find commercial markets for this breakthrough product in chemical research. By the 1970s, the NMR system had developed into the magnetic resonance imaging technology for body scanning known universally as MRI ("nuclear" by now being a tainted word). Demand for MRI scanners exploded in the early 1980s, and as they scrambled to enter the market, the world's leading medical equipment companies were forced to come to this modest-sized UK company for the scanner's most costly component, a magnet with a very strong and homogeneous field. MRI scanners were at that time the most expensive piece of hospital machinery around, costing $2m or more, of which the magnet represented a quarter.

Oxford Instruments prospered massively. Over the first half of the 1980s, turnover rose each year by an average of 45 per cent and profits soared by as much as 70 per cent, to £17.2m. Then in 1987 a sharp reduction in profits seemed to confirm City cynicism that it was a one-product company lucky to be in the right place at the right time. But Oxford had already spun off a company called Oxford Magnet Technology, six months before the group floated in 1984. Its management had reckoned – wisely in the light of rising costs and of emerging US and German competition that broke its monopoly – that the medical imaging business needed a distinct corporate identity and focus. OMT took over as the group's main generator of revenue and profits while the original OI acted as the corporate seedbed of technology and new business ideas.[10]

There were other promising middleweight technology-based companies in the 1980s such as UEI Electronics Quantel, a world leader in advanced digital imaging techniques for TV, and Amishaw, designers of precision metrology and inspection equipment. But while the technologies these companies pioneered went from strength to strength, many of the businesses themselves did not. Successful transition from single-product, high-tech start-up to multi-product company with market strength still remains rare in the UK two decades on.

The Thatcher government was aware of the problem. While it reined in financial support for the traditional lame ducks of industry, it was sympathetic to aiding the launch of new technology businesses. In 1982, "Information Technology Year", the new minister for information technology at the Department of Trade and Industry, Kenneth Baker, said it was unrealistic to expect technology industries "to grow in the marketplace without government prompting and assistance".[11] The leg-up was provided through the National Enterprise Board and National Research Development Council, both of which were eventually turned into a new state-owned company in 1991, the British Technology Group. BTG was a distinct success story, licensing new technologies for commercial exploitation and helping to create cutting-edge companies such as CellTech and Inmos.

Britain had, of course, produced high-tech pioneers 20 years earlier. Alan Sugar (see panel) produced his first Amstrad computer in 1968. It passed the million mark in sales in 1973, and Sugar took his company public in 1980. But it was not until 1985 that the Amstrad word-processor made him a household name. Its simplicity and cheapness introduced a whole new public to the age of the PC.

Clive Sinclair, bearded and intense and everyone's idea of the obsessive inventor, had made a splash in the 1970s with his pioneering pocket calculator and pocket-sized TV, launched in 1979. But somehow Sinclair's clever inventions and his Radionics company never quite had their day. Lord Ryder, chairman of the National Enterprise Board, had backed the pocket flat-screen television strongly, claiming it was the saviour of the British TV industry. But Ryder then left and the marketing drive never took off. Some 20,000 "Microvisions" were sold, not enough to make the TV mass-market, and the NEB claimed that it lost nearly £8m on the project.

The ZX80 micro-computer was again ahead of its time, and the cheapest on the market, but again the market

Sir Alan Sugar and Anita Roddick: they did it their way

Two of Britain's best-known entrepreneurs rose to household-name status in the 1980s, though their very different businesses had been founded years earlier. Alan Sugar, the rough-edged son of an east London tailor with a fondness for bad language and for starting his working days by "having a good shout" at his staff, set up Amstrad (a contraction of Alan Michael Sugar trading) in 1968, selling TVs and hi-fis from a battered van.

The great discovery of his early years, he has said, was that he could make more money selling non-exclusive goods if he manufactured them himself. In the 1970s, he moved into computers but his big breakthrough came in 1985, five years after listing Amstrad on the Stock Exchange, with the launch of the PCW 8256, an idiot-proof word-processor that introduced hundreds of thousands of people to computer skills. This was followed in 1986 by the PC 1512, an IBM-compatible PC

that, at a time when most similar products cost more than £2,000, retailed for just £399. Within six months, it had captured 25 per cent of the European PC market.

Sugar's ambition was always to make electronics accessible to the mass market. His aspiration to do the same for mobile phones when they still cost three

"A good shout": Sir Alan Sugar has never cared about his image. Below, left: Anita Roddick, for whom campaigning on ethical issues means more than cash management

figures was ahead of its time, but most of his products have made profits and he is reputedly worth around £600m. He even made money in the volatile world of football clubs, buying an £8m stake in Tottenham Hotspur in the 1990s and later selling two-thirds of it for £22m. In the 2000s, he is piling money into property. "I do all my gambling in electronics, but on the other side of my business I gotta be safe," he has said, thinking of his family's security.[15]

Anita Roddick's Body Shop, founded in 1976 with her husband Gordon, and taken public in 1985, brilliantly caught the tide of environmental concern and the craze for natural products that swept the 1980s and 1990s. Roddick, the daughter of Italian immigrants to Sussex, has always been an entrepreneur on a mission; most recently, the cause has been fair trading between the prosperous West and the developing world. Her favourite saying is: "If you think you're too small to have an impact, try going to bed with a mosquito."

At its peak, Body Shop had more than 1,300 shops in 66 countries, most of them operated

by women. Although they were run as franchises, Roddick did not charge franchise fees. Instead, the company earned its profits from wholesaling the products to the shops.

Roddick remains a celebrity entrepreneur, but over the years her campaigning vision overwhelmed her business perspective, to the extent that Body Shop's offices became plastered with posters calling for the boycott of Shell products and the like. "Business can and must be a force for positive social change ... it must actively do good," she told a Chamber of Commerce meeting in Mexico in 1995. But other retailers were by now on the environmental bandwagon, and investors grew disenchanted with Roddick's heart-on-sleeve attitude and her free admission that "finance bores the pants off me".

Having tried but failed to take the company private so as to direct its profits into social causes, she finally stepped down as CEO in 1998, but she remains co-chairman with her husband, and a powerful voice for the Body Shop's crusading values.[16]

Ahead of his time: Sir Clive Sinclair's inventions often missed their market. Below, his C5 electric car was never taken seriously by the media or the public

wasn't ready. Sinclair, undaunted, tried to launch a miniature electric town car, the C5, but it became a bit of a national joke. Ultimately, Sinclair was to remain a brilliant ideas man, hampered, in true British style, by lack of marketing skills.

As well as entrepreneurial dash, the 1980s saw the development of an aggressively acquisitive corporate culture that occasionally put business in the headlines for all the wrong reasons. Both of the principal scandals of the time – those surrounding Blue Arrow and Guinness – were a direct product of the culture of growth through debt-financed hostile acquisition that dominated the big corporate scene in the mid-1980s. In the last quarter of 1985, takeover bids topped £7bn, more than in the whole of the preceding year. Even before the financial deregulation or "Big Bang" that hit the City in 1986, large international investment banks were providing predatory companies with the opportunity to finance costly bid campaigns played out in the full glare of the media. The financial press

became an additional weapon, placing the target company or competitive bidder under intense pressure, and Big Bang put a turbo-charge behind the process.

An example where no underhand tactics were involved but where the target company's attempt to resist had no chance was the $4bn bid by Nestlé for Rowntree Mackintosh in 1988. Rowntree seemed to have all the cards it needed to repel unwelcome boarders. It was an historic old confectionery company, with a basket of popular brands such as Smarties, Quality Street and Kit-Kat. It also had a long reputation, stemming from its Quaker family origins, as a caring employer. But it relied too heavily on the public appeal of these assets to fight an offer that was financially irresistible to its shareholders. Nestlé made a dramatic opening bid of more than twice the share value and finally paid £10.50 a share compared with the pre-bid value of £4.80. Nor was Rowntree's management equipped to fight the new kind of media-oriented war: its chairman, Kenneth Dixon, was rarely available to speak to the press and failed to overcome Nestlé's arguments about the weaknesses in Rowntree's international business. Short of hard fact, the press began to speculate about boardroom dissension, and the battle was lost.

Takeovers in the 1980s were battles of wills, fought out under a very public spotlight. In an environment still largely lacking in external regulation, the scope for manipulation by the parties was immense, and ambition often outran common-sense. Tony Berry's strategy at Blue Arrow in trying to acquire such a large target as Manpower was unrealistic, akin to a snake trying to imitate the python by swallowing an animal several times its size. As with the Royal Mail case of 1931, it led him into basing the fateful rights issue on an exaggerated statement of the company's assets. Manpower was acquired, but as the dubious accounting became exposed, there was a boardroom coup ousting Berry, and Manpower bought itself out of the deal.

Deregulating the City in 1986 – 'Big Bang' – injected foreign competition and shook up the Stock Exchange

Ernest Saunders' downfall was owed to a different set of weaknesses, where personal aspirations corrupted an otherwise sharp business judgment. Before being headhunted into Guinness in late 1981, Saunders had been a marketing man much lauded for his skills, with a background in J. Walter Thompson, Beecham and – crucially – Nestlé, where he oversaw the controversial marketing campaign that supported the company's drive to sell powdered baby milk in developing countries.

It is unclear whether Guinness really wanted him as a brand marketing expert to help expand the appeal of its famous but traditionally based core product, or a general manager with a remit to overhaul the board. Saunders had had no real general management experience but on the basis of glowing testimonials from Beecham's Sir Ronald Halstead and Nestlé's chief executive Arthur Furer (whom he later invited to join the Guinness board), and in the light of Guinness's falling profits and dividends, he was able, within three months, to push the existing managing director Tony Purssell into a deputy's position and to assume the top job himself.

Saunders' turnround strategy was a classic of its time. First, cut out the non-core, largely loss-making businesses that have provoked the crisis; second, rationalise the core business; third, rebuild from the new, leaner base. Within two years, 149 Guinness-owned companies had either been shut down or sold, using criteria very similar to those followed by Jack Welch in his overhaul of General Electric on the other side of the Atlantic. A new hard-hitting advertising campaign targeted Guinness at the young 18-35 pub-goer who would normally drink ale. Costs were ruthlessly cut at the company's plants in north-west London and Dublin, involving the loss of 1,000 jobs, and the price to the publican was reduced.

The ever-confident Saunders – although he later said he always felt "below the salt" when consorting with the aristocratic Guinness family – may have inflated the commercial results of these first two prongs of his strategy, though they were much praised at the time. But it was the third prong – diversification and growth from a newly rationalised base – that led directly to the 1987 catastrophe. Saunders planned to turn Guinness from a UK-oriented brewing company to an international beverage-based conglomerate. Early "non-core" acquisitions such as Martin the Newsagent in 1984 and Champneys health spa resort were secondary to his desire to acquire a broad portfolio of top drinks brands.

Saunders' basic instincts were, once again, correct. They anticipated George Bull's and Allen Sheppard's focus on branded foods and drinks at GrandMet and the subsequent strategy at Guinness that led to the creation, with GrandMet, of Diageo in the 1990s. They also played well to his proven expertise and experience in building brand equity. But the the initiatives he took were risky in both speed and scale, given that, before the Martin acquisition, he had never conducted a takeover before.

In 1985, Saunders launched a £330m bid for whisky distillers Arthur Bell. It was a logical choice but the bid was eight times bigger than Saunders had yet tried, and Bell's chairman, Raymond Miquel, was in no mood to accept. A well-publicised and hostile campaign for control of Bells was played out all that summer. It ended on 23 August when Guinness won a 70 per cent shareholding following an increase of the bid to £370m.

In the same way as Berry's successful acquisitions of Reliance, Brook Street Bureau and Hoggett Bowers led him into over-ambition with Manpower, so Saunders' triumph with Bells prompted him to turn his eye on United Distillers. In the "anything is possible" atmosphere that permeated the investment community at the start of 1986, Distillers was the prize catch for a branded drinks company, owning not only prime whisky brands such as Dewars, Johnnie Walker, Haig and Buchanans but also famous gins such as Booth's and Gordon's and cognacs such as Hine. It also had Cossack vodka and Pimms to its name.

What raised the stakes to dangerous levels was not only that proceedings were highly publicised – speculation about a Guinness bid for Distillers dominated the quality press throughout early January 1986 – but also that they were conducted in the teeth of a bitter counter-bid by James Gulliver, founder of the Argyll Group.

Saunders' opening bid, worth £2.2bn, had the support of the Distillers board, which saw the Argyll bid as hostile and unwanted. But Gulliver, who had long nursed ambitions to acquire the company, immediately launched a bidding war. A vicious battle ensued that involved the referral of Guinness's bid to the Monopolies Commission, not once but three times. There was a row over Distillers' agreement to pay Guinness's bid costs, which forced the Stock Exchange to bar arrangements where a company paid another's bid costs above 25 per cent of the profits, and a legal suit was initiated by Guinness for alleged injurious falsehood and defamation in Argyll Group's bid advertising.

In the end, supported by the cream of the City's establishment, Guinness won a majority of the Distillers shares and announced victory on 18 April. But in the process, both before and after the takeover, Saunders had illegally connived in a share-support scheme whereby wealthy investors were persuaded to purchase Guinness shares to keep the company's stock market value artificially high. This was contrary to Section 151 of the Companies Act 1985. There was also enormous share buying from overseas. Between them just two institutions, Schenley Industries and Bank Leu of Switzerland bought almost £200m of Guinness shares. A fifth of the company's entire share capital changed hands in a matter of weeks.

The share ramp only came fully to light when US corporate raider Ivan Boesky confessed in November 1986 to insider trading in the US. Investigations into his case by the American Security and Exchange Commission (SEC) uncovered the fact that Guinness had invested £69m into the Boesky fund. Press reporting of the subsequent DTI investigation revealed that a further £7.6m had been paid to the merchant bank Henry Ansbacher, prompting the resignation of its managing director Lord Spens early in the New Year.

Caught out: three Guinness share-rampers who paid the price. From left to right: Ernest Saunders, CEO, who was jailed; property-to-cars tycoon Gerald Ronson, also jailed, and philanthropist Jack Lyons, who escaped imprisonment but lost his knighthood

In the fall-out, two British tycoons – one of them the creator of the property-based Heron Group, Gerald Ronson – admitted they had received over £5m each from Guinness for help with the Distillers bid. And Sir Jack Lyons, a highly respected philanthropist, was found to have accepted £2m. Two members of Guinness's bankers, Morgan Grenfell, were sacked under pressure from both the Chancellor and the Bank of England. Saunders himself was fired from Guinness in January 1987 and indicted for fraud the following May. He was convicted in 1990 of false accounting, theft and conspiracy and sentenced to five years' imprisonment, but this was halved on appeal. In the event he was released from open prison after serving only 10 months because doctors said he was suffering from Alzheimer's disease, a degenerative condition. He subsequently made a remarkable recovery and has since pursued a career as a consultant while managing to negotiate a £75,000 annual pension from Guinness. In 1996, the European Court of Human Rights decided that his trial had been unfair because he had been compelled to answer DTI inspectors' questions.

Despite immediately repaying the money Guinness had paid him, Ronson was sent to open prison for six months. Lyons was spared prison on health grounds but suffered the bitter indignity of having his knighthood

removed – an extremely rare penalty. Lord Spens, the chief executive of merchant bankers Henry Ansbacher, who was forced to resign but cleared of fraud, always maintained that there was nothing wrong with the Guinness deal. He said in 1997: "Takeovers are not genteel affairs, as the inspectors would have it. They are very, very serious, life and death businesses."[12]

The Guinness and Blue Arrow scandals resurrected questions about boardroom probity that had been lying dormant since the Lonrho controversy of the early 1970s. In the US, a stream of notorious actions by over-dominant CEOs had been raising similar concerns among investors, such as the revelation that Occidental Petroleum had used some shareholder funds to endow an art museum in the outgoing chairman's name. Institutional investors in particular had built up resentment at the erosion of shareholder rights, particularly the introduction of "poison pills" – anti-takeover measures that made it financially impossible for an outsider to bid a reasonable price for a company. In 1984, a US court had ruled that these could be pushed through by management without consulting shareholders. Five years later, shareholders in Time and Warner were denied the chance to vote on the deal that put the two companies together, which was restructured from a stock-based merger to a debt-financed acquisition. Nor were they consulted on a higher bid from Paramount, which was rejected by Time for strategic reasons.[13]

In Britain, too, institutional investors were preparing to flex their muscles. They played an important part in the sackings of Ernest Saunders and Tony Berry, and – perhaps unfairly in the wake of the 1987 stock market crash – in the ousting of those at the head of poorly performing companies. George Davies of Next and Sir Ralph Halpern of Burton Group were among the high-profile chairmen and CEOs elbowed out. Halpern, whose flamboyant private life entered tabloid folklore when a former girlfriend testified to his "five-times-a-night" ability, had expanded Burton from an old-fashioned men's tailors into a high-stepping fashion group before vanquishing Mohamed Al Fayed's House of Fraser in 1985 in a bitter battle to take over Debenhams, the department store. But he paid the price for sliding share value.

Alliances of institutional shareholders and rebellious non-executives were becoming more powerful in levering out top managers with whom they were dissatisfied. James White's enforced departure at Bunzl, a manufacturing and distribution group whose share price had collapsed in the late 1980s, was engineered in a way that became familiar in the 1990s. One assertive non-executive at Bunzl sounded out an informal alliance of big investors, and White and two other senior directors had to go.

Robert Horton, who had successfully turned around BP's Standard Oil business in the US through a ruthless programme of cutbacks and sell-offs resembling those of Welch at GE, ran into savage resistance when he tried a similar approach as chief executive in London and he, too, was forced out by an alliance of unhappy non-executives and institutional investors. Horton, once memorably described by a female management consultant as looking "like a man who opens doors with his chest", proved far too pugnacious

for the board of one of Britain's industrial icons. His later successor as CEO, John (now Lord) Browne, was just as focused and steely, but in the accepted British style disguised it under an urbane, cerebral manner. Browne remains Britain's most admired CEO year on year.

The way boards had operated for decades in Britain was about to change dramatically as the 1990s opened with corporate governance high on the agenda and the Cadbury Committee preparing the report that would damn the combined chairman/CEO role and stress the desirability of having independent directors. In 1981, an unnamed director of a public company described the methods by which his board reached agreement as "a sort of dinner party at which issues are discussed in a gentlemanly fashion and a consensus emerges". The opinion of each director was only canvassed for major decisions; minor ones were thrown open to general comment, and agreement was determined by "a murmur of assent" round the table.

In practice, it was often easier to obtain "a murmur of assent" to something involving £10m than a purchase involving £1,000, said one non-executive, explaining that it came down to how familiar people were with the object of the expense. "Everyone has got an idea of the colour of the bicycle shed, but whether this type of plant is better than that type of plant, they are a lot less ready to comment on." Non-executives often felt that minority dissensions tended to be muffled for the sake of consensus. "I don't think we have ever actually said: 'I really don't think this should happen, and I want that recorded in the minutes'," said one.[14]

Such pliant acquiescence might have been expected to become less common in the last decade of the 20th century, but in practice dominating chief executives would still prove able to pursue disastrous policies without any effective challenge from the board, as the shareholders of Marconi – to name the worst case – would discover at ruinous cost.

masters of the universe?

66 I think everyone agrees... that the Internet will change everything. But we will not agree when it will change each individual business. Act on it too early and your market will not be ready. Act on it too late and your competitors may have stolen a march on you. 99

Dr. Andy Grove, chief executive and president, Intel Corp, addressing London Business School in 1997

9

Poster people: Martha Lane Fox and Brent Hoberman became media stars when they launched lastminute.com, an online booking agency, in 1998. After a rocky ride, it survived the dotcom crash and went into profit in 2003

B usiness in the final decade of the 20th century was dominated by two revolutionary themes that went hand in hand: globalisation – unleashed in dramatic fashion by the breaking down of the Berlin Wall in 1989 and the accompanying collapse of European communism – and the conquest of time and space embodied in the internet.

So swift and heady was the wealth generated by Web-based businesses in the second half of the 1990s, and so intoxicating the business plans written more in blind faith than on hard facts, that parallels with the South Sea Bubble and Dutch tulip mania should have been obvious. But no-one seemed to remember their school history lessons: the stock prices of the "dotcoms" soared; Wall Street analysts fed the frenzy; e-business entrepreneurs became overnight multi-millionaires. It looked as though the bull market would run for ever, just as in the overheated summer of 1929. The collapse in value of the technology sector a year or so later due to massive over-capacity and the revelations of corporate wrongdoing in Enron and WorldCom, two icons of internet business, topped by the catastrophic terrorist attacks of September 11, 2001, led to a sustained plunge in global markets ominously reminiscent of 70 years earlier.

But all this lay in the future as the 1990s opened, with the exception of some early-warning signals that more curbs were needed on over-dominant CEOs, and the first signs of shareholders becoming more willing to take action. Concern in Britain about boardroom probity had largely subsided since the Guinness and Blue Arrow affairs of the 1980s and the earlier controversy at Lonrho, when Prime Minister Edward Heath had called Tiny Rowland's conduct

Eastern promise: breaking down the Berlin Wall in 1989 opened up eastern Europe for business

of the company "the unacceptable face of capitalism". Institutional investors, however, were becoming more unforgiving of poor performance during the 1980s. By the end of 1990 a string of chairmen and chief executives had walked the plank as a result of the institutions taking action in alliance with independent directors.

The idea of non-executives as pro-active guardians of shareholder interests was first aired in a paper from the Association of British Insurers in 1990 and given shape in an ISC report in 1991 called "The Role and Duties of Directors: a Statement of Best Practice". The central message of both publications – support for the unitary board but with a strengthened role for non-executives, especially in determining CEO compensation, and a recommendation against combining the posts of chairman and chief executive – became the basis of the first great report on corporate governance in the 1990s, from the committee headed by Sir Adrian Cadbury, former chairman of Cadbury Schweppes.

The Cadbury Code, as it came to be known, suggested voluntary guidelines for good governance. These included separation of the chairman/CEO roles, the appointment of at least three independent directors by the whole board, a three-year limit to executive contracts and a remuneration committee with a majority of NEDs. It was greeted with a good deal of scepticism: some eminent chairmen such as Sir Owen Green of industrial conglomerate BTR never believed in non-executives anyway, and take-up of the guidelines was slow. But Cadbury had the backing of the institutions and gradually the City and Stock Exchange adopted it as a benchmark of good boardroom practice.

Boardroom education, another major step forward in governance, was pioneered in the 1990s by the Institute of Directors, which also introduced the first professional qualification, the chartered director. This marked a significant break with the old-boy-network approach that had characterised British board appointments for decades, and other cultural changes would gradually bring more diversity and balance in the boardroom – of nationality, functional skills and gender.

Cadbury, which had concentrated on the financial aspects of governance, was followed by two other major inquiries into best boardroom practice, chaired by Sir Richard Greenbury of Marks and Spencer (himself a famously autocratic chairman) and Sir Ronald Hampel of ICI. Cadbury-inspired trust structures, based on separated chairman and CEO roles with externally nominated non-executives, were also adopted by public-sector governing bodies in hospitals, police authorities and education boards.

Meanwhile, new horizons of opportunity were opening up for business as the demolition of the Berlin Wall and the end of the Soviet Union and its satellites literally and symbolically broke down geographic barriers that had divided Europe since the Second World War. Even China, the last major communist nation, would move closer to a market economy in the 1990s, inviting closer trading links with the West and a flood of inward investment as colonial Hong Kong, the epitome of capitalist success in South-east Asia, prepared to revert to Chinese rule in 1997.

Hong Kong handover: China claims its capitalist prize from Britain

Needless to say, however, it was not British companies that leapt immediately into action in Eastern Europe to scoop up bargain acquisitions and gain a low-cost manufacturing springboard in the region, but General Electric of the US and Asea Brown Boveri, the Swedish-Swiss engineering combine put together in 1988 by Percy Barnevik, Sweden's answer to the dynamic Jack Welch of GE.

ABB realised as soon as the Wall came down that infrastructure and industry in the former Warsaw Pact countries offered major long-term opportunities for the group's power plants, electrical switching systems, locomotive manufacture and robotics – both in terms of filling domestic needs and furnishing low-cost manufacturing

Cadbury's code: Sir Adrian Cadbury gave his name to the first UK corporate governance recommendations

capabilities. It established a bridgehead in eastern Europe as early as 1989 and by 1996 could boast nearly 80 companies in some 20 east European states including the Ukraine.

It also poured hundreds of millions of dollars into knowledge transfer and education to develop local management talent, setting up three in-house business schools offering mini-MBA courses tailored to local needs in Warsaw, Brno in the Czech Republic and Moscow. Where other companies, including GE, went initially for Hungary with its high skills base and emigré connections (including investment wizard George Soros), ABB sized up the demographics and realised that Poland offered better potential with its 38 million people (to Hungary's 10 million), its deep-rooted Catholic culture and the fact that many of its leaders had studied in the West.[1]

And where were the British while ABB's multicultural managers were making inroads in the east? While a few companies such as Cadbury Schweppes and Pilkington got going early, in general Britain's entry into Eastern Europe was patchy, poorly co-ordinated and late. At the start of 1995, UK direct investment in the more developed countries of Hungary, Poland, the Czech Republic and Slovakia totalled only $575m, a negligible sum in comparison with investment not only from Germany and the US but also with that from Austrian, French, Dutch, Belgian and Italian industries. But it should be pointed out that two of the UK's biggest multinationals active in these markets, Unilever and Shell, skewed the figures because they were classified as Dutch companies.

Paul Reynolds of the Adam Smith Institute, a London-based think tank, was scathing at the time about "slothful" British companies, observing sardonically: "The Germans are there, the Americans are there – and there is usually some British trade mission with a bunch of bow-tied idiots getting drunk." Andrew Warren, an executive partner with consultants Coopers and Lybrand, commented in 1995 that Eastern

Europe was "talking to everyone but British companies". He added: "Medium-sized companies are very ignorant compared to their European counterparts. I am amazed how little they know and how forbidding they find it."[2]

Two areas in which British companies did make an early splash were branded food and drink products and retailing. Cadbury Schweppes sent its regional development director Matthew Cadbury to Eastern Europe in 1993 and decided to invest £20m in setting up a greenfield chocolate factory in Wroclaw in Poland. In 1994, after selling 280 million chocolate bars within Russia, the group committed a further £75m to establish a production plant near St. Petersburg. The company benefited from lower labour costs than in the UK and cheaper basic ingredients (in the Ukraine, sugar cost less than half the UK price) and managed to overcome what Matthew Cadbury described in 1995 as "an unbelievable amount of bureaucratic confusion". He added: "I can safely say that we haven't paid any bribes to anyone in Poland and in spite of that we have built a factory from scratch in a year when people in Poland told us we were insane and it would take at least three."[3]

The initial involvement of the supermarket group Tesco – typical of that of many companies in the early days – was through acquisition. In June 1994, it acquired for £15m a 57 per cent stake in the 43 stores operated by the Hungarian chain, Global. Tesco claimed that the profitability of the Hungarian stores leapt 40 per cent in less than two years following the deal, even before introducing check-out scanning and computer-controlled distribution. The investment was the start of one of the most successful expansions into Eastern Europe by a UK company. Tesco now has 53 stores under its own banner in Hungary, 66 in Poland (13 acquired from the local HIT chain), 17 in the Czech Republic and 66 in Poland. It is also the second biggest private employer of staff in Hungary, with 11,000 people working across all its operations.

Globalisation, married to technology, would spread much wider during the rest of the 1990s and into the new millennium, with more UK companies, especially manufacturing firms, setting up lower-cost production facilities in eastern Europe and South-east Asia. Recently, such quintessentially British brands as Hornby model trains and Wedgwood pottery have transferred manufacturing processes to China. There has also been rapid growth in the number of back-office functions and call centres in the Indian sub-continent as British and US financial institutions outsource to lower-cost regions – training local employees to speak in the idiom a caller would expect in Walsall or Westminster. This has obvious implications for white-collar workers back home: it has been estimated that 200,000 call-centre and similar service-sector jobs could migrate out of Britain in the next five years.[4] In 2003, western firms' outsourcing of IT and other business processes to India accounted for a quarter of the subcontinent's total revenues of £5.7bn from software and services.

Jan Leschly, CEO of SmithKline Beecham: the merger with Glaxo made it the world's biggest pharmaceutical group

THE CHANGING CENTURY

A snapshot of Britain:

1990: Britons took to the streets to demonstrate against the Community Charge, which replaced the household rates. The charge was levied on every member of a household eligible to vote – hence its common name, poll tax. According to surveys, three-quarters of the country thought it unfair. Police were called into town halls from Newcastle to Plymouth. Effigies of prime minister Thatcher were burned outside council offices. In the Commons, for the first time in 30 years, the sitting was adjourned because of grave disorder

1990: France joined Austria, West Germany and the Soviet Union in banning beef imports from Britain – this was the beginning of the bovine spongiform encephalopathy (BSE) controversy

1990: Britain applied to join the ERM, but the Cabinet remained divided on Europe. Geoffrey Howe, the former foreign secretary, who was now deputy prime minister, wanted to take part in talks towards a single currency, to which Thatcher was opposed. Howe eventually resigned, giving a speech to the House in which he spoke of a conflict of loyalties – loyalty to his prime minister and

loyalty to the party and the country. A leadership battle was now on

1990: On Wednesday, 28 November, Margaret Thatcher resigned. Her only crumb of comfort was that her successor was not, as had been predicted, her arch-rival Michael Heseltine, but "her man", John Major

1991: The new prime minister abandoned the poll tax

1991: At a meeting in Maastricht in the Netherlands, Major won the right to avoid implementing the social chapter and an agreement that Britain would not have to sign up for the single currency on January 1, 1999

1991: Desert Storm broke out. The UN passed a resolution allowing the Iraqis to be ejected in Kuwait (invaded in August 1990) and American and British troops went in. This was the first Gulf War

1992: The former chorus girl Betty Boothroyd became the first female speaker of the House of Commons

1992: The April election returned the Conservatives to power – albeit with a reduced majority. For Labour, the result marked a watershed; the party now knew that in order to win an election it need to embrace Tory reforms. Neil Kinnock resigned, to be succeeded by shadow chancellor John Smith

The rapid globalising of industry has also manifested itself in international merger and takeover activity, with French companies moving into the British privatised utilities market, UK food and drink companies taking over US businesses and major players in global sectors such as pharmaceuticals consolidating through mergers. Within just a few years in the early 1990s, Britain's venerable Beecham company, famed for Beecham's pills and powders, and America's Smith Kline merged; then that combined company merged again with Glaxo Wellcome, itself a merger of two old-established UK firms founded on baby food and medical research. Glaxo SmithKline (GSK) is now the largest pharmaceuticals group in the world, but the historic Beecham and Wellcome names have disappeared and the group's head office is now in the US, not London.

Today, the names of many FTSE companies reflect a revolution in global ownership. Reckitt Benckiser is a good example. Known from 1938 to 1999 as Reckitt and Colman, originally two 19th-century family companies founded respectively on laundry products and English mustard, the business had used acquisitions to gain a firm foothold in the huge US household cleaning market but had fallen victim in the 1990s to profit warnings and downgradings. In 1999, after a restructuring in which the Colman's Mustard brand was sold off to Unilever, it merged with the German industrial chemicals company Benckiser, which had relocated to the Netherlands and was listed in Amsterdam. Reckitt Benckiser, headquartered in Slough, is now the world's biggest maker of household cleaners and boasts a healthy profit stream.

Inextricably entwined with globalisation and the fall of communism, and certainly hastening both those processes, was the rise of the internet in everyday use and the floodgates of information it opened through the World Wide Web, which was pioneered as a "pro bono" public service by the brilliant British electronics engineer Tim Berners-Lee. Businesses that were nervously toying with the notion of getting "wired

1992: The crime statistics showed that in England, Wales and Scotland there were some six million crimes known to the police. Ten years earlier, there had been only half that number

1992: The prime minister told the Commons that the Prince and Princess of Wales were to separate. Prince Charles was the third of the Queen's four children to announce that his marriage had failed

1992: Unemployment was 2.6 million and rising. Privatisation of nationalised industries meant job cuts; when, for example, the Central Electricity Generating board was privatised and restructured as National Power, one third of the 17,000-strong workforce expected to be made redundant

1992: Peter Brooke, the national heritage secretary, proposed an exhibition to mark the end of the century: the ill-fated Millennium Dome project was conceived

1992: The number of people who had been killed since the Northern Ireland troubles began in 1969 passed the 3,000 mark. The Anglo-Irish (or Hillsborough) Agreement of 1985 had, it seemed, achieved little. Unionists had called for a general strike throughout the province in 1986 and boycotted the new Northern Ireland Assembly, set up by James Prior in 1982. Now the IRA began a new campaign, bombing the City of London

1992: David Owen, the former British foreign secretary, and Cyrus Vance, the former US secretary of state put forward a peace plan for what was now known as the former Yugoslavia. The Vance-Owen plan, which envisaged 10 provinces, each with a high degree of autonomy, and recommended the eventual demilitarisation of the country, was ultimately rejected by Radovan Karadzic and the Serbs

1992: Britain withdrew from the Exchange Rate Mechanism after a wave of buying and selling by currency speculators

1993: Unemployment was back to its mid-1980s level of three million. Nonetheless, there were shoots of recovery: withdrawal from the ERM had boosted exports and inflation was down to 1.3 per cent, the lowest for 30 years

1993: Britain ratified the Maastricht Treaty, a step further towards closer European political and financial union and a step further away from Cabinet unity

1993: The first British soldier was killed in Bosnia, shot by a sniper in Gonji Vkuf

British brain behind the World Wide Web: Tim Berners-Lee

up" at the start of the decade were soon aware that the electronic revolution could leave them seriously stranded, if not defunct, unless they joined it whole-heartedly. It was not only a matter of better, quicker tools for financial control, sourcing of supplies and closer relationships with customers, but of whole new business models "online".

Tesco, the ever-innovative supermarket chain once associated with "pile it high, sell it cheap" trading, took the market lead here, as it had in globalisation. Its online trading model, using existing stores for sourcing orders rather than purpose-built warehouses in some remote industrial site, avoided the mistakes of cost and over-expansion that brought down one ambitious US venture in the online grocery sector, WebVan, and streaked ahead of the faltering early efforts of its UK rivals.

But of all the products associated with the electronics and telecommunications revolution of the 1990s, it was the mobile phone that most transformed the way people lived, establishing massive new aspirational markets beyond mere telephony and spawning shoals of entrepreneurial new businesses. Rarely has a product developed so swiftly and visibly, from the heavy brick-like objects with long aerials seen in the 1988 film Wall Street (whose owners could only make them work by taking them into the open air) to the tiny fashion objects that were being carried in everyone's handbag or shirt pocket by the millennium.

THE CHANGING CENTURY

A snapshot of Britain:

1993: Two children were killed when an IRA bomb went off in Warrington; the following month a bigger bomb went off in the City. In the province, there were renewed IRA attacks. Pressure was on the government to negotiate – no matter how unpalatable the idea. Just before Christmas, John Major and the Taoiseach Albert Reynolds made the Downing Street Declaration: they would invite Sinn Fein to take part in talks about the future of Ulster provided it renounced violence. The IRA gave its response by planting a bomb in Londonderry

1994: John Smith died of a heart attack; Tony Blair became Labour leader

1995: John Major, feeling the split in the Cabinet was making his position untenable, resigned as leader of the Conservative party, inviting others to put their hats into the ring. The Euro-sceptic John Redwood rose to the challenge – but was defeated in the ensuing leadership contest

1995: At a special conference at the Central Hall in Westminster, 65 per cent of the Labour party voted to abolish Clause Four

1995: Major and the Taoiseach John Bruton announced that they would start talks involving all the political groups in Northern Ireland, including Sinn Fein. Meanwhile, an international commission would try to resolve the disarmament question. The US senator George Mitchell was seconded as the commission's chairman. (He had a tough task ahead: just a few weeks later, the IRA broke the cease-fire, killing four men)

1996: The European Commission imposed a worldwide ban on British beef exports as the government admitted there was a possible link between BSE and Creutzfeldt-Jakob Disease (CJD), widely known as mad cow disease. The EC's line did not soften for two years

1996: In February, the IRA exploded a bomb in London's Docklands. A few months later, they injured hundreds of people in the centre of Manchester

1997: Tony Blair's re-invention of the Labour party paid off at the polls. After an 18-year-gap, Labour were back in power – and back decidedly, winning 419 seats against the Conservatives' 165. It was the worst Tory result since 1832. John Major resigned, to be succeeded by William Hague

1997: Hong Kong, Britain's under lease since 1842, was handed back to China. It remains a semi-autonomous province, able to carry on more or less "business as usual"

1997: The Princess of Wales and her friend Dodi Fayed, son of the owner

Within three years in the middle of the decade, leaps in mobile technology not only enabled this miniaturisation but stretched standby time from a few hours to several days. Signal reception improved as base stations multiplied around the country, and a steady decline in the cost of integrated circuits reduced the price of a top-of-the-range phone to less than a quarter of the £800 it had cost at the start of the 1990s.

In 2003, a firm called Vertu, which described itself as "the first luxury communications company", launched the concept of the mobile phone as jewellery. The handset had a sapphire crystal screen and ruby bearings and was offered in stainless steel, gold or platinum at prices ranging from $4,900 to $19,450. It quickly became a must-have accessory for Hollywood actresses and pop stars. Gwyneth Paltrow was the first customer; Madonna and Mariah Carey followed; Jennifer Lopez was reputed to own three.

In the UK, the four main network operators were: Cellnet, a joint venture between BT and Securicor; Vodafone, floated off from its parent Racal in 1991; Mercury One-2-One, a joint venture between Cable and Wireless and US West; and Orange, an offshoot of the Hong Kong-based Hutchison Whampoa, which in the second half of the decade increasingly challenged Vodafone as UK market leader. The catalyst for the explosion in competition was pre-payment, which allowed people to buy telephone time off the shelf in the same way that they bought sweets or magazines. Under managing director Hans Snook in the late 1990s, Orange invested nearly £1bn in covering its geographic base with 6,000 stations in less than three years, 50 per cent more than Vodafone at the time.

By the end of the 1990s, however, Orange was still only third in the British market, with a 22 per cent share. Although it was the fastest-growing UK mobile company,

of Harrods, were killed in a Paris car crash. The 36-year-old princess was arguably the most famous, most photographed woman in the world. Her death and public reaction to it was one of the most analysed events of the year: why, it was asked, were millions of people in Britain and the rest of the world mourning a woman they had never met?

1997: Scotland and Wales voted for devolution in referenda held in September. Scotland got a parliament; Wales an assembly

1998: The Good Friday Agreement was signed. For the first time, Unionists and Republicans had come together to try to find a way out of the "troubles". There was to be a

new, elected power-sharing Northern Ireland assembly and, crucially, institutions that would link Northern Ireland and Eire. In addition, promises were made to release Republican and nationalist prisoners, to examine ways of reforming the Royal Ulster Constabulary and to begin the process of decommissioning weapons. The agreement was endorsed by a referendum in the province but appeared precarious: by the end of the year, the first promise had been fulfilled, the last had not

1998: The government published the Strategic Defence Review, which restructured Britain's armed forces. The review made clear that the end of the cold war did not mean the end of the nuclear threat. Britain

kept its nuclear forces, aware that in addition to the US, Britain, Russia, France and China at least 10 other states either had or were developing nuclear weapons. Its policy seemed completely vindicated by events in May: India exploded five nuclear warheads in a test programme; Pakistan responded by exploding five more

1999: In November, the Northern Ireland Assembly at last began operating under Ulster Unionist leader David Trimble. Failure to resolve completely the issue of decommissioning, however, led to its suspension a few months later. It was reconvened when the Provisionals indicated they would put their weapons beyond use. It

was not until October 2001, however, that they announced they had begun the process of disposing of their arms. In the meantime, Trimble had resigned over the arms issue; he was re-elected in November 2001

2000: For the first time, Londoners voted to elect a mayor. Their choice, Ken Livingstone, exasperated the government, which had backed another candidate, Frank Dobson. Livingstone, known as Red Ken, had headed the left-wing Greater London Council, abolished by Thatcher in 1986

Sources: Christopher Lee: This Sceptred Isle, Twentieth Century, BBC and Penguin Books, 1999; Patrick Robertson: The New Shell Book of Firsts, 1994, Headline Book Publishing; Guardian Unlimited; BBCi

Dealmaker extraordinary: Chris Gent (left) built Vodafone by acquisition into a world-beater

its future was caught up in a frenetic round of mergers within the European industry. In October 1999, Germany's Mannesmann group bought Orange for £19.8bn. Vodafone remained top of the league with over a third of the market, its prestige augmented by the takeover of AirTouch Communications of San Francisco. Vodafone AirTouch could then boast nearly 28 million customers worldwide: it now has 120 million.

After a £175bn hostile takeover of the Mannesmann group in 2000, Vodafone became one of the biggest companies in Europe by market value. The company's CEO, Chris Gent, was knighted the following year. His record £10m bonus for the Mannesmann deal sparked a furious shareholder debate over executive packages that has yet to subside, but when he stepped down as Vodafone CEO in the summer of 2003, his chairman Lord MacLaurin, the former head of Tesco, said he would "go down as one of the most influential business leaders of the past decade".

In a fascinating reprise of the famous 1940s prediction by IBM founder Thomas J. Watson Sr that the world market for computers would be about six, the US telecommunications giant AT&T had asked McKinsey in the early 1980s to estimate the number of cell phones that would be in use globally by 2000. The consultancy noted all the problems with the new devices – weight, short battery life, spotty coverage, high cost and so on – and concluded that it would be around 900,000. The actual figures zoomed from 500,000 in 1990 to 20 million by the end of the decade.

Mobile phones as a business created many millionaires in the Sunday Times annual "Rich List", notably Charles Dunstone of Carphone Warehouse. Dunstone is a classic example of the entrepreneur who saw the future and made it work. He opened his first mobile phone shop on London's Marylebone Road in 1989, when he was in his mid-twenties. There were then only two mobile operators in Britain and the brick-like phones themselves were still restricted by cost and weight to a few business users. Dunstone and his partner caught the wave of the mobile revolution as it happened, and it made him a fortune of £200m. By 2003, the group had 1,100 shops, half of them outside Britain, and the chubby, shirtsleeved Dunstone, still only 38, was eyeing up the Goliath of BT, preparing an assault on the residential telephone market. Other independent telecoms operators, including the ubiquitous Tesco, were joining in the preliminary skirmishes.

Multi-millions from mobiles: Charles Dunstone of the Carphone Warehouse

Not very mobile: early cell-phones were heavy, erratic and expensive, but business loved them

While mobile phones became a stable platform from which to launch substantial businesses, the dotcom frenzy of the late 1990s generated paper millions overnight for the founders of companies that never made any profit in their short lives. A madness seemed to overtake venture capital providers and ordinary investors in the last two years of the decade. They heard only what they wanted to hear about the promise of the internet, and transferred this unquestioningly to business plans that, Enron-like, were built on the illusions of notional future revenue.

In 1997, Andy Grove, the chairman of microchip giant Intel, told a lecture audience at London Business School that in five years' time all companies would be internet companies, "or they won't be companies at all". Few absorbed the caveat that he made in the same lecture: "I think that everyone agrees theoretically that the internet will change everything. But we will not agree when it will change each individual business. Act on it too early and your market will not be ready for what you have to offer. Act on it too late and your competitors may have stolen a march on you."

Whether or not bad timing was the reason, many dotcoms collapsed well before the whole sector imploded in 2001. Most of the over-hyped start-ups of the late 1990s were still losing money after a year in business. A league table of 20 UK e-commerce companies drawn up by the management consultancy Bain and Co. for Management Today in November 1999 was re-assessed a year later. A staggering 85 per cent had made no profit at all. The compilers of the survey commented: "The burn-rate at the bigger enterprises, such as boo.com, is millions each week, but this no longer raises eyebrows. Not making any money is now an accepted way of life in e-commerce."[5]

High in this anorexic list were two of Britain's most publicised e-companies: lastminute.com, a late-booking travel and entertainment specialist, and boo.com, a trendy online sportswear retailer. Both were darlings of the business press and attracted massive investment – in boo's case, £74m was pumped in from the likes of Benetton, the Italian fashion company, J P Morgan and Bain Capital, while lastminute's IPO raised £125m in a share issue that proved completely unrelated to the company's assets or performance at that time.

The youth and photogenic qualities of their founders undoubtedly helped to provoke public interest. Boo.com, one of the most talked-about start-ups of 1999, was founded by two young Swedes called Ernst Malmsten and Kajsa Leander, who had successfully sold a previous internet venture. Boo's offices were in Carnaby Street, one-time heart of the "Swinging Sixties" London fashion scene, and its mission was to sell trendy sports and designer wear online in 18 countries, with exciting innovations such as virtual changing rooms and 3D images. Even before launch, the hype surrounding the pair (who made the cover of Fortune magazine) valued the company at an astounding $390m. But within a year, plagued by technical glitches and difficulties with the website that drove customers away, boo.com was haemorrhaging money. When the market for internet stocks dived in April 2000, the company was doomed, and in less than a month it had collapsed.

Lastminute.com's founders were even more of a PR dream: Martha Lane Fox, a glamorous blonde from a wealthy family that had made its fortune as upmarket estate agents, and the clean-cut South African Brent Hoberman, a management consultant who came up with the idea for the business. The pair met while working for the same PR company in London, though Lane Fox was in fact Hoberman's second choice as partner. They launched the company in 1998 and as well as proving a magnet for investors' cash a year later, it attracted non-executives of the calibre of Allan Leighton, former chief executive of Asda and one of the corporate stars of the decade.

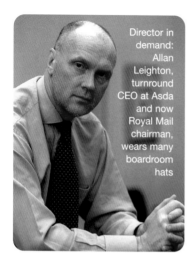

Director in demand: Allan Leighton, turnround CEO at Asda and now Royal Mail chairman, wears many boardroom hats

Like boo.com, lastminute also launched on a frenzied wave of hype and investors' money, but again technical problems constantly aggravated customers trying to book tickets for pop concerts or a discounted business-class trip to Sao Paulo. At times, as the technology crash sent other internet companies into oblivion, it looked as though Lane Fox and Hoberman would join those other paper tycoons worth hundreds of millions one day and nothing the next. But the business survived and in 2003 at last looked like making a modest profit.

The overriding lesson of the dotcom disasters – shared in spades by US companies at the heart of the internet boom in Silicon Valley – was that the basic rules of management, from sound business plan to rigorous budgeting and flexible strategy, do not change just because of some cool technological wizardry.

The lack of reality checks in the minds of the dotcommers was partly due to the breakneck speed with which e-mail and internet use established itself in the late 1990s. A survey of 400 managers, directors and chief executives carried out by BT in conjunction with Management Today in November 1998 found that use of e-mail among the respondents had risen from virtually zero five years earlier to a staggering 98 per cent. Nine out of 10 now also regularly accessed the Web. At the same time, however, companies revealed a curious blind spot about their own corporate sites. Few felt they were reaping tangible rewards. Most confined themselves to using the new medium for electronic versions of their existing marketing literature.

The jury is still out on whether many online companies are using the technology to transform the business proposition they offer customers, or merely refine it round the edges.

There is also doubt as to how far aspiring e-businesses realise that customer expectations themselves are being changed by the internet. In an interview in 2000, Eric Salama, group strategy director of the marketing services network WPP, discussed customer service in the context of the technological revolution. Ten years ago, he said most people seeking a financial product such as a mortgage would insist on seeing a representative of the provider face to face. "Now, a growing number of people don't feel this need. They will use the Net to shop around to find the best supplier offering the most advantageous rate.

"Nevertheless, most people still want a human being to speak to at the end of a phone before they make the deal, and this is likely to remain the case for some time. This is why banks like First Direct, whose transactions are based on phone contact, are still rated more highly in terms of customer service than banks where transactions are conducted entirely online. The information… could be provided through the computer but it is a comfort factor to speak to someone."[6]

Meanwhile, the "old" or "legacy" economy marched on. A big new industrial star of the decade was a traditional old-style inventor who had struggled for years to get his ideas accepted and finally broke through to millionaire-dom – James Dyson. It was a piquant irony that 1993, when Dyson launched his revolutionary bagless vacuum cleaner based on dual-cyclone technology, was also the year that Hoover launched possibly the most disastrous sales promotion in history – offering free flights to the US with each cleaner sold, but then retracting the offer when hundreds of thousands of customers claimed tickets. Two years later, Dyson's cleaner overtook sales of the leading Hoover model.

Today, the Dyson brand not only dominates the market but is starting to replace "Hoover" as a synonym for vacuum cleaner. In some ways, this is poetic justice. Hoover and leading competitor Electrolux were both offered Dyson's technology and both rejected it. Electrolux disapproved of the one aspect of the dual cyclone technology that broke with the past – the fact that the cleaner required no bag. The need to buy bags was something Dyson's competitors relied on to generate after-sales profits. Both Hoover and Electrolux tried to kill the technology at birth, despite (or more probably because of) the fact that the dual cyclone represented the greatest leap forward since electric-powered suction did away with the need for manual bellows.

The experience embittered Dyson. His autobiography Against All Odds, published in 1997, is notable for naming the people who stood in his way, executives who tried to rip him off, friends and even family who failed to have faith. He embodies all the contradictions of the British inventor turned commercial success; brilliantly good at business but hating its values, a champion of new technology and philosophy grounded in old-fashioned loyalty and integrity. His insistence on total control over all aspects of his company – no mergers, no redundancies, no smoking, no fry-ups in the canteen, no suits and ties, staff encouraged to cycle rather than drive to work – inspires admiration in some, accusations of crankiness in

Household name: James Dyson with ground-breaking bagless vacuum cleaner and latest washing machine

others. But even Dyson has recently had to bow to global economic forces, flout traditional concepts of local loyalty and move his manufacturing out of Britain to the Far East.

More entrepreneurial dynamism was injected into old-economy Britain in the 1990s from sources in the old empire. The image of Indian business as the open-all-hours, cash-and-carry corner shop run by Mr Patel was dispelled completely as Asian entrepreneurs took centre stage in the mid-decade boom. In the Sunday Times "Rich List" of 1996 two of Britain's 11 billionaires were Indian. The long list of millionaires included: Nat Puri, a Punjabi maths graduate who arrived in Britain in the 1960s to work in the engineering industry and whose wholly-owned Melton Medes Group in the east Midlands boasted assets of £126m; Raj Bagri, who ran the London Metals Exchange and whose MinMetco trading company, recently handed over to his son Apury, was worth £65m; and Ramrikrishnan Hinduja, a scion of the UK Asian oil-to-trucks trading conglomerate worth £1bn.

British Asian entrepreneurs today span all sectors and generations. Bombay-born Gulam Khaderboy Noon arrived in Britain in 1971 and, horrified at the poor quality of ready-made Indian food in the supermarkets, launched his own chilled-food company, Noon Products. Combining authentic recipes and preparation with modern mass-manufacturing

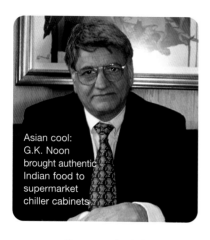

Asian cool: G.K. Noon brought authentic Indian food to supermarket chiller cabinets

methods, his products won own-brand contracts to supply Sainsbury and Waitrose as well as selling under the Noon label. By the end of the decade, Noon had a business turning over £50m a year.

"My hopes are pinned on the second generation," he commented in 1997. "They see themselves as British by birth and European in their culture." He might have been referring to Shami Ahmed, managing director of The Legendary Joe

Bloggs jeans company, founded when Ahmed was only 24. Ahmed's personality-led approach to brand leadership transformed his business into one of the UK's leading providers of smart-but-casual clothes. "People need to know what we are doing," he says. "Market demand is led by what you are as well as what you offer."

The billionaire Hinduja brothers were later tarnished by suspicions that their applications for British passports were expedited because of their donations to the Labour party, and by an acrimonious court case in India over their business dealings there. In contrast, Lord Paul, founder of the substantial Caparo engineering group and another 1960s immigrant, remained a pillar of New Labour – despite eloquently criticising the Blair government's laissez-faire attitude to the plight of British manufacturing.

THE CHANGING CENTURY

Facts from the business archives:

1990: Robert Maxwell launched the first pan-European newspaper, The European. (Publication ceased in 1998)

1990: Sony introduced Digital Audio Tape (DAT) recorders to the UK domestic market; DAT was another leap forward in sound quality

1991/1992: Three executives in the machine tool company Matrix Churchill stood trial for breaching government guidelines on the sale of arms-related equipment to Iraq (see box on sleaze)

1991: The tycoon Robert Maxwell died in mysterious circumstances; a month later it was revealed he had plundered £350m from the Mirror

Group Newspapers pension fund and left business debts totalling £1bn

1991: At the IoD convention, Gerald Ratner, head of the high-street jewellers, made a now legendary gaffe, describing one of his products as "total crap" – and another as "cheaper than a prawn sandwich". The speech wiped an estimated £500m off the value of the company and was Ratner's personal downfall: he left the company the next year. In 2002, however, he was back with a plan for an online business

1991: The supermarkets Tesco, Sainsbury's, Asda, Safeway and Gateway started to open on Sundays

1992: Cliff Stanford founded the internet services provider Demon, one of the first companies to offer affordable internet connectivity to UK users. Demon was set up for

£30,000; six years later, it was sold to Scottish Telecom (now known as Thus) in a deal worth £66m. It remains one of the biggest ISPs in the country

1992: Classic FM, the first national commercial radio station based in mainland Britain, hit the airwaves

1992: Ciba-Geigy Pharmaceuticals offered new hope to British tobacco addicts, introducing Nicotinell, the first nicotine patch in the UK

1993: BSkyB launched QVC, Britain's first home-shopping satellite TV channel

1993: Amstrad unveiled the PenPad, the world's first Personal Digital Assistant. It was able to convert handwritten notes into typescript

1994: In America, Jeff Bezos founded a book store with a

difference – the online-only retailer Amazon. By the end of the decade, it had become one of the biggest names in the world in e-commerce

1994: The Electronic Telegraph made its debut – the first national newspaper on the internet

1994: The National Lottery was launched under the auspices of the Camelot consortium. Under the deal, about 50 per cent of the proceeds went on prizes, 23 per cent went to good causes and 12 per cent in tax; Camelot got the balance

1994: The multi-millionaire financier Sir James Goldsmith founded the Referendum Party to campaign against closer economic and political union with Europe. He fielded 534 parliamentary candidates for the 1997 election and put £20m behind their campaign. (The move was

In transport services, the deregulations of the 1980s in aviation and long-distance bus and coach routes had produced two outstanding entrepreneurs, Michael Bishop and Brian Souter. Both expanded their operations hugely in the 1990s and continue to do so, their horizons seemingly limitless. Bishop had been obsessed by aviation since childhood and by the age of 21 had set up his own aircraft handling business for a local Manchester airline. When that was taken over by British Midlands Airways, a small company operating out of East Midlands Airport, he joined the new outfit and ended up running it by 1972, still aged only 30.

Priority No. 1 for a small airline is: where do we get the planes? The management buy-out of BM that Bishop led in 1978 was enabled by his discovery of an enormously rich dentist in California who had invested his wealth in

Low profile, high flier: the self-effacing
Sir Michael Bishop of BMI

opposed by fellow Euro-sceptic businessman Paul Sykes, who urged Goldsmith to withdraw his candidates in constituencies where a Conservative who opposed the single currency was standing.)

1995: London's oldest merchant bank Barings was brought down by the activities of "rogue trader" Nick Leeson, who single-handedly lost £17bn on the Japanese futures market. A court in Singapore subsequently jailed him for fraud

1995: More than 4,000 small shareholders converged on the AGM of British Gas to protest at the 75 per cent pay rise being offered to the then chief executive Cedric Brown. They got robust support from the unions, which even put an over-sized live pig, guzzling at a trough marked share options, on display outside the venue. They were ultimately

defeated by the City institutions, which backed the company, but left claiming a moral victory... the Greenbury report on directors' pay followed in the same year

1996: The government agency English Partnerships paid British Gas an estimated £28m for 294 acres of contaminated land in Greenwich. One hundred and thirty acres of the land, a former gasworks site, was to be expensively transformed into the Millennium Dome

1997: Nicola Horlick, the "City superwoman", first hit the headlines. Horlick had been suspended from her £1m-a-year job at Morgan Grenfell for allegedly plotting to defect to rival bank ABN Amro and take a number of colleagues with her. Hiring leading solicitors and PR executives to clear her name, she made counter-allegations of back-

stabbing and treachery. She went on to manage funds worth £1bn at the French bank Société Generale, before quitting City life in 2003

1999: Equitable Life, the world's oldest insurer, announced that it could no longer meet its financial commitments to its policyholders. A series of court proceedings followed and in July 2000 the company was forced to put itself up for sale. It was bought by the Halifax in 2001

2000: Jennie Page, chief executive of the Millennium Dome, resigned after a disastrous opening night (problems with security scanners meant several VIP guests were left stranded) and disappointing early attendances. A few months later, she was followed by the chairman, Bob Ayling. (The Millennium Commission had said it would not stump up any more money unless

Ayling, who had recently quit the top job at British Airways, went.)

2000: The Dutch clothing retailer C&A announced it was pulling out of the UK market. It had been a fixture of the high street for some 75 years and had 109 outlets in Britain and Ireland

2000: So-called soft-porn king Richard Desmond, chief executive of media group Northern and Shell, stunned the business world by buying Express Newspapers for £125m. The Daily Express, erstwhile bastion of Tory traditionalism and crusader for the British Empire, founded in 1900 by a rector's son, Arthur Pearson, was now in the same stable as such titles as Big Ones and Asian Babes

Sources: Patrick Robertson: The New Shell Book of Firsts, 1994, Headline Book Publishing; BBCi; Guardian Unlimited

two Boeing 707s. Bishop agreed to lease the 707s in return for a £2.5m loan to buy out BM. The dentist got 25 per cent of the company, and later sold out. Bishop and his managers got the remaining 75 per cent and are now very rich indeed.

Priority No. 2 is getting the slots and the routes. Bishop's real achievement was to anticipate and ride the deregulation climate of the early 1980s by lobbying hard for the right to fly from Heathrow on domestic routes head to head with BA. He didn't make Freddie Laker's mistake of being too urgent and high-profile in his pitch. Instead, he picked off routes such as Edinburgh, Glasgow and Belfast that were not then profitable and built up his clientele from a small base. The first two years of the Belfast route, for example, were a disaster financially, but passenger loads eventually doubled from 500,000 in 1984 to one million in 1997.

This "tortoise" strategy – hanging on in, never over-stretching the company and moving forward step by step with a five to 10 per cent increase in passenger growth each year – has enabled Bishop, now Sir Michael, to ride the notoriously cyclical nature of the industry that burnt out earlier innovators such as Laker and tour operator Harry Goodman. Unlike Richard Branson, he refused to play David to BA's Goliath and this kept his relations with BA cordial in the years when they could have swatted him out of the picture. Bishop took it as a compliment when Lord King, the BA chairman, referred to him patronisingly as "a quiet little operator and

Call me Stelios: EasyJet's exuberant founder

very straightforward to deal with".

BM may be quiet (Bishop leads a low-profile bachelor life and describes himself as "conventional on the outside, unconventional on the inside"); but it certainly isn't little. Bishop's profits trebled to £17.3m in the mid-1990s because he wasn't saddled with the debt he would have needed to emulate Virgin Atlantic. Now rebranded bmi (for British Midland International), the airline has vastly expanded its route map and may even be looking for a partnership with Virgin to challenge BA.

The major business revolution in aviation as the new millennium opened was the spread of cheap no-frills airlines on the model of Southwest Airlines in the US. Ryanair, an Irish venture run by the aggressive and unconventional Michael O'Leary, and EasyJet, a start-up by Greek-born Stelios Haji-Ioannou, another larger-than-life character, quickly made inroads into the big operators' holiday traffic, and even managed to register profits in the nervous aftermath of September 11. Despite the Iraq war, EasyJet almost doubled its number of passengers over the year 2002-2003.

Stelios, as he is known to all, is an exuberant entrepreneur who rapidly expanded his unique selling proposition, based on e-commerce, to internet cafes and car rental. EasyJet with its bright orange planes is now Europe's second largest discount airline after Ryanair, and its car rental business, offering only one type of vehicle, is priced 60 per cent below the industry giants. Equally brash and

Easy does it: cheap flights boom while the big airlines struggle

unconventional in an older business is Brian Souter of Stagecoach, the bus, coach and train operator. He projects a "just an ordinary man" image by habitually wearing an open-necked check shirt, anorak and track shoes and toting a plastic bag instead of a briefcase to media and PR events. Souter, whose near-20 per cent holding in the company he founded is now worth several hundred million, originally combined a part-time job as a bus conductor in Glasgow with work as an accountant. His sister and co-founder Ann Gloag was a nurse.

When the Conservative government passed the 1980 Transport Act, which deregulated long-distance coach and bus services, the pair borrowed £25,000 from their father to buy a second-hand bus in Perth and developed a luxury double-decker coach service between Scottish cities and London. Their big breakthrough came five years later in 1985 when the National Bus Company, the state-owned group that ran all non-municipal services, was broken up. Stagecoach hit the news by being the first company to buy a National Bus subsidiary. It went on to acquire three, in Hampshire, Cumbria and the Midlands as well as buying routes from Scottish Bus and London Buses.

From there, the company's ambitions seemed boundless. In 1992, encouraged by government attempts to inject private enterprise into British Rail, Souter leased two carriages to run an overnight service between Aberdeen and London and went on to take over South West Trains, one of the largest London commuter franchises. In 1997, he made his first international acquisition, the £110m purchase of Swebus, the principal Swedish bus operator. By the late 1990s, he was running bus operations in Kenya, Malawi and New Zealand and was targeting South Africa.

Souter's buccaneering risk-taking is matched by his hard-boiled attitude to both competitors and regulators. Even under the Major government, whose privatisation policies were the making of Souter, Stagecoach was hauled off to the Monopolies and Mergers Commission more times than any other British company of its vintage. In one much-cited case – a bid for a Darlington franchise – its behaviour was deemed to have been "predatory, deplorable and against the public interest".

Ann Gloag (centre) and Brian Souter (right), the sibling partners who built a transport empire on privatisation

Undaunted, as the Conservatives rushed through rail privatisation, Souter re-wrote the rules in 1997 by paying the vast sum of £825m for Porterbrook, one of the three privatised rolling stock leasing companies. This was in the teeth of government opposition and left Sir George Young, then transport secretary, fuming. Souter's aggressive hands-on direction is viewed with some nervousness in the City, but he claims that new managerial blood is what will keep the company dynamic. "The success of Stagecoach is in finding good busmen and railwaymen and making them into good businessmen," he commented in 1998. Meanwhile, his sister Ann Gloag had cashed in her share of the fortune and bought the historic Lovat Castle from the Scottish clan of that name. Now retired from the business, she pursues philanthropic interests.

Continuing the inexorable shift away from manufacturing, the biggest 1990s business successes (apart from Dyson) were nearly all in service industries – advertising, catering, leisure and entertainment. Even football clubs seemed to take their place among the business greats: Manchester United grew into a global brand, carrying the fame of Britain's soccer stars far beyond Europe's borders.

Manufacturing, indeed, seemed to be in ever-faster decline as the decade ended. It contributed just over 20 per cent to GDP in 1999 compared with 24 per cent in 1989. Thirteen times more people were employed in the courier business (71,000) than in the fishing industry (a mere 5,500). There were six times as many estate agents as there were people making boots and shoes, once staples of British manufacturing. As The Observer had put it the year before: "there are now as many people selling things in Britain as there are making them".

Couriers now outnumber workers in the fishing industry

THE CHANGING CENTURY

A snapshot of science and technology:

1990: Tim Berners-Lee, inventor of the World Wide Web, wrote the first web client (browser-editor) and the first web server

1990: The Japanese TV journalist Toyohiro Akiyama became the first paying passenger in space: TBS Television paid $37m for him to accompany the Soviet crew of Soyuz TM II

1991: Helen Sharman of Sheffield spent seven days in space aboard the Soviet Union's Soyuz TM12. She was the first female astronaut from outside the US and USSR

1991: Britain got its first wavepower station. It was established near Portnaven, Islay Island, Strathclyde to produce electricity for local use

1992: The concept of the "virtual world" was born; in California, a company called Spectrum Holobyte

developed a 3-D futuristic videogame system for arcades and malls, which it called Virtual Reality

1993: The first French and British passenger trains ran through the Channel Tunnel. Both made a Folkestone-Calais round trip with invited guests; both ran late

1993: At Great Ormond Street children's hospital, gene therapy was used to correct a hereditary condition in a one-year-old girl. It was the first time that the treatment, which repairs or replaces malfunctioning genes with healthy ones, was given in Britain

1993: A superglue for closing wounds, an alternative to needle-and-thread sutures, became available. It had been developed over eight years by medical scientists at Bradford University Bio-Materials Research Unit

1993: Nature magazine announced that Professor Daniel Cohen of Centre d'Etude du Polymorphisme

Humain, Paris, had produced the first map of the human genome. (The genome is the sum of all the DNA in a particular organism)

1994: In San Diego, Prodigy Services Co. (a joint venture between IBM and Sears) launched the first interactive TV service, enabling viewers to call up additional information, vid-clips, stills etc. associated with the programme they were watching

1996: Scientists at the Roslin Institute in Edinburgh published research on cloning. The following year, the result of their work, Dolly the sheep, was born

1997: Pixar Animation Studios, co-founded in 1986 by Steve Jobs of Apple Computer, brought out the first feature-length computer-animation film, the award-winning Toy Story

2000: A quarter of the UK population and nearly half of British businesses now had internet connections. In the four weeks before Christmas 1999,

more than three million users had shopped online, a three-fold increase over the same period in 1998. The markets for online grocery, book and CD shopping were growing rapidly*

2000: Broadband, the technology that allows high-speed, always-on access to the internet, at last became available in the UK; BT launched its ADSL service, hot on the heels of Telewest's Blueyonder. (In the US, broadband had been introduced two years previously; high costs were delaying its roll-out in the UK)

2000: WAP-enabled mobile phones, promising internet access, were launched in Europe; users, however, found the technology slow. They had to wait another year for faster, General Packet Radio Service (GPRS) handsets

See also: business facts box

Sources: Patrick Robertson: The New Shell Book of Firsts, 1994, Headline Book Publishing; BBCi; BBC News Online

*From surveys published in 2000 by Forrester Research and by NOP

Britain's most admired boss

John Browne (right), the chief executive who transformed BP in seven years from third-ranking oil major into the world's seventh largest company through an aggressive acquisition chase, is that rarity in business – a man with apparently no enemies. For four years he has been voted Britain's most admired manager. A US oilman calls him "the Sun King of the oil industry".

Browne shares with Jack Welch, for many years America's most admired CEO, a single-company career, having joined BP (where his father also worked on leaving the army) straight from taking a high-flying first in physics at Cambridge. (He also has a master's in business studies from Stanford.) But in every other way he is different from the tough Irish-American, whose image has been besmirched by questions over the accuracy of General Electric's legendary profit record and by an adulterous affair with a business journalist. (Welch got expensively divorced in his first year of retirement.)

For one thing, Browne is a finance man to his fingertips who demands accountability from every manager in BP. For another, he is a famously self-contained bachelor at 54 who lived with his mother, a Romanian-born survivor of the Holocaust, until her death in 2000. To the fascination of oil industry executives and not a little ridicule in the press, she acted as his consort and hostess at BP events. He regards a circle of close friends as his "surrogate family" and apart from a range of cultivated interests – he collects pre-Colombian art and has a passion for opera – he appears married to the company. Rich Cuban cigars (though he won't smoke them in the US, respecting the political embargo on Havanas) appear to be one of the few indulgences arising from his considerable salary.

Browne rose with apparently effortless ease through BP, being singled out early for the top in its fast-track management development system. He became group treasurer and then, in 1989, head of the company's exploration division, where his rigorous pursuit of performance targets, innovative outsourcing and radical cost-cutting transformed BPX from a money-eating fiefdom into a business standing on its own two feet. When the top job beckoned in 1995, he was the youngest CEO (at 46) in BP's history.

Realising that BP's scale behind Exxon and Shell made it "too small to prosper," Browne began a spectacular series of annual acquisitions – Amoco in 1998, Atlantic Richfield in 1999, Burmah Castrol in 2000 and Veba in 2001. From a market capitalisation of £24.6bn in 1995, the company was worth more than £108bn seven years later. Browne rose even faster in personal status, being knighted and made a "people's peer" within two years of New Labour's election in 1997.

Browne's success is attributed by those who know and work with him to his extraordinary intellectual calibre – often radical in its thinking – coupled with a phenomenal appetite for hard work and the ability to excite others with his vision. But he demands delivery: "if you cannot keep up and perform, you are dead," says a former senior BP director. He is a problem-solver by nature and runs BP, says his university friend Professor Peter Hennessy, the constitutional historian, "like a research scientist".

Browne's frequent visits to 10 Downing Street and the well-known mutual admiration between him and the prime minister, mean BP is sometimes derisively dubbed "Blair Petroleum". But Browne, clean-handed as ever, eschews political donations and his personal politics are unknown. He will step down at the statutory age of 60 and will certainly be in avid demand for a range of public roles. But his prime job before he reaches that birthday in 2009 will be to ensure a smooth succession at BP. Following the Sun King will be difficult, but leaving the monarchy without a capable heir would tarnish a uniquely brilliant image.

Black or white? Chancellor Norman Lamont had a bad day on September 16, 1992, but leaving the ERM was good for business

At the same time, the export/import deficit had risen alarmingly in 1998/1999, from £20.6bn to £27bn. This was in spite of a distinct boost for exporters in 1992 when Britain was forced out of the ERM system of European monetary alignment. (John Major's Conservative government saw the day of withdrawal from ERM as "Black Wednesday", but much of business, rejoicing in the renewed competitiveness of sterling against European currencies, called it "White Wednesday".)

One leading figure in the service sector who could celebrate the new millennium in buoyant style was Martin Sorrell, founding head of one of the world's top three advertising groups, WPP. Operating profits grew by 43 per cent, and WPP acquired Young & Rubicam, America's most prestigious marketing group, for a cool $4.7bn in the biggest takeover in advertising history. On top of that, Sorrell was knighted. Two decades earlier, Sir Martin's company, bought off the shelf as a shell for his advertising ambitions, had been a small business making supermarket shopping baskets: WPP stands for Wire and Plastics Products.

It took just 15 years for the diminutive Sorrell to build WPP to the position it holds now: as this was being written, Sorrell was again on the acquisition trail in his ambition to make WPP the world's biggest advertising group. He had already acquired some of the biggest names in advertising. Long before capturing Y&R in 2000, he had snapped up J. Walter Thompson in 1987 – the first purchase of a listed American advertising agency by a foreign rival – and Ogilvy & Mather two years later. WPP now has 40 separate companies and employs 20,000 staff worldwide.

Sorrell has not been afraid to use hostile takeovers when he has needed to – a livid David Ogilvy called him an "odious little shit" at the time of the O&M acquisition. In the process, he has taken risks that would have raised the hair of the most acquisitive Wall Street trader. Already over-leveraged after buying JWT – 16 times WPP's size – his decision to pay for Ogilvy & Mather with cash and convertible shares, coupled with a plummeting share price during the 1990 recession, nearly pushed him over the financial edge. When he was forced to surrender a large slice of his company to the banks, nobody would have given him odds for survival. A decade later, he is much admired for his business skills and his company's debt is well under control.

Like many tycoons dismissed as ruthless number-crunchers intent on squeezing maximum financial rewards out of their company's mixed fortunes, Sir Martin nurses surprisingly old-fashioned values. A down-to-earth pragmatist, he runs WPP from a modest two-storey building behind a Westminster Cleansing depot off London's Berkeley Square. He deplores the "erosion of loyalty" between agency and staff in the advertising business, bemoaning the fact that "nobody is willing to serve an apprenticeship any more". He never takes anything for granted. In an interview for The Economist in 2001 he commented: "I never feel secure. I started WPP with two people in a room and I worry that we can go back to that."

Much hand-wringing went on in the latter part of the 1990s about the shrinking of Britain's management talent pool and general lack of business leadership. Apart from the indestructible Richard Branson (knighted in the Millennium New Year Honours), there were few charismatic individuals at the head of public companies, and a cluster of high-profile vacancies remained unfilled. It seemed that headhunters had to turn to foreign-born chief executives for the required qualities, and a mounting number was brought in at eye-popping remuneration packages to take charge of British commercial institutions. At Barclays Bank there was Canadian Matt Barrett; at the ailing Marks and Spencer the Belgian Luc Vandevelde; at BT the Dutchman Ben Voorwayen; at Safeway supermarket group the exotically named Argentinian Carlos Criades Perez; at the Pearson group, publishers of the Financial Times, the American-born Marjorie Scardino.

When native talent did deliver spectacular results, it was pursued by many boards seeking a touch of the magic, and, as with Lord Browne of BP, written about endlessly with fascination and awe. (See panel.) A prime example of the achieving CEO who quickly became a serial director/chairman on many boards was – and is – Allan Leighton, who succeeded the former McKinsey consultant Archie Norman in 1995 as CEO of the northern supermarket group Asda. Norman and Leighton completed such a turnround of the fading business – and introduced such an Americanised culture, with the CEO wearing a badge proclaiming "I'm Archie [or Allan]. Happy to help" – that the group was eventually taken over by the US giant discounter Wal-Mart.

The transformation of Asda, widely credited to Norman, in fact owed much to new work practices brought in by Leighton and modelled on his experience at Mars, the US confectionery group. Such innovations as the "one-team" management style (no surnames, open

Turnround talent: Marjorie Scardino was one of many foreign CEOs who shook up British boardrooms

plan offices, everyone termed a "colleague" regardless of rank) are pure Mars. (The approach was quickly adopted by the previously hierarchical Sainsbury's as the group's old-style management saw how Asda delivered the goods.) Leighton's back-slapping style also complemented Norman's incisive but remote approach to strategy. An external adviser working with both men commented: "Archie was a brilliant communicator and myth-maker, but only with the press and the City, not so much with his own staff. That is what Allan is brilliant at."

As Asda grew to new strength, another British retailer was taken ill. The decline of Marks and Spencer, revered for decades as the epitome of good British management, was a shock that could not be attributed to any one factor – unlike the more sudden and blameworthy collapse of Marconi – unless it was the fatal complacency that comes with too long a run of market dominance.

In May 1998, Marks & Spencer still supplied Britons with a quarter of their suits, almost all of their bras and a third of their sandwiches. It was a British institution and the country's most profitable retailer. In 1998, its annual report showed profits of £2bn and its share price hit a record high of 664p. But in October of that year, it was forced to report the first fall in profits since the start of the decade and, by the end of 1998, its share price had dropped by 32 per cent. Two years later, the share price had fallen to less than 180p.

Bad news kept coming. Long-term chairman Sir Richard Greenbury retired a year early in February 1999 and his successor, Peter Salisbury, lasted only 18 months. Perhaps the lowest point, in PR terms, came when a thousand trade unionists from France, Spain and Belgium demonstrated outside the company's flagship store at London's Marble Arch over the proposed closure of stores on the continent. Worst of all, customers were turning their backs on M&S garments, those classic standbys that had been a byword for value and quality. Some commentators doubted whether the company would survive at all.

The turning point was the appointment of chairman Luc Vandevelde in February 2000, although the bottom-line benefits were not seen for a further 18 months. By that time, the company had an entirely new set of executives up to and including the managing director, Roger Holmes, who came from Kingfisher, the former Woolworths.

As a rise and fall story, the M&S saga has few business equals. So what happened? The answer is that the very strengths on which the company's success was consolidated under the Sieff family in the 1930s – strong central control and a top-down attention to detail – had rebounded on it. Centralisation always brings the dangers of complacency – and by the mid-1990s M&S was very vulnerable. Its early lead in pioneering up-market ready-made meals was being eroded by catch-ups Tesco and Sainsbury. Its insistence on buying almost all of its clothes from domestic suppliers, a patriotic asset in Thatcher's 1980s Britain, seemed irrelevant to a more cosmopolitan generation and allowed competitors who imported more cheaply to compete aggressively on price.

In a lecture on innovation in 1997, M&S's deputy chairman Keith Oates conceded that the company was almost wholly dependent for new ideas on its suppliers, and by then many of Marks' UK suppliers were out of touch with the new global fashion market. Its centralised buying system also meant that one bad judgment had widespread consequences, as when M&S buyers decided that grey was the colour of the year for female fashion. British women stayed away in droves.

Nor had M&S's ventures abroad delivered on their

An icon falls: French employees of Marks and Spencer rage against the closure of stores in France

THE CHANGING CENTURY

"Sleaze": a brief history

1992: The Matrix Churchill trial (see business facts box) collapsed after Alan Clark, defence procurement minister, admitted it was possible he had given the Machine Tool Trade Association the impression that companies could get round government guidelines on the export of weapons by stressing "the civil applications of their equipment even though they knew that it could be used for military purposes". His testimony exonerated the Matrix Churchill directors but put government departments on trial: a judicial inquiry, led by Sir Richard Scott, followed

1994: At the end of the year, the Guardian newspaper ran a story suggesting that the Department for Trade and Industry minister Neil Hamilton and another Tory MP Tim Smith had been bribed by Harrods owner Mohamed Al Fayed to table questions in the House of Commons. So began the cash-for-questions scandal

1995: New revelations of bribery and corruption: the Guardian newspaper and Granada TV's World in Action programme alleged that a Saudi businessman had paid for Jonathan Aitken, then chief secretary to the Treasury, to stay at the Paris Ritz hotel. Aitken began a suit for libel, which spectacularly failed in 1997. Two years later, he was jailed for 18

earlier promise. Clothes sold in its overseas stores were often too expensive because they had details such as buttons finished in Britain. Although the Paris stores had been a rip-roaring success, particularly (and ironically) in the food department, growth elsewhere in Europe was slow. Brooks Brothers, the prestige US acquisition, was losing money and attempts to reposition the M&S brand as high-fashion in Asia had not worked at a time when the region was about to go belly-up economically.

All of this, reflected in a 23-per-cent fall in half-year profits at the end of 1998 (the first in M&S's 30-year history as a public company), would have been enough to trigger nervousness in the investment community. But that year a lot of the company's scraggy corporate governance chickens also came home to roost. Despite chairing a committee on corporate governance in 1995, Sir Richard Greenbury, chairman and chief executive, had been dismissive about the new benchmarks of boardroom probity. Interviewed in 1990, when his assumption of the combined role had provoked widespread criticism in the City, he commented: "The idea that the chairman does the long-term stuff and the chief executive does the short-term stuff is rubbish, business school rubbish."

Now, for the first time, the unquestioning loyalty he demanded from the board – stitched into his office cushion were the words "I have many faults, but being wrong isn't

Never wrong? Sir Richard Greenbury ran M&S on traditional lines, but changing times and tastes brought disaster

one of them" – slipped out of control. Away in India, he was unable to prevent an unseemly power struggle going public over who should succeed him as chief executive. Keith Oates even appealed to M&S's NEDs when executive directors indicated they would prefer Peter Salisbury.

The composition of the board at the time was a telling indication of the company's inward-looking character. Sixteen of the 22 directors were insiders. Of the six non-executives, one was a former executive and a member of the founding Sieff family. As The Economist commented in a critical profile of Greenbury in November 1998: "With M&S now selling financial services and going overseas, the narrowness of M&S's senior managers and board directors is a weakness… Taking their lead from Sir Richard himself, M&S executives

months after admitting to perjury. (The scandals of 1994-1995 led to the establishment of the Nolan Committee, now the Committee on Standards in Public Life)

1996: The Scott Report was published. It confirmed that Conservative ministers had concealed from Parliament the sale of weapons to Iraq

1998: New Labour, whose victory speeches had promised to serve the people in honesty and integrity, was itself tainted by scandal. It was revealed that Bernie Ecclestone, the Formula One boss, had made a donation of £1m to the party – just ahead of a government decision to exempt motor racing from an EU directive on banning tobacco

sponsorship of sports

1998: Peter Mandelson resigned as Trade and Industry Secretary in December 1998 after revelations in the Guardian about an undisclosed home loan from Paymaster General Geoffrey Robinson. Ten months later, he was back as Northern Ireland Secretary, a post he quit in 2001

after allegations that he had used his influence to push through British passport applications for the Indian billionaire Srichand Hinduja. (The Hinduja brothers had pledged £1m in sponsorship for London's Millennium Dome, a project once overseen by Mandelson)

Sources: BBCi; Guardian Unlimited

the bug that never was

It was the great doomsday event that never happened. Three years on, who gives a thought to the Millennium Bug? Certainly not the army of computer nerds and specialist consultants who in the run-up to the century's end predicted a meltdown that would turn the clock back 100 years, as the world's software instantly and simultaneously mistook the year 2000 for 1900.

The new century, according to the worst predictions, would dawn with police, hospitals and other emergency services paralysed, the banking system locked up, governments (to say nothing of nuclear reactors) in chaos and aeroplanes falling out of the sky, as the electronics they all depended on stopped working. The looming nightmare was blamed on cheese-paring 30 years earlier at the start of the computer age, when to save data memory, software was written with mechanisms that gave two digits instead of four. This would naturally affect year identification when the century changed. It was supposed that when midnight struck on Millennium Eve the world would be sent on a one-way time-travel passage to disaster.

Bug fever reached a pitch in 1997 when a leading news magazine asked on its front cover, "Could two measly digits really halt civilisation?" and answered itself, "Yes, yes – a thousand times yes!" Estimates of what the problem would cost the world's companies and governments to fix varied from $600bn (The

Gartner Group) to $3.6trn (Boston Software Productivity Research). Experts in Cobol, the original computer language, were hunted like the Holy Grail and told they could write their own cheques.

Independent Canadian software expert Peter de Jager warned companies: "It is going to cost you a whole truck-load of money, but you have to fix the problem if you want to continue doing business in the 21st century. The business case is simple: do it or you are dead."

When the time came, nobody died – in air crashes or as a result of any failed computers. But did the truck-load of money that business threw at the problem make any difference? Perhaps in embarrassment at yielding so expensively to panic, no-one has yet come up with a definitive answer.

Would the lights go out? Predictions of millennial doom never happened

have failed to understand much of what is happening outside their green and white shop window, let alone outside Britain's borders."

Not surprisingly, when the first foreign and "outside" chairman in the company's history was appointed, his first priority was not only to bring in the best designers to create a fashion brand beyond St. Michael, but to establish a more balanced board of insiders and outsiders. Vandevelde also ordered a complete overhaul of the parochial, top-down culture. Pivotal in the company's long road to recovery was a two-day workshop in the summer of 2000 by London Business School professor Lynda Gratton. Held at Lord's cricket ground and attended by 500 managers, it threw every previous tenet of M&S management into the dustbin and replaced them with new freedoms of action, using skill tests to find out how comfortable managers would be with the change. It proved the most successful management development event ever run by the company.[7]

At the time of writing, Marks and Spencer appeared finally to have hauled itself out of the mire, and a further imaginative appointment to its executive team in 2003 (as head of homeware) was that of the Italian Vittorio Radice, whose transformation of Selfridges department store in London had been the toast of the business press.

The 1990s was a heady decade for business, and not only in the over-hyped dotcom sector. Many young entrepreneurial talents emerged in service industries as diverse as microchip design, youth entertainment, broadcasting, food and biotechnology. Not all survived: the former disc-jockey Chris Evans, who bought Richard Branson's Virgin Radio (on which Evans had been the star attraction) in 1997 from under Capital's nose and formed an ambitious media group eyeing up everything from digital licences to national newspapers, fell victim five years later to a spectacular personal burn-out.

An even more youth-focused business, the Ministry

of Sound, was founded in 1991 by James Palumbo (left), son of the property developer Lord Palumbo. After turning a south London warehouse into the capital's first "superclub", Palumbo (who personally hates rave music) has expanded his brand into an extraordinary range of businesses, from compact discs and magazines to clothes and travel. By the year 2000, with the aid of a £24m stake bought by venture capital firm 3i, the CD business had turned into Britain's largest independent record label, valued at £160m. While the club and record business remained a successful core, in other areas there were suggestions of over-expansion, and in 2003 Palumbo yielded the hands-on reins to a new, strategy-oriented chief executive who would concentrate on developing the brand worldwide.

The Ministry of Sound began as a "rave" superclub in a warehouse. Now it's a big brand business, from clothes to CDs

Yet another "son-also-rises" story was that of Luke Johnson, son of the historian and right-wing journalist Paul Johnson. Born in 1962, Johnson had an eclectic career as adman, assistant to the subsequently disgraced Tory MP Jonathan Aitken, investment adviser and media analyst, before finding his metier as a restaurant entrepreneur. He made Pizza Express fashionable for its striking and well-designed premises, launched a heavily branded mussels-and-chips chain called Belgo and audaciously capped this by co-acquiring the historic and super-chic Ivy restaurant in London's theatreland.

Johnson's rocket-like success in a business in which he had little or no track record is based on two things: a solid understanding of financial management ("good cashflow, low waste") and a

"Good cash-flow, low waste": Luke Johnson's formula for restaurant success

phenomenal personal network built up from the days when he grew up with the likes of Robert Maxwell and Rupert Murdoch as his parents' dinner guests. In time, he could challenge Sir Terence Conran as restaurant king of London. The indestructible Conran, meanwhile, who started with the cheap and cheerful Soup Kitchen in the 1950s, gave us Habitat, a new concept in British design and furnishing, in the 1960s and went on to launch quirky and upmarket restaurants, also had a good decade. He brought back Quaglino's, a favourite dine-and-dance spot of the 1930s, as a fashionable West End restaurant and opened many other big, trendy eating places in old bank buildings around the capital.

Sir Robin Saxby: his chip-design company is essential to 80 per cent of the world's mobile phones

British technical innovation in electronics had its triumphs, too, demonstrating that a one-time cottage industry such as ARM Holdings, the chip designer, could grow from a 12-person business to one that provides the intelligence inside 80 per cent of the world's mobile phones, as well as hand-held computers, digital cameras, cars and set-top boxes. Built on the basis of licensing its advanced technology rather than manufacturing, the business proved strong enough to weather the savage technology crash of 2000-2002. Chairman Sir Robin Saxby is one of the most impressive of a new generation of strategically-minded technical wizards.

In this sense, Saxby has followed the path of David Potter, founder of Psion and, like James Dyson, a gifted inventor whose understanding of markets has turned him into a highly successful businessman. Psion – the acronym reflects Potter's determination to launch his own business and stands for Potter Scientific Instruments Or Nothing – was founded in 1984 with a personal organiser technically streets ahead of the competition at the time. The business was floated in 1987 at just over 53 pence per share; by the late 1990s, after Potter's dominance of the market for hand-held computers, the price had multiplied tenfold.

In 1998 Psion entered a joint venture with global giants Nokia and Motorola to develop software that could compete in the smart phone market with Microsoft's CE system. Daring joint ventures transformed Psion during the 1990s into one of the UK's few global companies in the technology sector. In 2000, Potter oversaw key ventures with IBM (creating business applications based on Psion's EPOC software) and Motorola (to launch new mobile internet access devices). Psion also joined forces with Palm, Nokia, Motorola and IBM to develop a new standard (SyncML) allowing different high-tech devices to talk to each other – a key innovation to challenge the global domination of Microsoft.

In other areas of technology, however, notably the hyper-active telecommunications industry into which investment was being poured at the end of the 1990s, over-capacity would soon spell disaster on a global scale.

In the year 2000, the plug was pulled on a decade of dreams and great expectations, and trillions of new wealth – both corporate and personal – went down the drain.

Innovation is not enough: David Potter of Psion has mastered the arts of successful global marketing

tomorrow's world

" What the stockmarkets want is companies with size, substance, value, the best management teams and the best product pipelines. "

Sir Christopher Evans, leading biotechnology entrepreneur, on the future of the industry, April 2003

10

Only a paper world? The vulnerability of economies and stockmarkets has been sharply exposed since the year 2000

he first true year of the 21st century and the third millennium, 2001, was an annus horribilis for America and its economy, inescapably the driver of all its global trading and investment partners. First came the shocking unravelling of Enron and WorldCom, two icons of innovative business models that had been hailed in business bestsellers and on the conference circuit by eminent management gurus. Then, before the worst of the accounting legerdemain and management venality had been fully exposed, the nightmare of September 11 exploded on a vulnerable business world in both the US and Britain. It said much for the basic stability of US economic management and investors' level-headedness that after the New York Stock Exchange closed for five days amid the rubble of the twin towers, there was no panic of the kind that precipitated the Wall Street Crash of 1929 and the onset of the Depression.

Some industries, of course, were devastated – airlines dived into bankruptcy, all businesses linked to travel and tourism suffered, insurance companies buckled – and business confidence was affected on a massive international scale. But stockmarkets were more deeply disturbed by the revelations that more US companies, and a major auditor (Arthur Andersen), were revealed to have been implicated in dubious accounting, than by the new kind of terrorism stalking the West.

Acquisition, as ever, had been the catalyst for disaster, both at the former gas utility Enron and the hubristic telecoms company WorldCom. The source of all WorldCom's subsequent problems was a high-profile shut-out bid for MCI in 1998. Bernie Ebbers, the flamboyant southerner who had founded WorldCom as a tiny start-up in Jackson, Mississippi, in 1983, was a master of buy-out wizardry, using his own shares to pay prices for companies that made other potential investors blanch.

Kenneth Lay of Enron was regarded with, if anything, greater awe as a dealmaker. The story of how he turned a stodgy gas provider into a soaring new-economy company by preaching liberalisation and deregulation was a widely admired business-school case study. Like Ebbers, Lay was the master of take-no-prisoners buy-ups and had a highly sophisticated approach to managing risk. As with WorldCom, the results were breathtaking: the company's sales leapt from $4.6bn at the start of the decade to $40.1bn at its end, most of it coming from trading deals in energy. And, just as with WorldCom's acquisitions, each Enron success pushed the odds longer against the likelihood of a viable return.

The signs that both companies, and their backers, were losing touch with reality were already becoming apparent at the turn of the millennium. When Enron duly collapsed in a welter of bad debts in 2001, the fall-out tainted not only the immediate players but also other businesses that had tacked their sails very close to the wind. Even the mighty GE's shares fell in the autumn of 2002 as investors, so long bedazzled by Jack Welch's apparent ability to increase profits at 15 per cent a year for nearly two decades, finally began to ask questions.

Perhaps the most dramatic loss of credibility was that experienced by the internationally respected accountancy firm Arthur Andersen. Once it became clear that the US partnership had shredded Enron documents in an attempt to cover up Andersen's complicity, UK companies serviced by Andersen's auditors wanted explanations. Despite a herculean effort to plead that Andersen UK should not be singled out for blame over Enron, UK managing partner John Ormerod was forced into negotiations with KPMG to take over the practice. It was lucky for Andersen's sister consulting firm that it had already separated from the AA partnership and re-branded itself as Accenture.

On trial still are not only the auditing practices used by North American and UK firms but also the management culture that shaped and inspired them for nearly 20 years.

Once Andersen's files were opened in Britain, they provoked fraud investigations involving three of its clients. There had also been involvement in the 1970s De Lorean motor vehicle scandal in Northern Ireland, a gigantic fraud involving government grants. Despite this, an extensive campaign to cosy up to New Labour had resulted in Andersen staff working closely with Gordon Brown's Shadow Treasury team in the mid-1990s on a business-friendly economic agenda (known around the City as "the prawn cocktail offensive"). Andersen gained official contracts, including (perhaps prophetically) the audit of the monumentally wasteful Millennium Dome project and work on further privatisations.

In 2002-2003, the accountancy profession in Britain mounted a frantic attempt at damage limitation, arguing that the broader, less pedantic British approach would have prevented an Enron-like disaster. It also pointed out that Britain has much tougher rules than the US to limit the creation of special-purpose entities removed from the balance sheet. But Sir David Tweedie, chairman of the International Accounting Standards Board and former head of Britain's Accounting Standards Board, was sceptical

100 YEARS LATER...

In the IoD's centenary year, 2003:

- On March 20, after fruitless attempts to obtain a UN mandate to remove Saddam Hussein's regime by force, a coalition led by the US and Britain launched war on Iraq. Although President Bush and Prime Minister Blair cited earlier UN resolutions in support, France, Germany and Russia were implacably opposed. Mass protests erupted across Britain – in London, over a million people marched. The Commons ratified the war decision after what was said to be the biggest anti-government revolt in a century

- On May 1, Bush declared the war over. The regime had fled heavily-bombed Baghdad. But the leader remained at large and US/UK occupying forces were subjected to continued loss of life through guerrilla attacks. By September, no "weapons of mass destruction," the supposed

Tony Blair after giving evidence in the Hutton Inquiry, 28 August, 2003

casus belli, had been found. Bush appealed to Congress for another $75bn to foot the bill

- British weapons expert Dr. David Kelly took his own life after being named as a source for a BBC report that the case for war had been "sexed up." Blair and defence secretary Geoff Hoon, along with others in government, the civil service and the BBC, faced a public inquiry

- A by-election at Brent East, a die-hard Labour seat, fell to the Liberal Democrats: the war was cited as a key factor, along with failure to deliver better public services. While New Labour retained a wide poll lead over the Tories, other surveys revealed a heavy loss of trust in Blair over the war

- Osama bin Laden, the al-Qaeda leader, appeared in supposedly new video footage to mark the second anniversary of the September 11 terrorist attacks in New York. He praised the pilots who had flown into the twin towers, killing some 3,000 people

- British Airways and Air France announced that they were taking Concorde out of service

- institutional investors in pharmaceuticals company GlaxoSmithKline voted down a £22m "golden parachute" pay package for chief executive Jean-Pierre Garnier

- Derek Higgs, commissioned by the government to review "the role and effectiveness of non-executive directors", published his report in the wake of the Enron and WorldCom scandals. He met criticism from some business leaders, who accused him of being too prescriptive, of placing an unrealistic burden on NEDs and of marginalising the role of executive chairman. His recommendation that a non-executive chair the nomination committee was dropped outright, and other proposals had to be qualified or clarified. Nonetheless, in July the Financial Reporting Council, responsible for the combined code on corporate governance, accepted the "spirit and substantial content" of his report. Among the main recommendations: that independent non-executives make up at least half the board; that they are rigorously selected and assessed once a year; that senior independent

enough to comment in the spring of 2002: "History is full of people who said 'it couldn't happen here' and came to regret it. I do not plan to repeat that mistake."

Is Britain in danger of repeating other mistakes in the business history of the past 100 years? This small island has always punched above its weight in ideas and innovation, but, as events in the first half of the 20th century showed, it has often shown a marked reluctance to sustain that creativity in the marketplace, relying instead on a native ability to pull chestnuts out of the fire at the last minute.

Sunrise, sunset: The sun rising over the Millennium Dome on its last day of opening to the public, 2 January, 2001

directors listen (by way of formal meetings) to the concerns of major shareholders

- the UK's largest personal injury claims company, the Accident Group, collapsed, taking around 2,500 employees with it. Many workers were sacked by brusque text messages to their mobile phones, informing them that their salaries would not be paid

- Corus, the company that owns the former British Steel, announced that thousands of jobs had to go to stem losses of £400m (see main text)

- the Employment Act 2002 came into force, extending paternity and maternity leave, and giving parents with children under six or disabled children under 18 the right to have requests to work flexibly seriously considered

- across the country, firefighters went on strike for more pay. (The dispute, which began at the end of 2002, was not

settled until June, when the Fire Brigades' Union urged members to accept a 16 per cent offer, in return for limited changes to working practices)

- London mayor Ken Livingstone imposed a congestion charge of £5 a day on motorists coming into the centre of the capital between 7am and 6.30pm

- Chinese brands were being identified by researchers and commentators as the next "big thing" in global business. Among those tipped for possible greatness were Haier household appliances and Legend computers. Such brands were already giving the multinationals a run for their money in their home market; next stop, Europe?

- seven astronauts died aboard the US space shuttle Columbia. A report into the accident subsequently called for sweeping reforms at NASA, calling the agency's safety culture "reactive, complacent and dominated by

unjustified optimism"

- a medical team at King's college, London, announced that, for the first time, embryonic stem cells had been grown in the UK. The cells were to be used to research treatments for Parkinson's disease and diabetes

- broadband technology was making it big in Britain: the number of internet subscribers with permanent connections grew by 170 per cent in the 12 months to June

- according to the CBI and Atos KPMG Consulting, 87 per cent of UK companies were using e-business technologies to improve efficiency*

- the UK population was about 59 million**

- average life expectancy was 73 for men and 77 for women

- GDP was around £800bn**

- manufacturing accounted for 22

per cent of output, agriculture, forestry and fishing 2 per cent, services 66 per cent*

- more than a third of young people were going to university or college – a rise of roughly 25 per cent since the 1960s. (The government was hoping to increase the proportion to 50 per cent by 2010)

- women accounted for 46 per cent of the workforce**

- full-time average earnings were more than £350 a week***

- a second-class return from London to Glasgow cost between £37.00 and £192.00, depending on booking and travel times

- a four course, à la carte dinner at the Savoy cost approximately £85.00 (excluding wine)

*2002 report, Reality Bites **2000 figure ***1997 figure

Sources: Craig Lindsay: A century of labour market change: 1900 to 2000, Labour Market, March 2003; The Office for National Statistics; Guardian Unlimited; BBCi

Creative workshop of the world? Nick Park's triple Oscar-winning films starring his clay animation figures Wallace and Gromit are part of a £60bn "creative economy"

Spitfires and Hurricanes built in time for the Battle of Britain. Massive centralised effort created whole industries such as chemicals and machine tools from scratch at breakneck speed in 1914 and 1939, but the crisis had been largely self-inflicted by managements content for too long to rely on importing cutting-edge German technology as the easiest road to profit.

Today's boundaryless, global trading is far less fraught with risk of that kind, though some would argue that Britain has abandoned too much of its manufacturing capacity to foreign imports. And the UK is more of a creative workshop than ever before, in industries that have only been recognised as significant to the economy in the period immediately surrounding the millennium. Industries such as computer animation, advertising, film special effects and games design are part of a creative and media sector that the DTI calculates is worth around £60bn in revenues and which employs more than 1.4 million people, five per cent of the total UK workforce. When a brand name such as Disney is alone reckoned to be worth $32bn, or 61 per cent of the company's entire market capitalisation, something revolutionary is going on.[1]

Yet, as William Sargent, joint chief executive of the computer animation company Framestore CFC and chairman of the Small Business Council, wrote in Director magazine in May 2002, "the creative industries are held back by an inability to commercialise ideas. Britain is perceived to have been responsible for about 40 per cent of the world's innovation since World War II, but has actually exploited very few ideas ... very little of the wealth created flows back to the UK". Plus ca change! The problem today, as Sargent identifies it, has to do with loss of control over intellectual property rights and the means of global distribution – we create the ideas but the big beneficiaries are, for example, the all-powerful Hollywood studio network and the Japanese electronics giants.

Thus, twice in 25 years Britain let a likely enemy (first the Kaiser's Germany, then Hitler's) corner key industries in world markets, leaving itself dangerously exposed when war did come. In 1940, this resulted in the supreme irony of having to depend on Nazi-engineered machine tools to get

There have been gains for the UK in the political arena, in that both major parties now want to foster a healthier, less tax-burdened climate for new business and are willing to invest in support networks such as Business Link. Yet there is still a perceptible anti-business culture in Britain, reaching from the ancient universities down to the saloon bar, and this has unfortunately been given a new lease of life by the rampant peer-group greed of some chief executives. Even where there is no overt hostility to business, the mass of Britons display a sad lack of interest in the mechanics of successful entrepreneurship, unlike the aspirational Americans. A writer in the Financial Times recently cited the difference between the two nations in treating work as a subject matter for fiction. In the US, from Sinclair Lewis in the 1920s to Tom Wolfe in the 1980s and 1990s, novelists have written knowledgeably about the world of business and how it works: in British literature, at least since Dickens and Trollope, this has been so rare as to be almost invisible. Modern British novels tend to revolve around personal preoccupations and insecurities, chiefly to do with relationships and class.

Nonetheless, this is still a nation of resilient small businesses, as it was in the early 1900s. There are nearly four million small firms in Britain, only 7,000 of which employ more than 250 people. Many of them are traditional businesses, in which the influence of the founding family remains strong: in 2003, Scotland's Entrepreneur of the Year (and a contender for the UK-wide award) was Robert Wiseman of Wiseman Dairies, a business founded in 1958 by his father with five milk rounds and eight employees. Today, it is Scotland's largest milk producer and employs 3,000 people. But the SME sector, reckoned to employ 12 million people in the UK, is also well represented at the cutting edge of scientific innovation. According to David Irwin, founding chief executive of the Small Business Service, half of all innovations since World War II have come from start-ups and smaller firms. Some of these have gone on to become global leaders in their field, such as ARM Holdings of Cambridge, which designs the chips for electronic gadgets ranging from mobile phones to digital cameras.

Britain's science-based industries have come into their own in the 1990s and early 2000s and, in contrast to a century ago, are internationally competitive in their cost base as well as in quality. Two sectors were identified in 2003 through patent filings as the most innovative: pharmaceuticals and biotechnology, and aerospace and defence. These two accounted for 46 per cent of all corporate R&D spending, and aerospace/defence scored highest for innovation on the basis of patents issued in the US, with 7.4 measured against a US base of 100.

Nanotechnology, the mechanics of constructing and manipulating molecules tens of thousands times thinner than a human hair – is another evolving industry in which Britain is doing well but spending far less on research than Japan, the US and some other European countries. The science has already been responsible for such products as light but powerful tennis rackets made with carbon fibre 10,000 times tougher than steel, advanced dental fillings, cosmetics and a self-cleaning type of glass, made by Pilkington.

Biotechnology, a wave-of-the-future industry, which was destructively over-hyped just before the millennium and which crashed along with many others that had yet to prove themselves, is capable of great things, hooked as it is to such transformational research as the Human Genome Project. UK biotech companies account for £9bn of the £70bn global industry, but Germany has more of them.[2] The British industry knows that it needs to gather its resources and consolidate if it is to carry serious clout in the world. In the late summer of 2003, after a number of mergers and acquisitions, big investing institutions appeared to be developing more interest in the sector. Biotechnology shares were outperforming the market in both Europe and the US in 2003.[3]

Europe has about 100 quoted biotech companies and some 1,700 private ones, according to Sir Christopher Evans, the UK's leading biotech entrepreneur. "All 1,700 will want cash at least once or twice in the next four or five years, which means a total cash call privately of between £3bn and £5bn," he said early in 2003. "That money cannot be supplied ... If the flotation market did open again during

Biotech boffin to City dealmaker: Sir Christopher Evans advises small biotech companies to "merge now... or get murdered later"

the next five years, only the very best companies could float, which I think would be only three or four per cent of the 1,700. What the stockmarkets want is companies with size, substance, value, the best management teams and the best product pipelines."[4]

Evans, the son of a Welsh steelworker in Port Talbot, achieved academic distinction in microbiology and biochemistry before studying genetic engineering at the University of Michigan. In the 1980s, he set up his first company, an enzyme manufacturing business, with £1.3m backing from British Sugar. Enzymatix was one of the first

UK biotech companies and in 1992 became the core of Evans' entrepreneurial ventures when he sold off and floated parts of it to form Celsis and Chiroscience, two other successful companies.

Chiroscience merged with Celltech in 1999 to create the UK's leading biotech company. Evans by this time had already founded the biotech venture capital business Merlin Biosciences, and was a very rich man from the sale of shares in his companies. One of his former City advisers said: "He's one of the quickest learners I've ever met. He went from biotech boffin to City operator like a Ferrari going from 0 to 60."

Knighted in 2001, Evans believed that 2003 would see the start of major consolidation in the sector and was determined to be in at the off when it happened. "Small is no longer beautiful in this marketplace," he said in 2003. "Merge now for mass, money, molecules and management, or get murdered later." Undaunted by a spectacularly volatile stockmarket (by New Year's Eve 2002, the FTSE100 had fallen for three consecutive years), he has said: "When the market is really rough, that's when I work at my best."[5]

While the "new economy" slowly crawled back out of its stockmarket grave in 2003, surprising resilience was emerging from one of the oldest of Britain's traditional industries, which had been a pillar of the economy when the 20th century began. Warship building, which seemed destined to bleed to death as defence budgets were cut after the end of the Cold War, made a surprise comeback in 2003 with the news that Europe's most automated yard was being constructed on England's south coast with a string of orders in the pipeline. The company proposing to invest the best part of £100m in new facilities at Portsmouth carried a venerable name in defence manufacturing, Vosper Thorneycroft, now fashionably shortened to VT. It looked confidently to the future with two massive Ministry of Defence orders under its belt; one for a new destroyer and the

Vosper Thorneycroft chief executive Paul Lester: war and terrorism are creating new markets for an old industry

other for a £10bn contract to build and maintain two new aircraft carriers.

"World events are creating markets," said VT's chief executive, Paul Lester, in the wake of the US-UK led invasion of Saddam Hussein's Iraq in the spring of 2003. The terrorist threat from organisations such as al-Qaeda has also led to a boom in demand from several governments for offshore patrol vessels. "Shipbuilding used to be a sunset industry, but not any more," observes Lester, who sees growth in this area continuing well into the next decade.[6]

Despite persistent predictions of the death of British manufacturing, small specialist players such as Rotork, which makes valve actuators (and where the vacuum-cleaner inventor James Dyson began his working life) continue to dominate global niches. Even in big companies, there is confidence in the ability to innovate out of difficulties. Kevin Smith, who took over as chief executive of historic GKN in January 2003, is one of manufacturing's positive thinkers. The inheritor of 250 years of history, he would not have been out of place in the clattering Guest, Keen and Nettlefold workshops of a century ago that provided industry the world over with nuts, bolts and screws.

Smith started work straight from school in a textile mill and rose to be group managing director of British Aerospace (BAe), Britain's biggest manufacturer, before moving to the car components and aerospace giant. Almost the first thing he did was to move the head office back from a grandiose townhouse in London's clubland to its administrative base in Redditch, Worcestershire, a town historically associated with the manufacture of small steel products such as nails and sewing needles.

GKN faces global challenges common to its sector: a struggling volume car industry; aerospace orders hit by the decline in airline travel; periodic rows with government over defence procurement. But innovation, as always, is the key, and GKN has a powerful weapon in its 42-per-cent command of the market for drivelines, the mechanism that links a car's wheels to its engine. Following an Italian joint venture, it is also the world's biggest helicopter maker, and is positioning itself to make inroads into the key US defence market, where there is massive investment in helicopters. In this area, Smith aims to raise the group's revenues fivefold in five years.

Old company, new customers: GKN is the world's biggest helicopter manufacturer

Having left school himself "with a few O levels and not much else", Smith believes the future of manufacturing is "at the intellectual end; at the highly complex, value-added end". GKN, he says, is "well known for engineering and manufacturing competence, but is less well known for its strong technological capability that can be applied on top of that".[7]

Smith's theory is being validated at other traditional manufacturing firms. Johnson Matthey, once a name synonymous with heavy steel products, has invested in a promising business making fuel cells, miniature electronic devices that convert hydrogen and oxygen into electricity that is free from pollution. The fledgling business, with just 100 employees in mid-2003, was set up in Swindon to be near Johnson Matthey's main R&D centre in Reading.

Such marriages of scientific innovation and old manufacturing skills could prove increasingly important in 21st century British factories, and there is no shortage of high skills in certain areas of engineering. JCB, the world-class manufacturer of earth-moving equipment, which is still privately owned by the Bamford family, bucked the perception of decline in British engineering in the autumn of 2003 by

launching one of the first new engines for more than a decade to be entirely designed and built in the UK. It will replace engines for medium-sized off-road vehicles previously supplied by Perkins of Peterborough, which is now owned by JCB's US rival, Caterpillar. Cosworth Technology, another high-end engineering company involved in the JCB project, said there had been few equivalent innovations since Jaguar's AJ26 engine in the mid-1990s.

In the industry on which all engineering and much of manufacturing depend, however, a long and chequered history appeared to be approaching its end in 2003. Steel, which a century ago was dominated by family-run firms such as Baldwins of Bewdley, became in the post-war decades a political football between Labour and Conservative governments. Alternately nationalised and denationalised, the industry was eventually privatised as British Steel in 1987 and, having undergone radical restructuring and modernisation, appeared well placed to beat its European competitors. But the familiar story of low-cost imports from China, India and post-Communist eastern Europe overwhelmed its profitability, and attempts to drive into new specialised markets could not reverse decline. In 1999, British Steel merged with the Dutch firm of Hoogovens to form Corus, the world's fourth largest steel company, with annual sales of £10bn and a market value of more than £4bn.

The bright promise soon tarnished. In less than four years, that market value had shrunk by

Family business bucks the trend: JCB, headed by Sir Anthony Bamford (right), remains a world engineering innovator

a calamitous 97 per cent and the company had posted losses of £2.4bn. The UK side, hit by the strength of sterling against the euro, was forced to cut production by a fifth in three years. Unlike the role-model examples of Unilever and Royal Dutch/Shell, this Anglo-Dutch merger did not work well in management terms. Although meant to be "a merger of equals", the Dutch perceived the process of decision-making to be tilting towards the British half. "The Dutch way of doing things emphasises consensus while the British style is to give orders and say 'let's get on with it,'" said Leo Berndsen, chairman of the supervisory board.

Attempts by the British management to recoup money by selling off the aluminium side of the business were stymied by the supervisory board, which feared all the money would vanish into a British pit. In an extraordinary challenge, the British chairman, Sir Brian Moffat, and chief executive Tony Pedder took the supervisory board to court, only to have the case thrown out by the Dutch judge, who decided that the board had not acted irresponsibly or solely in the interests of the Dutch operation. The verdict was greeted jubilantly in the Netherlands as stopping the British from "selling the family silver", echoing Harold Macmillan's telling phrase about privatising state assets. Pedder resigned, but Moffat pressed on, trying to restructure yet again and cut costs by cutting jobs. The company was also faced with refinancing itself. After the court debacle, its market value – once £4.1bn – was put at just £125m.[8]

Steel is an industry under siege in many Western economies: in the US, Bethlehem Steel, "the bedrock of American industry", as its last CEO Steve Miller put it, followed 18 other steel companies into bankruptcy. In 2003, it was finally sold off to International Steel Group, losing its historic name and most of the financial security of its 95,000 pensioners. Miller doubts that in 20 years any raw steel will be produced in either Europe or North America; it is likely to come instead from China and Brazil, where costs are low.

The future in metal

Corus chairman Sir Brian Moffat: Anglo-Dutch misunderstandings multiplied troubles in the steel giant

Globalism presents manufacturers everywhere in the West with an equal measure of opportunity and threat. One month hundreds of small businesses are reported to be closing their doors under the onslaught of cheap components from abroad (more than 150 Midlands engineering companies have shut down in less than two years); soon afterwards, James Dyson is boldly likening his newly relocated manufacturing operation (in Malaysia) to that of Apple or Sony, both of which benefit from lower-cost manufacturing outside the US or Japan while still being regarded as key parts of their homeland economies.

Service industries, of course, remain the dominant sector in all advanced economies, and in 2003 the much-quoted "24/7" lifestyle, led by well-paid but time-pressured professionals, has thrown up a whole new cluster of potential businesses. An industrial research group called the Future Foundation has identified 53 per cent of the adult population as welcoming the 24-hour society and the prospect of 24-hour services to match. Of these, 25 per cent are "fast-laners", adults who are under 30, childless and have

Convenience living: Tesco was an early mover in 12-hour opening

a hedonistic view of the 24-hour culture, wanting all-night restaurants, shops, bars and places of entertainment (and, of course, reliable public transport) available on tap. A slightly larger group (around 27 per cent) is "convenience-driven", couples in the 30-50 age bracket – often two working parents – who complain of time pressures and seek 24-hour services as a pragmatic way to ease their clock-driven lives.

The Greater London Authority (GLA) under mayor Ken Livingstone is ambitious to follow big North American cities such as Seattle and San Francisco and to transform the British capital into a 24-hour city. The idea is to resuscitate street life after dark in the central or "downtown" districts and their neighbouring areas. In continental Europe, Copenhagen has been a role model for such development for some 20 years, while Barcelona followed up its year as host city to the Olympics in 1992 by creating 150 new public squares. In the UK, Manchester has led the way, regenerating its declining industrial heritage with a throbbing night-time economy of bars, clubs, restaurants and entertainment. During the 1990s, thanks to a more relaxed approach to licensing and planning laws, it increased the residential population of its central

district tenfold and turned itself into a major magnet for students (the city is home to more than 100,000) and free-spending gay people.

In London, the GLA estimates that some 500,000 young people go clubbing regularly on Saturday nights – more than all the weekly visitors to London's top 10 tourist attractions put together. The capital's growing tourism and entertainment sector now employs more than 300,000, or eight per cent of the UK's total workforce. Extending public transport services to 3am or 4am to encourage more suburbanites to come into the centre would, the argument goes, open up new opportunities for people to work unsocial hours in pubs, restaurants, take-aways, bars, cafes and supermarkets – as well as creating more jobs in the transport sector itself and in policing and security.

Already, a research centre in London's University College has charted the capital's evening economy as reaching out well beyond the West End – into fashionable or busy residential areas stretching from Islington, Earl's Court and Chelsea in inner London to Hampstead and Kingston upon Thames on the city's fringes. At the time of writing, the GLA was lobbying for 24-hour licences to be granted to selected venues in designated "Entertainment Management Zones".

Global corporations in nocturnally revitalised business districts would doubtless find it easier to operate around the clock and across time zones. But it remains to be seen whether the British psyche would welcome the breaching of the night-time "frontier", as the US sociologist Murray Melbin calls it. Melbin compares the hours of darkness to the frontier of the Old West, likening the shortage of land in the 19th century to the shortage of time in the 21st. "A frontier is a new source of supply for substinence or profit," he writes. "It is a safety valve for people who feel confined".

Leisure and pleasure, it seems, will be a driving economic combination in an increasingly hedonistic society of rising incomes. A book published in 2003 by the economist Roger Bootle endorsed this with predictions of many new business opportunities in added-value services, ranging from personal training and grooming to more comfort in air travel. He forecasts that holidays will follow the pattern of rising standards seen in the food industry, where significant numbers of consumers are moving their buying criteria from low cost to premium quality.[9]

Wherever the new business wealth of Britain is generated, and whatever the future of existing enterprises – whether in the old or new economies – one aspect of running a company will be fundamentally changed from that of the 1900s, where this historical journey began. Society at large, and especially the shareholding part of it – whether individual investors or fund managers responsible for others' mass savings – now demands much more from business than the simple measures of satisfactory products and dividends.

Now it's personal: services such as fitness training are in high demand

The corporate governance movement, little more than a decade old, is rapidly gathering pace and power on both sides of the Atlantic, fuelled by the misuse of boardroom responsibility that has been exposed since the year 2000 in such companies as Enron and WorldCom (now MCI) and by growing resentment at the perception that too many senior executives look after themselves and each other in their financial packages rather than experience a genuine risk-and-reward culture. In the US, a tough new code, specifically aimed at cleaning up MCI's financial governance, is being shaped under the auspices of a former chairman of the SEC, Richard Breeden. Its 77 recommendations are expected to have a widespread impact on corporate America, now that US investors have the bit between their teeth, but they are bound to be resisted by many CEOs as an unacceptable curb on traditional entrepreneurial freedoms.

In the UK, where the modern corporation as an entity was invented in the Companies Acts of the mid-19th century, the pressures to improve corporate governance will bring about 21st-century innovation in the way companies are structured and run. The Higgs report (see box) is the latest in a mounting pile of recommendations for best practice in the boardroom. The legal responsibilities being laid on non-executives, and the demands these make on their time and knowledge, are expanding as independents are being urged to take a more pro-active role in board decisions. There are some fears that – rather as in modern government – the demands of the job will inevitably mean that the pool of suitable candidates will shrink.

Non-executives are now expected to involve themselves not merely in the performance of the company, but in matters as diverse as health and safety of employees, environmental concerns, risk management and the treatment of outsourced labour in distant developing countries. The days when they were chosen as "people like us", to fit in like clubmen (they were usually men) with the chairman and the rest of the board, are fading fast. That sort of selection process in any case could hardly produce the calibre of independent judgment now being demanded. The increasing emphasis on boardroom professionalism, promoted through such initiatives as the IoD's chartered director qualification,

An age of anti-business protest: left, Greenpeace campaigns for 'green fuel' at higher prices; right, May Day anti-capitalist demonstrators at Oxford Circus in London in 2001

is another nail in the coffin of the old-boy network.

The world of 1903 business looks wonderfully simple from the perspective of 2003: cheap labour, low taxes, advancing technology, captive imperial markets, freely convertible currency, few trade unions, complete freedom to manage and to disclose only as the board decided – not to mention mutually back-scratching practices that today would be condemned as insider dealing or worse. We live in an infinitely more transparent and complex world, where technology demands at least as much as it offers, where corporate ethics and good practice are becoming a matter of active shareholder concern, where public trust in the probity of directors is falling alarmingly and where the management of people and resources requires a range of high-quality skills. (The trust problem is becoming acute: a MORI poll commissioned by the Financial Times in late summer 2003 found that four out of five respondents believed that directors of large corporations cannot be relied on to tell the truth.)

Management as an art or science was in its infancy in 1903: today, it is the stock-in-trade of some of the world's highest-rated educational institutions. Today's leading managers have a far sharper and longer vision than their predecessors of a century ago, many of whom were content to rest on the dusty laurels of the country that gave birth to the Industrial Revolution but failed to exploit the technological opportunities of the 1900s.

No chief executive or owner-manager today could spend half the year on holiday as William Morris, Lord Nuffield, did as late as the 1930s (though in the end that contributed to his downfall); few would be free, in any case, from the tugging umbilical cords of mobile telephony and e-mail. But if the management of business is so much more demanding and stressful, and so much more scrutinised than in past decades, so the challenge is that much greater and more fulfilling. As the poet Robert Browning wrote, in a time before women were given the chance to achieve: "A man's reach should exceed his grasp/Or what's a heaven for?"

appendix

GROSS DOMESTIC PRODUCT
1900-2000

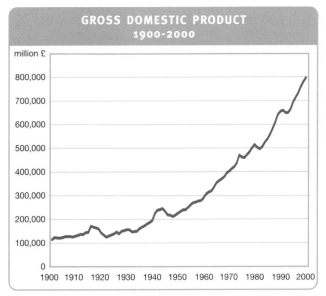

Source: United Kingdom National Accounts – The Blue Book

PROPORTION OF PEOPLE IN EMPLOYMENT WHO ARE MEMBERS OF A TRADE UNION 1900-2000

Sources: Trade union membership levels: British Labour Statistics Historical Abstract 1886-1968;
Department of Employment; Certification Officers' Annual Reports
Employment levels: One Hundred Years of Economic Statistics; Labour Force Survey

NUMBER OF PEOPLE IN EMPLOYMENT
1900-2000

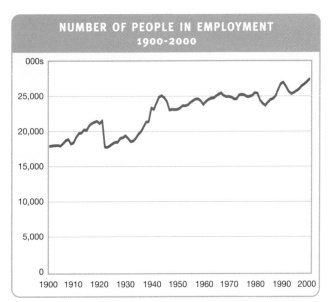

Sources: The Economist Publications Ltd.; Labour Force Survey

NUMBER OF WORKING DAYS LOST DUE TO LABOUR DISPUTES 1900-2000

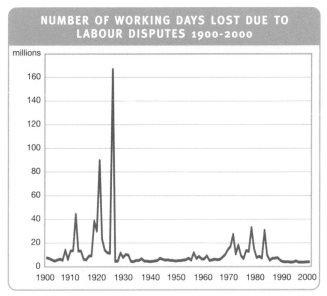

Source: Social Trends 30, Office for National Statistics

GROWTH RATES OF AVERAGE EARNINGS 1940-2000

— The index of Liesner's hourly earnings
— Average Earnings Index

Sources: The Economist Publications Ltd.; Average Earnings Index

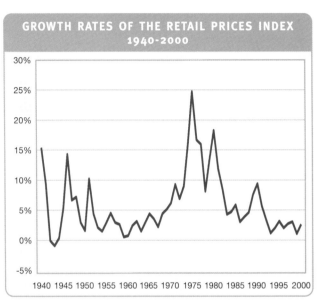

GROWTH RATES OF THE RETAIL PRICES INDEX 1940-2000

Sources: The Economist Publications Ltd.; Average Earnings Index

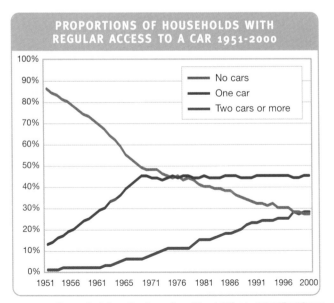

PROPORTIONS OF HOUSEHOLDS WITH REGULAR ACCESS TO A CAR 1951-2000

— No cars
— One car
— Two cars or more

Sources: Family Expenditure Survey; General Household Survey; National Travel Survey

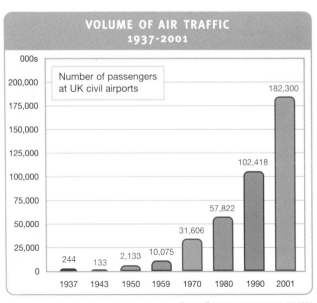

VOLUME OF AIR TRAFFIC 1937-2001

Number of passengers at UK civil airports

1937	1943	1950	1959	1970	1980	1990	2001
244	133	2,133	10,075	31,606	57,822	102,418	182,300

Source: British historical statistics; UK 2003

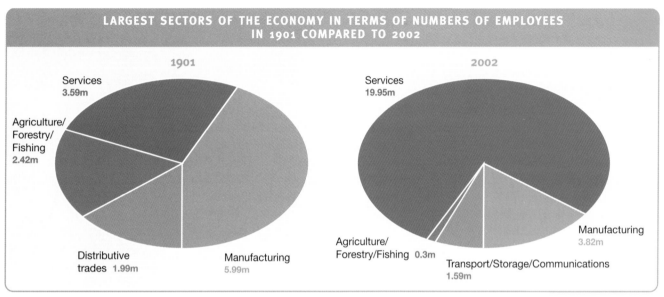

LARGEST SECTORS OF THE ECONOMY IN TERMS OF NUMBERS OF EMPLOYEES IN 1901 COMPARED TO 2002

1901

Services
3.59m

Agriculture/
Forestry/
Fishing
2.42m

Distributive
trades 1.99m

Manufacturing
5.99m

2002

Services
19.95m

Agriculture/
Forestry/Fishing 0.3m

Transport/Storage/Communications
1.59m

Manufacturing
3.82m

Source: One hundred years of economic statistics, The Economist, 1989; Whitaker's Almanack 2003

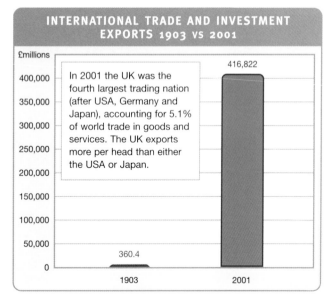

INTERNATIONAL TRADE AND INVESTMENT EXPORTS 1903 vs 2001

£millions

In 2001 the UK was the fourth largest trading nation (after USA, Germany and Japan), accounting for 5.1% of world trade in goods and services. The UK exports more per head than either the USA or Japan.

416,822

360.4

1903   2001

Source: UK 2003, the official yearbook of the UK

COMPANIES AND BUSINESSES

The UK has 3.7 million businesses.

At the end of March 2002 there were 1,491,500 'live' companies registered in Great Britain with the Registrar of Companies.

Small firms

☐ 43% of the private sector workforce work for companies employing fewer than 50 people.

☐ 2.6 million businesses are sole traders or partners without employees.

☐ 748,000 businesses employ one to four people.

Together these 3.3 million enterprises account for 89.3% of the number of businesses, 22.7% of business employment and 15.4% of turnover.

In 2001 there were 345,000 business start-ups in the UK.

Source: UK 2003, the official yearbook of the UK

chapter one

1. Correlli Barnett: The Collapse of British Power (Eyre Methuen, 1972)

2. David S. Landes: The Unbound Prometheus (reissue, Cambridge University Press, 2003)

3. Business History, December 1960. S.B. Saul: The American impact on British industry, 1895-1914

4. Business History, January 1966. Derek Aldcroft: Technical progress and British enterprise, 1875-1914

5. Martin Adeney: Nuffield – a Biography (Robert Hale, 1993)

6. Business History, January 1971. R.J. Irving: British railway investment and innovation 1900-1913

7. David Kynaston: The City of London, Vol. II, Golden Years, 1890-1914 (Chatto and Windus, 1995)

8. Business History, December 1960. S.B. Saul: The American impact on British industry, 1895-1914

9. Business History, December 1962. S.B. Saul: The motor industry in Britain to 1914

chapter two

1. Carol Kennedy: ICI – The Company That Changed Our Lives, (Hutchinson 1986, new edition Paul Chapman Publishing, 1993)

2. B.W.E. Alford: Lost opportunities: British business and businessmen during the First World War. Published in Business Life and Public Policy, ed. N. McKendrick, 1986

3. Business History, April 1990. Panikos Panayi: German business interests in Britain during the First World War

4. David Kynaston: the City of London, Vol. III, Illusions of Gold, 1914-45 (Chatto and Windus, 1999)

5. Gerard J. DeGroot: Blighty: British Society in the Era of the Great War, (Addison Wesley Longman, 1996)

6. Carol Kennedy: Business Pioneers, (Random House Business Books, 2001)

7. Kynaston: the City of London, Vol. III

8. A.J.P. Taylor: English History, 1914-1945 (Oxford University Press, 1965)

9. Alford: Lost opportunities

10. DeGroot: Blighty

11. ibid

12. Journal of European Economic History, 1982. Boswell and Johns: Patriots or Profiteers? British businessmen and the First World War.

13. DeGroot: Blighty

14. Arthur Marwick: The Deluge: British Society and the First World War (The Bodley Head, 1965)

15. Boswell and Johns: Patriots or Profiteers?

16. ibid; T.C. Barker: The Glassmakers, Pilkington 1826-1976 (Weidenfeld and Nicolson, 1977)

17. DeGroot: Blighty

18. Alford: Lost opportunities

19. Adeney: Nuffield - a Biography

20. Marwick: The Deluge

21. Business History, April 1990: Panikos Panayi: German business interests in Britain in the First World War

22. Marwick: The Deluge

23. Alford: Lost opportunities

24. Taylor: English History, 1914-1945

25. Alford: Lost opportunities

26. ibid

27. ibid

28. Marwick: The Deluge

29. ibid

chapter three

1. Economic History Review, 1996. Greasley and Oxley: Discontinuities in competitiveness: the impact of the First World War on British industry

2. Economic History Review, Vol. XXX No. 2, 1978. Rodney Lowe: The erosion of state intervention in Britain

3. Peter Clarke: Hope and Glory, Britain 1900-1990 (Allen Lane The Penguin Press, 1996)

4. Barnett: The Collapse of British Power

5. B.W.E. Alford: Lost opportunities : British business and businessmen during the First World War. Published in Business Life and Public Policy, ed. N. McKendrick, 1986

6. Marwick: The Deluge

7. Kennedy: ICI – The Company That Changed Our Lives

8. Business History, April 1986. Lewis Johnman: The largest manufacturing companies of 1935

9. Economic History Review, Vol. XXVII, No. 2, 1974. Leslie Hannah: Managerial innovation and the rise of the large-scale company in inter-war Britain

10. ibid

11. Economic History Review, Vol. XVI, No. 1, 1974. Leslie Hannah: Takeover bids in Britain before 1950: an exercise in business reality

12. Business History, April 1986. Lewis Johnman: The largest manufacturing companies of 1935

13. Adeney: Nuffield – a Biography

14. Economic History Review, February 1992. Bowden and Collins: The Bank of England, industrial regeneration and hire purchase between the wars

15. Business History, January 1990. Sue Bowden: Credit facilities and the growth of consumer demand for electric appliances in the 1930s

16. Business History, April 1986: Johnman: The largest manufacturing companies of 1935

17. Correlli Barnett: The Audit of War (Macmillan, 1986)

18. Economic History Review, Vol. XXXVI, No. 4, November 1983. Mark Thomas: Rearmament and economic recovery in the late 1930s

19. Barnett: The Collapse of British Power

20. Barnett: The Audit of War

21. Barnett: The Collapse of British Power

22. Barnett: The Audit of War

chapter four

1. Peter Hennessy: Never Again: Britain 1945-51 (Jonathan Cape, 1992)

2. Angus Calder: The People's War, Britain 1939-45 (Jonathan Cape, 1969)

3. Kennedy: Business Pioneers; Calder: The People's War

4. Calder: The People's War

5. Kennedy: ICI – The Company That Changed Our Lives

6. ibid

7. Hennessy: Never Again

8. Calder: The People's War

9. ibid

10. Hennessy: Never Again

11. ibid

12. Business History, January 1987. John Hendry: the teashop computer manufacturer

13. Hennessy: Never Again

14. ibid

15. Paul Addison: Now the War is Over, a social history of Britain 1945-1951 (BBC/Jonathan Cape, 1985); Hennessy: Never Again

16. Hennessy: Never Again

17. Correlli Barnett. The Lost Victory: British Dreams, British Realities 1945-1950 (Macmillan, 1995)

18. Barnett: The Lost Victory

19. Addison: Now the War Is Over

chapter five

1. Hennessy: Never Again

2. Juliet Gardiner: From the Bomb to the Beatles: the changing face of post-war Britain 1945-65, (Collins and Brown, 1999)

3. Miriam Akhtar and Steve Humphries. The Fifties and Sixties: a lifestyle revolution, (Boxtree, 2001)

4. Clarke: Hope and Glory

5. David Kynaston: The City of London, Vol. IV, A Club No More, 1945-2000 (Chatto and Windus, 2001)

6. Director files, 1950

7. ibid

8. Clarke: Hope and Glory

9. Akhtar and Humphries: The Fifties and Sixties

10. Akhtar and Humphries: The Fifties and Sixties

11. Kennedy: Business Pioneers

12. Barclays Capital

13. Director files, 1950

14. ibid

15. Clarke: Hope and Glory

16. Andrews and Brunner: Productivity and the businessman, Oxford Economic Papers Vol. 2 (1950); Business History, April 1998. Broadberry and Crafts: The post-war settlement: not such a good bargain after all

17. Gardiner: From the Bomb to the Beatles

18. Akhtar and Humphries: The Fifties and Sixties

19. Gardiner: From the Bomb to the Beatles; Economist, January 1959

20. Clarke: Hope and Glory

21. Kynaston: The City of London, Vol. IV

22. Hennessy: Never Again

23. The Guardian, December 22, 2001

24. Gardiner: From the Bomb to the Beatles

25. The Advertising Statistics Yearbook, 2002 (The Advertising Association)

26. ibid

chapter six

1. Akhtar and Humphries: The Fifties and Sixties
2. Gardiner: From the Bomb to the Beatles
3. Robert Heller: British Railways After Beeching, Management Today, June 1967
4. TV documentary: Car Junkies, BBC2, February 23, 2003
5. Dave McAleer: Beatboom! Pop Goes the Sixties, Hamlyn, 1994
6. McAleer: Beatboom!
7. Pretty Polly corporate website
8. Designing the Decades, BBCTV, 2003
9. Christopher Lee, This Sceptred Isle, 20th Century, BBC and Penguin Books, 1999, citing The Castle Diaries, 1964-1967
10. Management Today, April 1966; Nov 1966
11. Grand Prix Hall of Fame; GP Encyclopedia; www.grandprix.com; Director, March 1970
12. Kynaston: The City of London, Vol. IV

chapter seven

1. The Economist, January 18, 1974; March 9, 1974
2. Management Today, December 1973
3. Management Today, February 1974
4. The Economist, February 2nd, 1974
5. The Economist, March 9, 1974
6. Carol Kennedy: Interview with Philip Sadler of Ashridge Management College
7. Management Today, January 2003
8. ibid
9. Management Today, December 1974
10. Management Today, August 1973

chapter eight

1. Management Today, May 1987
2. Michel Syrett and Jean Lammiman: From Leanness to Fitness (IPD, 1997)
3. Financial Times, April 15, 2003
4. Department of Employment
5. Institute of Manpower Studies
6. Management Today, March 1987
7. ibid
8. ibid
9. Management Today, March 1988
10. Management Today, January 1987
11. Management Today, October 1981
12. Nicholas Kochan and Hugh Pym: The Guinness Affair, 1987; BBC News online, November 28, 1997
13. Business International, 1991. Nicholas Kochan and Michel Syrett: New Directions in Corporate Governance
14. Management Today, May 1981
15. Sunday Times, March 16, 2003
16. www.ltbn.com

chapter nine

1. Carol Kennedy: ABB's sun rises in the east, Director, September 1996
2. Management Today, October 1995
3. ibid
4. Sunday Times, June 8, 2003
5. Management Today, November 2000
6. Michel Syrett and Jean Lammiman: Creativity (Capstone-Wiley ExpressExec guides 2003)
7. The Economist, November 21, 1998; Kochan and Syrett: report on corporate governance; Syrett and Lammiman: Management Development (Capstone-Wiley ExpressExec guides, 2002)

chapter ten

1. John Howkins; The Creative Economy, (Allen Lane The Penguin Press, 2001)
2. Financial Times, July 18, 2003
3. Financial Times, August 18, 2003
4. The Times, April 4, 2003
5. ibid
6. The Times, May 19, 2003
7. The Times, April 18, 2003
8. The Sunday Times, March 16, 2003
9. Roger Bootle: Money for Nothing: Real Wealth, Financial Fantasies and the Economy of the Future (Nicholas Brealey, 2003)